# Inhale
# Exhale

## BREATHE: NEW LIFE

*A Rhythm of Reflection, Restoration, and Release*

# Dedication

To the *Springs of Life-Giving Water Church* and a rich legacy of leaders whose lives and transitions helped to develop pastoral ministry in me:

Dea. Harold Walker, Dea. Juanita Alston, Deacon Noel Clark, Deacon Janet Gregory, Deaconess Bea Bailey, Mother Lucille Brantley, Mother Mary Hanna, and Mother Annie Hudson.

# Table Of Contents

# Introduction

Welcome to BREATHE: NEW LIFE—a sacred rhythm of reflection, restoration, and release. This is more than a devotional. It is a spiritual breathing space, an invitation to inhale what is holy and exhale what is heavy. These meditations were born in the trenches of life and faith—where the Spirit meets the soul in stillness, where tired hearts are gently revived, and where each breath becomes a testimony of survival and grace.

In a world that moves too fast and pulls us in too many directions, BREATHE: NEW LIFE offers you permission to pause. Whether you're a weary pastor, a bold believer, or someone navigating grief, uncertainty, or transition, this book is your companion through the wilderness and the wellspring. Each entry is a daily altar—an opportunity to sit with Scripture, name your truth, and receive divine breath anew. This journey doesn't demand perfection; it simply asks for presence.

So, inhale. Receive the breath of God that restores. Exhale. Release what no longer serves your spirit. And as you turn these pages, may you find a rhythm of living that is slow, sacred, and strong. Let's walk together—through healing, through hope, through the hard places—and into new life.

# SPEAK OVER YOUR LIFE

## JANUARY

# January 1

*Thou hidest thy face, they are troubled:*
*thou takest away their breath, they die, and return to their dust.*
*Thou sendest forth thy spirit, they are created:*
*and thou renewest the face of the earth.*
Psalm 104:29-30

The new life for your new year rests in your ability to see, hear, and act out your Word of life. Just because you have a Word for your life does not mean there will be no challenges; however, what it does mean is that as you engage your Word, there are opportunities for empowerment to overcome those challenges and reach your expected end. Your steps have been ordered by the Lord, meaning your Word of life has been ordered, commanded. Therefore, as you enter new eras of your experiences, you are obligated, under orders to follow through, despite and in spite of the challenges before you. The challenges of your life serve as obstacles to prevent, stall you, and/or cause you to give up; however, giving up is not an option if you want to reach your expected end. Thus, **Speak Over Your Life**, including your challenges, commanding them to your ordered steps. You can live in your abundant life, you being here, in the new year, a new experience is evidence that it is possible, ***Breathe: New Life***; forcibly exhale the old and expectantly inhale the new; your possibilities which create new opportunities for you to live abundantly!

# January 2

*Words satisfy the mind as much as fruit does the stomach;*
*good talk is as gratifying as a good harvest.*
*Words kill, words give life;*
*they're either poison or fruit—you choose.*
Proverbs 18:20-21

An essential element for living in life and life more abundantly, that which you believe should be, rests in your choices. Whether you choose right or left or no choice at all, indecision is a choice; you lay the foundation for what shall be. You cannot only rely on the fact that you have entered a new year and/or are situated in a new space for the newness of the year or experience will not land you in the place you should be, but you must also choose new life and act upon it. Whether you reach your expected end or not depends on the choices you make. Your choices are fueled by your **Speaking Over Your Life** into existence that which you believe should be. Speaking life to your circumstances opens you up, including your mind, thus creating a magnet, an antenna to attract and discern new possibilities, which leads to opportunities for what should be. **Speak Over Your Life** and *Breathe: New Life*, inhaling and exhaling forcibly to make room for new life, oxygen necessary to expand your lungs, your being, and becoming. Speak to yourself and your space and command the inhaling of the new and exhaling of the old, all things falling in line with what you believe should be for your life. Your words matter to your ability to imagine and conceive the new, and it will produce the necessary fruit that empowers you to live, *Breathe: New Life*.

## January 3

*Evildoers are trapped by their sinful talk,*
*and so the innocent escape trouble.*
*From the fruit of their lips people are filled with good things,*
*and the work of their hands brings them reward.*
Proverbs 12:13-14 (NIV)

To keep yourself on a pathway that leads to and nurtures your development in that which should be for your life, you must guard your conversation. Your conversation is one of the main fueling agents for your ability to achieve your Word of life. As you speak and allow it to be spoken in your life, you are equipping your mind to imagine possibilities that lead to opportunities for new life in your circumstances. You know how bad your circumstances may be and even their impossibility, what you need is the power to **Speak Over Your Life**, speak to your circumstances to *Breathe: New Life*. As you speak, your mind will follow, and as a result, you are empowered to overcome by translating your thoughts into necessary actions that lead you into your ordered steps for your circumstances, producing your life and life more abundantly.

## January 4

*From the fruit of their lips people enjoy good things,*
*but the unfaithful have an appetite for violence.*
*Those who guard their lips preserve their lives,*
*but those who speak rashly will come to ruin.*
Proverbs 13:2-3 (NIV)

Taking charge of your life also means what you allow into your life. Your speaking and conversations are critical to influencing your mind and, thus, your actions, making it incumbent upon you to guard what you say and the kind of conversations you engage in for the health and well-being of your life and promises.  Words do matter, and if you allow the negativity of words spoken in and through, as well as over your life, it will send the wrong message; kill your expectations, and assassinate your possibilities, making it less likely to seize opportunities for new life. **Speak Over Your Life** that which builds, nurtures, and produces, empowering and guarding your life to flourish in your circumstances to *Breathe: New Life*!

## January 5

*"If you grow a healthy tree, you'll pick healthy fruit. If you grow a diseased tree, you'll pick worm-eaten fruit. The fruit tells you about the tree.  "You have minds like a snake pit! How do you suppose what you say is worth anything when you are so foul-minded? It's your heart, not the dictionary, that gives meaning to your words. A good person produces good deeds and words season after season. An evil person is a blight on the orchard. Let me tell you something: Every one of these careless words is going to come back to haunt you. There will be a time of Reckoning. Words are powerful; take them seriously. Words can be your salvation. Words can also be your damnation."*
Matthew 1`2:33-37 (MSG)

Whatsoever you sow you will reap, meaning what you put in is what you will get out. We must be conscious and diligent about what we put into our lives, including what we **Speak over Our Lives** and/or what we allow to be spoken in our space and conversations. Whatever is spoken finds residence in our being and minds and, as a result, begins to form thoughts and ideas, which will produce fruit, both good and/or bad. If you guard your life and space, ensuring you do whatever is necessary to create a healthy, whole space, you will produce healthy, whole outcomes. However, if you allow trash, negativity, chaos, confusion to reign over your life and in your space, you will produce outcomes that reflect the heart of that substance. The words spoken over your life, which are healthy and whole, will bring about your ability to *Breathe: New Life*. As the positivity and soundness of your words go forth from you and your space, they take root in your mind, influencing your thoughts and ideas, moving you toward possibilities that create opportunities for you to receive new life. Guard your anointing, your chosen-ness, your Word of life by ensuring that you **Speak Over Your Life** and allow spoken over your life that which builds, nurtures, and produces new life: exhaling the old and inhaling the new; *Breathe: New Life*!

## January 6

*Fools are undone by their big mouths;*
*their souls are crushed by their words.*
*Listening to gossip is like eating cheap candy;*
*do you really want junk like that in your belly?*
Proverbs 18:7-8 (MSG)

10

Be careful about what you feed your spirit and thus your mind. The intake of junk, chaos, confusion, lies, deception, etc., will poison your thoughts and depress the gift of your promise, your Word of life. Guard your anointing, your chosen-ness, because God has declared that you live and live abundantly in and through your ordered steps, which is made possible as you exhale the junk and inhale that which brings new life. Ensure that you **Speak Over Your Life** and allow positive and empowering words to be spoken in your space, for it is in them that your mind and spirit will be strengthened to conceive and accomplish what God has ordained for your life. Go ahead and *Breathe: New Life*, releasing yourself from the negative and inhaling the required oxygen for your promise, the Words spoken over and in your life and space, building, nurturing, and producing new life!

## January 7

*Say ye to the righteous, that it shall be well with him:*
*for they shall eat the fruit of their doings.*
Isaiah 3:10

**Speak Over Your Life** because it is a mechanism that influences your mind; your thoughts and ideas, opening you up to opportunities to *Breathe: New Life* into your circumstances. Say what it is you want, and it will be well done, fruit to your being and mind, and as a result, openness to exhale the junk and negativity of life and inhale oxygen, giving possibilities that lead to opportunities for new life. What you say and what you allow to be **Spoken Over Your Life** and in your life is critical to you formulating ideas and thoughts that promote and fuel new life in your circumstances.  The fruit of your words produces actions that open up the way for you to experience the revelation of God and the ordered steps for the fulfillment of your promises, vision for your life, and of God Himself.  *Breathe: New Life* and walk into the revelation of your abundance and the power of God prevailing in and through your life!

## January 8

*We all stumble in many ways. Anyone who is never at fault in what they say is perfect, able to keep their whole body in check. When we put bits into the mouths of horses to make them obey us, we can turn the whole animal.*

James 3:2-3 (NIV)

The quest to *Breathe: New Life* by **Speaking Over Your Life** or allowing words spoken in your life alone is insufficient because you are human with limitations, thus, exhaling and inhaling, especially under pressure, will fall short at times.  However, as you are conscious of the fact that your words matter, you must correct in motion as you confront the challenges of your life.  Remember, bits in the mouth of horses, yet make them obey, and the same is true, work your words, correct when necessary, and drive your narrative.  The power of life and death is in your tongue; thus, what you speak and the atmosphere in which you allow to exist in your space empower you to conquer your fears and conceive the new for your circumstances, for your life.  Neither you nor I is perfect, therefore, we must be conscious while in motion through our everyday walking around experiences to move, have our being, and live in the power, the Spirit of our promises, vision,

Word for our life, for our circumstances. **Speak Over Your Life** and *Breathe: New Life* while in motion, exhaling the toxic and inhaling the necessary oxygen to bring new life to your life, to your circumstances.

## January 9

*Then he told this parable: "A man had a fig tree growing in his vineyard, and he went to look for fruit on it but did not find any. So he said to the man who took care of the vineyard, 'For three years now I've been coming to look for fruit on this fig tree and haven't found any. Cut it down! Why should it use up the soil?'" 'Sir,' the man replied, 'leave it alone for one more year, and I'll dig around it and fertilize it. If it bears fruit next year, fine! If not, then cut it down.'"*
Luke 13:6-9 (NIV)

The power to **Speak Over Your Life** and to ensure that you make consistent what you allow spoken in your space must be coupled with you feeding your words. Words alone will not do the trick, although you have the power of life and death in the tongue; that power must be activated, and to activate means to feed what you speak and allow what is spoken to be realized in your life. Feed your words with expectations that the spoken word is not just empty and void, but instead, you are actively looking for and doing what is necessary to bring to pass that which you have spoken. In addition to feeding your words expectations, it also demands encouragement, motivation, pushing forward of your words, including pushing out what is contrary (exhaling) and inhaling from all sources that give oxygen, giving life to your

13

words.  The process of exhaling and inhaling emancipates you from what is and/or what is acceptable in your present reality, opening the way to the exceedingly, abundantly, more than. *Breathe: New Life* by feeding your words with expectations, encouragement, and emancipation, freeing your words and yourself to new possibilities, which point you to opportunities for new life in your circumstances.


## January 10


*The apostles came up and said to the Master, "Give us more faith." But the Master said, "You don't need more faith. There is no 'more' or 'less' in faith. If you have a bare kernel of faith, say the size of a poppy seed, you could say to this sycamore tree, 'Go jump in the lake,' and it would do it.*
Luke 17:5-6 (MSG)


We often find ourselves in situations where we feel inadequate with what we have, even though we believe we can and should achieve what seems impossible. The reality is that you can just work with what you have!  **Speak Over Your Life,** and allow yourself to be spoken over your circumstances in a way that empowers you to use what you have where you are, pushing you toward the fulfillment of what should be.  Often, it is our fears of failing camouflaged by our feelings of inadequacy or undeserving of the endless energy and boundless strength required to overcome; however, to overcome simply requires you to believe, to feed that faith to push you across the finish line.   No matter how small, inadequate, or lacking you think you are, **Speak Over Your Life** feeds that faith and emboldens you to confront the challenges of your life, creating possibilities that point you toward the opportunity to conceive the new life that should be. **Breathe: New Life** by working with what you have (inhaling) and exhaling the toxins of doubt and fears to take the necessary actions for new life in your circumstances.

## January 11

*At the bottom of the mountain, they were met by a crowd of waiting people. As they approached, a man came out of the crowd and fell to his knees begging, "Master, have mercy on my son. He goes out of his mind and suffers terribly, falling into seizures. Frequently he is pitched into the fire, other times into the river. I brought him to your disciples, but they could do nothing for him." Jesus said, "What a generation! No sense of God! No focus to your lives! How many times do I have to go over these things? How much longer do I have to put up with this? Bring the boy here." He ordered the afflicting demon out—and it was out, gone. From that moment on the boy was well. When the disciples had Jesus off to themselves, they asked, "Why couldn't we throw it out?" "Because you're not yet taking God seriously," said Jesus. "The simple truth is that if you had a mere kernel of faith, a poppy seed, say, you would tell this mountain, 'Move!' and it would move. There is nothing you wouldn't be able to tackle."*
Matthew 17:14-21 (MSG)

The power of your Words is nullified if you do not believe them yourself. Your faith in what you **Speak Over Your Life** and allow to be spoken in your space fuels the power of the words to accomplish what you intend. Thus, as you speak, you must expect your words to be fulfilled by taking intentional action toward them, translating them into revelation. You can speak the words, let them be spoken in your space, and hang out with them, but not until you internalize them by feeding them your expectations and producing thoughts and ideas toward their fulfillment does the power of your words become activated. The disciples were all too aware and absorbed with the power of the word, Jesus Himself active in their lives; however, the words did not take root in their faith, believing what they said and heard, and as a result, when confronted with the challenge of revealing the word, it fell flat. Believe what you **Speak Over Your Life** by feeding the words with your expectations, producing thoughts and ideas for your actions, and *Breathe: New Life* into your circumstances, that which you have spoken and thus, believe!

## January 12

*Dear friends, do you think you'll get anywhere in this if you learn all the right words but never do anything? Does merely talking about faith indicate that a person really has it? For instance, you come upon an old friend dressed in rags and half-starved and say, "Good morning, friend! Be clothed in Christ! Be filled with the Holy Spirit!" and walk off without providing so much as a coat or a cup of soup—where does that get you? Isn't it obvious that God-talk without God-acts is outrageous nonsense?*
James 2:14-17 (MSG)

The challenge to **Speak Over Your Life** is also a demand to feed the words you speak so that they are neither hollow nor empty.

Feeding your words with expectations, encouragement, and emancipation sets your thoughts and ideas in motion, translating them into action and motivating you to receive and enhance new life in your situation. When we **Breathe: New Life**, we exhale the toxicity of our lives, making room for additional oxygen to fill our lungs, causing a contraction that expands our possibilities. Our words must translate into actions, making what we believe should be real, first in our minds, thoughts, and ideas, and then in our actions. **Breathe: New Life** to your situations by ensuring that you **Speak Over Your Life,** what should be, triggering your thoughts and ideas, laying a foundation for actions, for possibilities in which you are positioned to seize your opportunities for new life.

## January 13

*Is it not evident that a person is made right with God not by a barren faith but by faith fruitful in works? The same with Rahab, the Jericho harlot. Wasn't her action in hiding God's spies and helping them escape—that seamless unity of believing and doing —what counted with God? The very moment you separate body and spirit, you end up with a corpse. Separate faith and works and you get the same thing: a corpse.*
James 2:24-26 (MSG)

Your ability to **Speak Over Your Life** impregnates you with possibilities that lead to opportunities for a new life, including in your present circumstances. The process of the birth of new life is contingent upon planting seeds, and your **Speaking Over Your Life** cast forth seeds, seeds which must be fed and nurtured with your expectations, encouragement, and emancipation to the truth of your words.  Your speaking serves as a push, exhaling the toxicity of your life, of your circumstances, and inhaling vision, the truth of God's promises for your life and your circumstances.  The additional oxygen you inhale from your vision, thoughts, and ideas encourages you to engage in actions and possibilities focused on what should be for your life and circumstances.  Speaking your truth, engaging the wind of the spirit of truth, will lead and guide you into the revelation, the fulfillment of that truth.  By no means am I suggesting that just speaking alone will accomplish your expected end; however, it will go a long way in motivating you to action, blowing you into your ordered steps, and as a result, you can **Breathe: New Life**!

## January 14

*There was also another great eagle with great wings and many feathers: and, behold, this vine did bend her roots toward him, and shot forth her branches toward him, that he might water it by the furrows of her plantation. It was planted in a good soil by great waters, that it might bring forth branches, and that it might bear fruit, that it might be a goodly vine.*
Ezekiel 17:7-8

When you **Speak Over Your Life** and guard your space by screening what you allow to be spoken, you create a magnetic field that attracts what you speak and allows it to be spoken.  The magnetic atmosphere draws in what feeds and nurtures what you have spoken, laying the groundwork for your expectations, encouragement, and emancipation toward the fulfillment of what you believe should be.  There is no doubt that you can attract positive and progressive energy as you speak; the power of life and death is in the tongue, triggering thoughts and ideas, thus creating a radar, which identifies and draws on that which complements your words. *Breathe: New Life*, allowing the expansion of your lungs to attract, creating a magnetic field for those things that would bring you new life and bear much fruit.


## January 15

*Be patient, then, brothers and sisters, until the Lord's coming. See how the farmer waits for the land to yield its valuable crop, patiently waiting for the autumn and spring rains. You too, be patient and stand firm, because the Lord's coming is near.*
James 5:7-8 (NIV)


A lesson from the life of Martin Luther King: As you **Speak Over Your Life** and allow the positive and focused direction toward fulfilling your promises to be inhaled from your space, you must be consistent and persistent. Consistency allows for the words spoken to take root in your mind; your thoughts and ideas, making you alert for possibilities that lead to opportunities. The power of the spoken word resonates in your mind and spirit, and as a result, motivates, provides you with the resilience to be persistent even though you see no immediate results, and/or you face difficult challenges. However, the more you are consistent and persistent in what you have spoken and allowed to be spoken, you begin to see the budding of your fruit. Remember, as you diligently pursue what you believe should be, what you have been created and built for, God, the Creator of all things, rewards you; therefore, do not get weary in your well-doing. *Breathe: New*

*Life*, inhaling possibilities, thoughts, and ideas, and place those into motion while also exhaling your frustrations, fears, and doubts, allowing God in His Spirit of truth to carry you forth into the revelation and fulfillment of His promises for your life!

## January 16

*God told Jeremiah, "Up on your feet! Go to the potter's house. When you get there, I'll tell you what I have to say." So I went to the potter's house, and sure enough, the potter was there, working away at his wheel. Whenever the pot the potter was working on turned out badly, as sometimes happens when you are working with clay, the potter would simply start over and use the same clay to make another pot.*
Jeremiah 18:1-4 (MSG)

The weekend marks the celebration of Martin Luther King's birthday, which is worth celebrating. We celebrate King's accomplishments for our people, the nation, and the world. King dared to dream and, in dreaming, to **Speak Over His Life** and to garner other voices that echoed his dream and belief in what should be, particularly using the media to bring about moral conviction in his speech. King lived during an era in which Black people and Blackness were made to feel like second-class citizens, openly while also legally enforced; however, he dared to dream differently and speak that, putting into motion actions that transformed our community, the nation, and world. He **Breathe: New Life**. By no means did everything King spoke or dreamed become reality; however, it set in motion thoughts and ideas that translated into action items that are bearing and will bear fruit.

20

Jeremiah, the prophet to the children of Israel during their captivity, was alert enough to be open to possibilities that led to their opportunity to be free before freedom existed, and spoke those things, and as a result, put into motion thoughts and ideas for freedom. Stop cutting off your possibilities because they seem hopeless and are marred, pursue them, and seize your opportunity to act and live in that which you **Speak Over Your Life**. *Breathe: New Life*, inhale your possibilities and release, exhaling your frustrations, fears, and doubts about not succeeding or about thinking it is impossible, and live in your new life, remaking your circumstances to accommodate your spoken word of new life!

## January 17

*Now faith is the substance of things hoped for, the evidence of things not seen. For by it the elders obtained a good report. Through faith we understand that the worlds were framed by the word of God, so that things which are seen were not made of things which do appear.*
Hebrews 11:1-3

As you **Speak Over Your Life,** you build confidence in yourself and in what you believe should be, and, as a result, you build up and nurture your faith. **Speaking Over Your Life** sets in motion your mind to conceive thoughts and ideas that translate into actions, and thus, as you speak, you create that which is not as if it were, the very evidence of the possibility you seek. Please note that just because the possibility does not yield what you believe it should, or the final outcome does not match what should be, does not mean it has been a waste of time, thoughts, or ideas; the possibility produced fruit that leads to opportunity. *Breathe: New Life* is the outcome of you inhaling oxygen that feeds your bloodstream, providing energy and strength to all of your organs, and as you do so, you are refreshed and renewed to new life possibilities in your circumstance. In celebration of King's Day, *Breathe: New Life* by **Speaking Over Your Life,** what should be and allow the saturation of your mind, your dreaming, to conceive possibilities that will point to the opportunity for new life in your circumstances.

## January 18

*But without faith it is impossible to please him: for he that cometh to God must believe that he is, and that he is a rewarder of them that diligently seek him.*
Hebrews 11:6

**Speak Over Your Life** with the confidence it instills and pursue that which you have spoken as if it were. By no means; it's your speaking that drives your narrative, but it will also fuel your narrative of what you believe should be. **Speaking Over Your Life** fuels confidence and, as it takes root in your mind, expands your imagination to conceive new life. Do not allow yourself or anything else to convince you that what is impossible is impossible, with the active presence of God in your life and your willingness to be active as a co-creator with God, any and all things are possible. The possibilities may not be as successful as you want or think they should be; however, it is in the possibilities, the trying, that you gain access to your opportunity for a new life.  Go ahead and *Breathe: New Life*, in and through whatever your circumstances, sending oxygen through your bloodstream, which energizes you to diligently pursue, with the very present help of God, the exceedingly abundantly, more than.

## January 19

*I could go on and on, but I've run out of time. There are so many more—Gideon, Barak, Samson, Jephthah, David, Samuel, the prophets. . . . Through acts of faith, they toppled kingdoms, made justice work, took the promises for themselves. They were protected from lions, fires, and sword thrusts, turned disadvantage to advantage, won battles, routed alien armies. Women received their loved ones back from the dead. There were those who, under torture, refused to give in and go free, preferring something better: resurrection. Others braved abuse and whips, and, yes, chains and dungeons. We have stories of those who were stoned, sawed in two, murdered in cold blood; stories of vagrants wandering the earth in animal skins, homeless, friendless, powerless—the world didn't deserve them!—making their way as best they could on the cruel edges of the world.  Not one of these people, even though their lives of faith were exemplary, got their hands on what was promised. God had a better plan for us: that their faith and our faith would come together to make one completed whole, their lives of faith not complete apart from ours.*
Hebrews 11:32-40 (MSG)

No matter what you face, know that you have the power to overcome, **Speak Over Your Life**, and put into motion that which will not only empower you but also motivate you to take the necessary action to win. The strategy you use to overcome circumstances will often involve possibilities that may or may not lead to your outcomes; however, don't get weary, stay alert, be available, and be active for your opportunity. Seizing your opportunity paves the way for you to **Breathe: New Life**, inhaling and exhaling to bring about the necessary transformation to and for your circumstances. Believing in you is critical; thus, inhaling oxygen to provide you with endless energy and boundless strength, feeding your organs so that you live well and whole, confident about what should be for your life. The exhaling of toxicity makes room for the exceedingly, abundantly more than from inhaling oxygen; possibilities working in you. Remember, where you are, God has a better plan for you. Take up the possibilities that lead to a new life. Even if that possibility does not work the way you plan, it is your vehicle to **Breathe: New Life**!

## January 20

*Wherefore seeing we also are compassed about with so great a cloud of witnesses, let us lay aside every weight, and the sin which doth so easily beset us, and let us run with patience the race that is set before us,*
Hebrews 12:1

**Speak Over Your Life** for what you speak becomes magnetic to witnesses; people, places, and things that will affirm and confirm what should be. Yes, there will be naysayers; however, your magnetic field will draw support that encourages and offers possibilities that lead to new life in your circumstances. We are surrounded by a cloud of witnesses; however, those witnesses, people, places, and things, do not know what we are about or what we are striving for, make it known, and inhale the oxygen. Keep pressing on as you **Speak Over Your Life** and the difficulties you face; you will find possibilities that help you navigate and reach the place that should be in your circumstances. Remember, God is a very active presence in your life and in the world, and all things are subject to Him, making ways so that all things will work for your good. ***Breathe: New Life***!

## January 21

*The disciples were even more amazed, and said to each other, "Who then can be saved?" Jesus looked at them and said, "With man this is impossible, but not with God; all things are possible with God." Then Peter spoke up, "We have left everything to follow you!" "Truly I tell you," Jesus replied, "no one who has left home or brothers or sisters or mother or father or children or fields for me and the gospel will fail to receive a hundred times as much in this present age: homes, brothers, sisters, mothers, children and fields—along with persecutions—and in the age to come eternal life. But many who are first will be last, and the last first."*
Mark 10:26-31 (NIV)

Do not allow yourself to give up, continue to **Speak Over Your Life,** for with God nothing is impossible, and He promises that you will reap what you sow and do so a hundredfold. Your circumstances will not just change because you **Speak Over Your Life**, ***Breathe: New Life*** consistently and persistently, and you will be rewarded more than you can ever imagine or think. **Speaking**

**Over Your Life** triggers a process of thoughts and ideas that translate to actions that push you forward through or around your circumstances to your place of victory, that which should be for your life. Never think that your positive and progressive energy, as well as your strength, will go to waste; your rightful outcome may appear delayed, but nevertheless be steadfast; your blessing will be right on time and in increase, overflowing. *Breathe: New Life*, inhaling and expanding your lungs, setting in motion your exhale with greater force, making room for the more than, the what should be for your life. Hold on, help is on the way, and it will come like a rush of mighty wind, filling you and your space with new life!

## January 22

*And they said unto him, Where is Sarah thy wife? And he said, Behold, in the tent. And he said, I will certainly return unto thee according to the time of life; and, lo, Sarah thy wife shall have a son. And Sarah heard it in the tent door, which was behind him. Now Abraham and Sarah were old and well stricken in age; and it ceased to be with Sarah after the manner of women. Therefore Sarah laughed within herself, saying, After I am waxed old shall I have pleasure, my lord being old also? And the LORD said unto Abraham, Wherefore did Sarah laugh, saying, Shall I of a surety bear a child, which am old? Is any thing too hard for the LORD? At the time appointed I will return unto thee, according to the time of life, and Sarah shall have a son.*
Genesis 18:9-14

Often, we do not believe the possibilities before us are possible and, as a result, never even try to pursue them, shutting the door to awaiting opportunities for new life in our circumstances. **Speak Over Your Life** that which you believe should be, although it is challenging, pushing you beyond your limits of what you believe to be possible, it is necessary to transform your what is into what should be, your new life. Whether what you speak appears possible or not, you cannot allow it to affect your willingness to **Speak Over Your Life** what should be, it will be hard, but remember you are not alone, God is with you. Whatever you face or challenge that raises its head in rejection of what you speak, speak your truth as declared by God, the Creator and Master of all, it can and will be achieved as you seek to co-create with God that which should be. Go ahead and *Breathe: New Life*, inhale the possibilities with the difficulties, nothing with God is impossible or too hard, God is with you and will be with you to the end, the transformation of what is to what should be, your new life!

## January 23

*No test or temptation that comes your way is beyond the course of what others have had to face. All you need to remember is that God will never let you down; he'll never let you be pushed past your limit; he'll always be there to help you come through it.*
I Corinthians 10:13 (MSG)

The power of your words triggers your mind to thoughts and ideas that lead to action; however, the challenge is to **Speak Over Your Life** those words with confidence, as if what you have said were true. Actions are critical, and your actions are fueled by your faith, believing what should be despite what is. Fueling your words with actions toward what should be for your life does not mean you will do everything perfectly and without error, or that the people, places, and things of your life will just fall in line and cooperate. On the contrary, you must believe you can do this. Obstacles and difficulties are part of our journey, but they do not have to define us or prevent us from overcoming and living in what should be. We must always remember that we are not in our circumstances by ourselves, especially when we feel we are the only ones. God, the Creator and Master of life, is with you and a very present help in your time of trouble. Draw on God, I dare say the Spirit of God's Word, truth for your life, and allow it to generate your thoughts, impressing upon the mind ideas that lead you through your circumstances and empower you to victory. *Breathe: New Life*, allowing the oxygen of God's Spirit of possibilities to infiltrate your mind, thoughts, and ideas to expand your lungs, pushing out the negative and your shortcomings so that you might seize the opportunity for new life in your circumstances!

## January 24

*And not only that, but God himself is right alongside to keep you steady and on track until things are all wrapped up by Jesus. God, who got you started in this spiritual adventure, shares with us the life of his Son and our Master Jesus. He will never give up on you. Never forget that.*
I Corinthians 1:8-9 (MSG)

Often, the circumstances of your life have come to act as a deceiver, a cloud of distraction, preventing you from clearly seeing and realizing what your truth is of what should be. Your ability to **Speak Over Your Life,** what should be, clashes with the deception created by your circumstances; therefore, you must be willing to *Breathe: New Life* by speaking your truth in the face of the chaos of the deception. To speak your truth requires confidence and faith in what is your promise for life and life more abundantly, and in conquering the deception that it will not be achieved and/or received by taking action on your truth, with the understanding that you are not alone. God, Emmanuel, is with you and will be faithful to you throughout the process of bringing to pass that which should be, drawing on the supernatural and everlasting power of God, the Creator, Redeemer, and Sustainer of all life. Go ahead and *Breathe: New Life*, inhale the fullness of God's possibilities, and seize your opportunity for new life in your circumstances, inhaling the wind of God's Spirit, which guides you to His truth of what should be for your life!

## January 25

*I know what I'm doing. I have it all planned out—plans to take care of you, not abandon you, plans to give you the future you hope for.*
Jeremiah 29:11 (MSG)

**Speak Over Your Life** the truth of God's Word of what should be, your receiving life and life more abundantly in and through all things, no matter the storms of your life, they will cease and pass over. Receive your blessing by positioning yourself, which begins with you declaring, **Speaking Over Your Life,** to move you and your being in alignment with God's truth, your truth of what should be.  Although life and your circumstances may not cooperate the way you feel they should or even line up to produce the outcome of your abundant life, do not worry or be afraid, God knows what He is doing, just *Breathe: New Life.*  Inhale the possibilities amid your difficulties, for God is in and through all things, waiting to lead and guide you through or around your circumstances to His opportunity of escape for His promise to your abundant life.  God has laid out your way, your journey, beforehand, and created you and everything about you for that journey.  Trust God and yourself, and *Breathe: New Life*!

## January 26

*And we know that all things work together for good to them that love God, to them who are the called according to his purpose. For whom he did foreknow, he also did predestinate to be conformed to the image of his Son, that he might be the firstborn among many brethren. Moreover whom he did predestinate, them he also called: and whom he called, them he also justified: and whom he justified, them he also glorified.*
Romans 8:28-30

**Speak Over Your Life** that which should be as promised by God, although it may appear impossible and difficult to achieve, you have a promise; be confident and pursue it with everything you have.  To pursue that which you believe should be is not an easy task; you will get weary, frustrated, and want to give up, but you must remember that the One who promised is also responsible for ensuring that you are empowered to accomplish it. Empowerment is something that springs forth from within; you must believe first and then pursue it, leaving the how to the Author and Finisher of your faith to work out all things for the good. If you are willing to go, to pursue, God is willing to work it all out for you; it is His plan that has been predestined for your life. God, in His creation of you, built you for your journey, and thus, all that is required is simply responding to His call, His promises, for your life. I do not know why or how God does what He does, but I am confident that He can and will do what He has declared because He is inseparable from His Word and thus, faithful to His Word, Himself, for His revelation to come forth. **Speak Over Your Life** as if what should be is and *Breathe: New Life*, inhaling the Spirit of God, empowering you from within to receive all He has promised, for it has already been done!

**January 27**

*What God did in this case made it perfectly plain that his purpose is not a hit-or-miss thing dependent on what we do or don't do, but a sure thing determined by his decision, flowing steadily from his initiative.*
Romans 9:11 (MSG)

When we are on one accord with what should be for our lives as established by the Creator, the giver of life, we are well equipped; we are built for the journey to accomplish that which should be. Therefore, **Speak Over Your Life** as if it were, planting seeds within your mind that develop thoughts and ideas that push forward through your being to actions, bringing to pass that which has been spoken as should be.  The power of you going forth to **Speak Over Your Life** triggers what is necessary to co-create with God, to ***Breathe: New Life***.  As we choose to inhale the oxygen of God's Spirit, His promises for our lives, we send it forth throughout our being to bring to pass the actions necessary to conquer what is in our circumstances in order to live in the new life God has prepared.

## January 28

*He has saved us and called us to a holy life—not because of anything we have done but because of his own purpose and grace. This grace was given us in Christ Jesus before the beginning of time, but it has now been revealed through the appearing of our Savior, Christ Jesus, who has destroyed death and has brought life and immortality to light through the gospel.*
II Timothy 1:9-10 (NIV)

You can **Speak Over Your Life** the truth of God's promises for your life because God has already done it to fulfill His purpose and plan.  No matter how good we try to be, it will never be enough to make up for the difference of God's love, grace, and mercy to us; He blesses us not because we have earned it but simply because He wills it to be so.  Understand God's love for us is everlasting, not just in the sense of time; it transcends time to eternity, covering and lasting, despite and beyond our shortcomings, mistakes, and choice of wrong turns.  What God has promised is everlasting, and all you and I have to do is receive it by believing and taking action on that belief.  Our belief, our faith, is nurtured and developed as a result of us hearing the word of our promise;

therefore, **Speak Over Your Life** that which God has promised you, despite and in spite of you. The circumstances of your life serve as distractions and/or deterrents. Speak your truth from God and confront your circumstances from a position in which you drive your narrative. **Speak Over Your Life**, giving command to your mind, thoughts, and ideas, translating them into actions to *Breathe: New Life*, moving you forward in what should be as promised by God!

## January 29

*But ye are a chosen generation, a royal priesthood, an holy nation, a peculiar people; that ye should shew forth the praises of him who hath called you out of darkness into his marvellous light:*
I Peter 2:9

*Breathe: New Life* to and in your circumstances because you have been chosen for your life and your life chosen for you, and as you engage it, you will discover your internal strength and power to secure that which should be, the promise of your life and life more abundantly. Life, for chosen people, does not have to be perfect, and/or all things, including people, places, and things, cooperate with what should be for your life, you have the power to co-create with God, serve as the priest of your household, commanding all things toward your ability to be fruitful and multiply. Although it may appear impossible and too hard for you, remember you are not in this alone. You have been built for your journey, and you also have the Creator and Master of life's journey with you to show forth, to reveal, to witness God and His Word as truth. **Speak Over Your Life** the truth of God's promises for you, and though it may seem peculiar, given your circumstances, God, who is with you and built you, He has already overcome the world and brought all things into subjection to you, commanding you to go and *Breathe: New Life*!

## January 30

*Walking down the street, Jesus saw a man blind from birth. His disciples asked, "Rabbi, who sinned: this man or his parents, causing him to be born blind?" Jesus said, "You're asking the wrong question. You're looking for someone to blame. There is no such cause-effect here. Look instead for what God can do. We need to be energetically at work for the One who sent me here, working while the sun shines. When night falls, the workday is over. For as long as I am in the world, there is plenty of light. I am the world's Light." He said this and then spit in the dust, made a clay paste with the saliva, rubbed the paste on the blind man's eyes, and said, "Go, wash at the Pool of Siloam" (Siloam means "Sent"). The man went and washed—and saw. . . . He replied, "I know nothing about that one way or the other. But I know one thing for sure: I was blind . . . I now see."*
John 9:1-7, 25

The challenge to *Breathe: New Life* in our circumstances hinges on our ability to see, to have a vision, for what could and should be for our lives. Life's circumstances, along with our own human limitations, tend to clutter our lives, often leaving us feeling hopeless or blind to how we can transform them for the better. Therefore, in order to **Speak Over Your Life**, exercising the power

34

of life which is in your tongue, you must be able to see, to have vision; the impressing upon your mind that which could and should be. We cannot allow the difficulties of our lives, whether of our own making or the result of external forces, to cloud our ability to see clearly and to drive our narrative. God has called us to a realm of possibilities that surpasses what is or what has been done. We are trailblazers as we make ourselves available unto God for Him to do the exceedingly, abundantly, more than we can ever ask or think by the power that works within us. Activate your power by being available to God's Spirit to see, lead, and guide you in that which God has already ordained for your life, your vision, thus inhale oxygen, expand your lungs, and send energy to your being to **Breathe: New Life. Speak Over Your Life,** your vision, the truth of life and life more abundantly for you in your circumstances, and trigger your process to see clearly, discovering and uncovering that which can and should be for your life, despite and in spite of all things!

## January 31

*The LORD is my light and my salvation; whom shall I fear?*
*the LORD is the strength of my life; of whom shall I be afraid?*
*When the wicked, even mine enemies and my foes, came upon me*
*to eat up my flesh,*
*they stumbled and fell.*
*Though an host should encamp against me, my heart shall not*
*fear:*
*though war should rise against me, in this will I be confident.*
*One thing have I desired of the LORD, that will I seek after;*
*that I may dwell in the house of the LORD all the days of my life,*
*to behold the beauty of the LORD, and to enquire in his temple.*

*For in the time of trouble he shall hide me in his pavilion:*
*in the secret of his tabernacle shall he hide me;*
*he shall set me up upon a rock.*
*And now shall mine head be lifted up above mine enemies round*
*about me:*
*therefore will I offer in his tabernacle sacrifices of joy;*
*I will sing, yea, I will sing praises unto the LORD.*
Psalms 27:1-6


**Speak Over Your Life** the Word of God's truth, for it provides light in your circumstances, equipping you to navigate the course toward your life and life more abundantly in and through the circumstances.  The distractions and deceptions of your circumstances seek to separate you from the new life that is yours, representing darkness to confuse and confound your ability to move forward in your abundance.  Lift up Your Head in the light of God's Word, promises for your life, and allow the light to scatter the darkness.  **Speak Over Your Life**, scattering your darkness and focusing your mind, thoughts, and ideas in dwelling, residing in your truth, promises from God with confidence to *Breathe: New Life* into your circumstances.  Choose to *Breathe: New Life* and the light of your Word, your promise from God will illuminate the way which has been prepared for you, lifting you, your head, and being, over and beyond the circumstances, pointing the way to your new life abundantly!

# *INHALE*

## FEBRUARY

## February 1

*For the LORD God is a sun and shield:*
*the LORD will give grace and glory:*
*no good thing will he withhold from them that walk uprightly.*
Psalm 84:11

In order to **Breathe: New Life,** we must be intentional in our everyday walking around life to **Inhale**.  As we **Inhale**, we bring in air, oxygen, life to our being, everything God intends for our lives; fueling our heart, which pumps blood to all of our organs to live. Walk in the sun, the light of God's truth for your life, **Breathing: New Life** with the expectation of receiving His favor and revelation toward your promise, your Word.  **Inhale**, God is ever present everywhere and in everything.  Look for Him; diligently pursue what He has promised, and you get Him, including His favor and revelation for new life abundantly.

## February 2

*Blessed are those you choose*
*and bring near to live in your courts!*
*We are filled with the good things of your house,*
*of your holy temple.*
Psalm 65:4 (NIV)

God has chosen you and has pre-ordered for you a full life package that will bring prosperity, the life and life more abundantly promised specifically for you. Therefore, the decision to choose what God intends for your life is entirely yours and awaits your action to fulfill your promise. God will not force you or trick you into receiving the life and life more abundantly He has prepared; you must be willing to exercise your free will to choose, to intentionally **Inhale** that which would bring about your abundance. Your choice, by no means, will be free from frustration and/or weariness or wrong turns and detours; however, as long as you choose to live in the abundance God has prepared for you, it is yours. **Inhale** the new life by breathing in the very presence of God in and through your circumstances, and as you ***Breathe: New Life*** is revealed and formed in your circumstances. The more you **Inhale** God and His presence, the more you receive the fullness of joy, and while also being at His righthand, you receive pleasures forevermore, ***Breathe: New Life***!

## February 3

*May the favor of the Lord our God rest on us;*
*establish the work of our hands for us—*
*yes, establish the work of our hands.*
Psalm 90:17 (NIV)

**Inhale** the beauty of the Lord, meaning His favor in and over your life, and go forward in taking action on what you believe can and should be. God, in creating humankind, and specifically you, built you with the intent of your receiving His grace, favor. God knew and knows that you and I are not perfect and will make mistakes, wrong choices, and at times be downright defiant; however, His unconditional love for us triggers the extension of His grace, favor over our lives. ***Breathe: New Life*** by **Inhaling** God's favor, which is readily available to you, making up for your shortcomings, that whatever you lack, and/or whatever is refused to you. Therefore, work what you believe can and should be, taking actions that move you forward and mature you to and in God's promises fulfilled for your life, and God will do the rest, establishing the works of your hands and working out all things for your good. Go ahead and ***Breathe: New Life*** in your circumstances, for you have the favor of God to turn the impossible into the possible, your crooked places into straight pathways, your chaos and confusion into your heaven and earth!

## February 4

*In the shelter of your presence you hide them from all human intrigues; you keep them safe in your dwelling from accusing tongues.*
Psalm 31:20 (NIV)

***Breathe: New Life*** to your circumstances as you seek to be in the presence of God, the presence of His Word of truth for your life, and with that Word of truth, you dwell, reside in the presence of God. God and His Word are inseparable, and so the more you *Inhale* that which is the Word of truth for your life, including everyone and everything that supports your visionnerring and your subsequent actions, you will be empowered to execute your truth, revealing God and thus, His presence in and over your life! God's presence in your life provides you with the necessary shelter and assistance required to overcome obstacles, difficulties, and impossibilities beyond your human limitations; to work wonders in your life.  Go ahead and take a deep breath.  **Inhale** God's presence and abide in the shadows of His ability to shelter, guide, protect, and cause you to be triumphant in and through all things.  As you **Inhale** the presence of God, God the Spirit flows through you, equipping and transforming your being for the new life that is yours, just ***Breathe: New Life***!

## February 5

*You who sit down in the High God's presence, spend the night in Shaddai's shadow,*
Psalm 91:1 (MSG)

The challenge to ***Breathe: New Life*** involves the willingness to **Inhale** the very presence of God in our lives and allow it to flow in our circumstances.  Our willingness to **Inhale** is a direct result of our having the power of choice, the free will to choose the path for our lives, and, in so doing, to shoulder the responsibility and accountability for our actions.  When we choose a path that leads to the presence of God, we have additional support to navigate life, including the often unknown and sometimes beyond our control.  God's presence provides us assistance from the One who is the Creator of all things and also manifests as the Redeemer and Sustainer of life.  God, Creator, Redeemer, and Sustainer are inseparable from the Word of truth declared by God for our lives; that which can and should be.  Thus, the more we **Inhale** the Word of truth and that which supports and assists us in executing that Word for our lives, the more we have the inseparable Creator, Redeemer, and Sustainer of life to assist beyond human limitations and what is perceived to be the impossible!

## February 6

*At the time God made Earth and Heaven, before any grasses or*
*shrubs had sprouted from the ground—God hadn't yet sent rain*
*on Earth, nor was there anyone around to work the ground (the*
*whole Earth was watered by underground springs)—God formed*
*Man out of dirt from the ground and blew into his nostrils the*
*breath of life. The Man came alive—a living soul!*
Genesis 2:5-7 (MSG)

**Breathe: New Life** is an intentional act in which you must make
the necessary move, take the necessary actions, seek to do that
which is necessary to receive the new life as it should be.  We
learn from creation that God created everything and ensured it
could be nurtured; however, He needed someone to work His
creation for it to be fruitful and multiply, and He chose us.  With
the establishment of creation and everything necessary to
produce, God created humankind as His agents, co-creators, to
bring to pass the abundance, the exceedingly, abundantly, more
than.  The truth of creation is also the truth of our existence.  God
has provided the necessary seed of abundance for our lives as
well as an internal nurturing element, His breath, Spirit, for our
abundance, but we must choose to act, intentionally take up our
assignment, and work our harvest.  No matter your circumstances,
within them there is your seed of abundance and within you an
ungrounded spring of living water, internal power, to create that
which can and should be for your life abundantly.   Work your
circumstances, for they are pregnant with possibilities, seeds that
will transform your circumstances and you to live in the fulfilled

promises of God for your abundant life.  **Inhale**, the breath of God, and receive His power transformed into your energy to harvest the yield of your abundance, for God has provided everything you need to *Breathe: New Life*, acting intentionally toward your harvest!

## February 7

*Later on that day, the disciples had gathered together, but, fearful of the Jews, had locked all the doors in the house. Jesus entered, stood among them, and said, "Peace to you." Then he showed them his hands and side.  The disciples, seeing the Master with their own eyes, were awestruck. Jesus repeated his greeting: "Peace to you. Just as the Father sent me, I send you."  Then he took a deep breath and breathed into them. "Receive the Holy Spirit," he said. "If you forgive someone's sins, they're gone for good. If you don't forgive sins, what are you going to do with them?"*
John 20:19-23 (MSG)

Our being intentional as we **Breathe: New Life** takes its toll on us physically as well as spiritually, often causing us to become weary in our well-doing and in need of restoration.  The weariness of life is natural, and you and I must be aware and know that there are times in which we need restoration, periods of rest, rediscovery, and reimagining.  Rest is critical to our forging ahead.  **Inhaling** that which can and should be for our lives, and as we do so, we rediscover the internal power of God's Spirit, manifested through our gifts, causing us to *Breathe: New Life*, reimagining our outcomes.  Therefore, we must seek the restoration of our souls and our spirits, which keep us alive and fuel our drive toward what can and should be in our lives. Life will be filled with roadblocks and deterrents, some known and some unknown; thus, we must always be refueling our courage to forge through our fears, to co-create and synergize with God, releasing power to overcome all things. **Inhale** the restoration of God's Spirit that provides you courage, synergy with God's Spirit manifested in you by exercising your gifts/abilities that produce power to inherit all things!

## February 8

> *He knows us inside and out,*
> *keeps in mind that we're made of mud.*
> Psalm 103:14 (MSG)

*Breathe: New Life* by **Inhaling** all of the empowering possibilities before you. God knew and knows both your internal and external thoughts and actions, and has ordered your steps, created possibilities for the fulfillment of His promise of life and life more abundantly. The challenge before you and me is to choose, choose to **Inhale** the Spirit of promise in and through our lived experiences as well as trust the power and promise of God within us, and we will become pregnant with possibilities. Remember, we are made from mud, which can be both hard and soft; therefore, do not think that each and every possibility is it, possibilities is the means of transporting you to your appropriate opportunity to co-create with God that which can and should be for your life. *Breathe: New Life* and possess your possibilities, mingling them with the power within you to transform them into energy coupled with God's leading and directing to position you for walking through your doors of opportunity for life and life more abundantly!


## February 9

*The body is put back in the same ground it came from.*
*The spirit returns to God, who first breathed it.*
Ecclesiastes 12:7 (MSG)


*Breathe: New Life* by **Inhaling** the essence of God, the breath of life, which is His Word of truth for you and your life abundantly. As you **Inhale**, you position yourself in spaces that empower you to transform your life and your circumstances into what can and should be for your life by receiving the breath of life, making you a living soul. Life is a journey of reconciliation, reconciling where you are to where and what God intends, His promises for your life and life more abundantly. Thus, when He created you, He did so with the intent that you be alive, despite and in spite of the mud of life. **Inhale** God's Spirit, the essence of His being, which connects you to God and God, which is inseparable from His Word, makes you a living soul, alive amid your circumstances for living in the what can and should be for your life. Go ahead and *Breathe: New Life* from the Spirit of God so richly dwelling in your space, manifested in people, places, and things as agents for your transformation, empowering you to bring forth new life!


## February 10

*Yet you, Lord, are our Father.*
*We are the clay, you are the potter;*
*we are all the work of your hand.*
Isaiah 64:8 (NIV)


**Breathe: New Life** by embracing God as the potter and you as the clay, allowing Him to lead and guide you through and in your circumstances to the very space He has ordained for your life and life abundantly.  Embracing God as the potter entails seeking to **Inhale** God's Spirit, taking full control of your life, filling your lungs, and allowing them to fully soak up His power.  The expansion of your lungs is a direct result of soaking up God's Spirit and guidance for your life, and as you synergize with God, you are empowered to bring new life to your circumstances.  Your lungs are sponge material, and as you **Inhale** God's Spirit, it will consume you, causing you to expand to a position in which you are empowered to seize opportunities, producing life and life more abundantly, all because you **Breathe: New Life**!


## February 11


*The Spirit of God hath made me,*
*and the breath of the Almighty hath given me life.*
Job 33:4


**Breathe: New Life** by embracing the breath of God that makes you alive, a living soul.  To be alive, live as God has commanded, we must constantly **Inhale** the Spirit of God, His truth declared for our lives to transform us and our circumstances into the likeness

48

of that which can and should be.  The more we **Inhale** the oxygen of God's Word manifested by His Spirit dwelling within, we are empowered through this synergy with God; energized to forge ahead through our circumstances to work through them for the good.  It is God's Spirit that has made us and caused us to live, *Breathe: New Life* by your intentional action of receiving more and more of God's Spirit, the essence of Him that makes us a living soul, transforming your space to produce your abundant life!

## February 12

*For we are his workmanship, created in Christ Jesus unto good works, which God hath before ordained that we should walk in them.*
Ephesians 2:10

**Breathe: New Life** by taking in God's ordered steps for your life, which have been beforehand prepared just for you.  Understand that you are unique, fearfully and wonderfully made for your journey and the fulfillment of God's promises for your life.  To reach your previously prepared destination, you must navigate the circumstances of your life with the energy to overcome them, exercising your God-given strength and power to have dominion over them and be fruitful and multiply.  Therefore, it becomes critical that you **Inhale** the appropriate oxygen that will expand your lungs with the fullness of God, His promise for your life, and as the natural process of **Inhaling** flows, it will break down, transform your circumstances for the good.  Remember, you are not alone.  *Breathe: New Life* of God's beforehand prepared promises, thus His very presence in your life, and allow the synergy of His spirit and your energy to empower you to overcome and inherit all things!

## February 13

*You, however, know all about my teaching, my way of life, my purpose, faith, patience, love, endurance, persecutions, sufferings —what kinds of things happened to me in Antioch, Iconium and Lystra, the persecutions I endured. Yet the Lord rescued me from all of them. In fact, everyone who wants to live a godly life in Christ Jesus will be persecuted, while evildoers and impostors will go from bad to worse, deceiving and being deceived. But as for you, continue in what you have learned and have become convinced of, because you know those from whom you learned it, and how from infancy you have known the Holy Scriptures, which can make you wise for salvation through faith in Christ Jesus. All Scripture is God-breathed and is useful for teaching, rebuking, correcting, and training in righteousness, so that the servant of God[a] may be thoroughly equipped for every good work.*
II Timothy 3:10-17 (NIV)

Life, from time to time, demands that we evaluate where we are to successfully get to where we should be. Evaluations help us navigate the demands of life and our circumstances, which often place us at crossroads, requiring us to go right, left, forward, backward, or remain stuck at the intersection. The challenge at the intersection is further complicated by traffic flow. Will we be able to merge into, handle the transition required to get us to our destination?  What is most helpful in challenging situations is to take deep breaths, to **Inhale,** driving the necessary oxygen into our lungs, which expand and force the oxygen out to our heart, causing blood to flow, transforming food (possibilities) along the way into energy toward opportunities for the body (your life) to operate appropriately at full capacity.  Therefore, since the challenges of life are constant, we must constantly evaluate our breathing, especially if we desire to *Breathe: New Life*. Just as is normal when we appear at our Doctor's appointment, the Doctor checks our breathing as a way to determine the flow and process, appropriate functioning of the lungs to process to the heart and thus the pumping of energy to the body to function appropriately, so too must we, as Paul instructs Timothy.  Check out what you are **Inhaling** to determine if it is free-flowing and causes you to learn, to develop from your experiences, know-with-all for you achieving that which should be.  Further, is there a free-flowing spirit that challenges you to not just be but flow in the traffic of your life to that which has been prepared for you, and in flowing in such a way that provides you with the opportunity for practical application of your Word of promise?  *Breathe: New Life* demands that we constantly evaluate what we are **Inhaling** to ensure that the free-flowing spirit of that which will make us advantageous in our circumstances to seize the opportunities to overcome and inherit all things!

## February 14

*Do you see what this means—all these pioneers who blazed the way, all these veterans cheering us on? It means we'd better get on with it. Strip down, start running—and never quit! No extra*

*spiritual fat, no parasitic sins. Keep your eyes on Jesus, who both began and finished this race we're in. Study how he did it. Because he never lost sight of where he was headed—that exhilarating finish in and with God—he could put up with anything along the way: Cross, shame, whatever. And now he's there, in the place of honor, right alongside God. When you find yourselves flagging in your faith, go over that story again, item by item, that long litany of hostility he plowed through. That will shoot adrenaline into your souls! In this all-out match against sin, others have suffered far worse than you, to say nothing of what Jesus went through— all that bloodshed! So don't feel sorry for yourselves.*
Hebrews 12:1-4 (MSG)

Critical to breathing, which impacts one's ability to operate at their maximum functioning capacity, is the quality of the air one breathes. Because of concerns about air quality, environmental controls are key to space development, especially in urban communities. The lack of quality of air lessens the ability for people to function at their maximum potential. Please note that there is no perfect atmosphere or space free of toxins; however, the higher the quality of the air breathed, the greater the chance that the body can function at its maximum potential. The same is true for living in the fullness of life and life more abundantly, and thus, the writer of Hebrews suggests that the quality of what we are **Inhaling** is essential as we run this race called life. The writer of Hebrews suggests that if we are to ***Breathe: New Life***, it will require a quality atmosphere to ensure we are fully equipped and energized, functioning at our maximum potential, to break down all things for the good to live in our life and life more abundantly as promised. Therefore, we should be filling our spaces as a result of discerning what and/or who brings about a quality of sustainability to our experiences, forcing us to act and build, not just for the now but for eternity. In addition, to discern whether or not the things we are **Inhaling** bring to bear a quality of vision, which focuses on getting us to our destination. And finally, a quality of motivation is the incentive to keep us pressing forward through all the obstacles of our lives. ***Breathe: New Life*** by creating spaces in which you are provided with a quality of air to **Inhale** so that you operate at your maximum potential toward your promises.

## February 15

*For everything that was written in the past was written to teach us, so that through the endurance taught in the Scriptures and the encouragement they provide we might have hope.*
Romans 15:4 (NIV)

The power of learning is very underestimated in our society because it may somehow offend our sensibilities, preconceived notions, and/or political/social principles. However, if your sensibilities, notions, and/or principles are so solid and you are so right, there is nothing you can learn, you can explore, and it will not take from you what you may believe. It very well may develop, nurture, and strengthen your belief. When you confine your spirit of learning, you limit your ability to grow, mature, and develop into that which can and should be, as well as see what can and should be bigger and more profound than you originally thought. ***Breathe: New Life*** happens because we are willing to **Inhale** a spirit of learning that makes room for us to stretch our thoughts and positions while at the same time strengthening us to move forward informed, strategic, and expanded to achieve that which can and should be for our lives.  Open yourself to expanded learning, including exposure and information gathering that is both affirming and critical, so you may be fully equipped and motivated, with hope, to fulfill your promises, despite and in spite of obstacles and persecutions.

## February 16

*If a man therefore purge himself from these, he shall be a vessel unto honour, sanctified, and meet for the master's use, and prepared unto every good work.*
II Timothy 2:21

***Breathe: New Life*** in which you **Inhale** from your atmosphere that which is empowering, purging yourself of the toxicity that exists in your life while also energizing to press forward in what can and should be for your life.  The process to **Inhale,** breathe in from your atmosphere; an intentional, creative space that is not perfect yet filled with quality and free-flowing material, which enhances your ability to produce endless energy and boundless strength toward what can and should be.   The quality of your intake determines the leverage you have to become an overcomer and transformer of your circumstances, empowering you to live in and through them.  In addition, the quality of your intake frees you to become more flexible and adjustable through the Spirit of God dwelling within, leading and guiding you to actions and pathways that create ways in your impossibilities: the creation of rivers in deserts and the making of crooked spaces straight.  ***Breathe: New Life*** by preparation, creating, and cultivating an atmosphere in which you can **Inhale** quality that also makes you flexible to be more than a conqueror, overcomer, and inheritor of all things.

## February 17

*Not that I have already obtained all this, or have already arrived at my goal, but I press on to take hold of that for which Christ Jesus took hold of me.  Brothers and sisters, I do not consider myself yet to have taken hold of it. But one thing I do: Forgetting what is behind and straining toward what is ahead, I press on toward the goal to win the prize for which God has called me heavenward in Christ Jesus.*
Philippians 3:12-14 (NIV)

Often, we find ourselves in bondage to our past, our mistakes, and/or our shortcomings, to the point that it prevents us from moving forward or even attempting to do so, and thus we give up on our chances to transform our circumstances.  If what we believe can and should be is to become a reality, we must be willing to move forward, even with our "baggage," expecting that the journey to our promise will unentangle us from that baggage. The key to our route of unentangling from the excess baggage we carry must be intentional, creating a conducive atmosphere, a space in which we **Inhale** that empowers and gives us the courage to press forward.  No matter where we are in life and what we are carrying, legitimate or not, we must continue to live, to ***Breathe: New Life***, otherwise, we will become complacent and thus, stop maturing in the fullness of what can and should be for our lives. God desires to do exceedingly, abundantly, more than we can ever ask or think, and therefore, it requires endless energy and boundless strength to press forward and stay in the game of life at all times. Stop allowing where you are, where you come from, what has transpired, or even present struggles to contain you; press forward through it all. Intentionally create an atmosphere, space filled with people, places, and things that empower and encourage you, and **Inhale** to *Breathe: New Life*, free-flowing and of quality that keeps you pressing toward the higher calling at all times!

## February 18

*Now it was not written for his sake alone, that it was imputed to him; But for us also, to whom it shall be imputed, if we believe on him that raised Jesus our Lord from the dead;*
Romans 4:23-24

*Breathe: New Life* is critical for transforming your present realities into what can and should be for your life. Building something new requires new insight, as well as the energy and strength to take on the challenge of moving from the comfortable and convenient to the unknown or never-before-experienced. Naturally, we all want to remain in spaces and places in which we are comfortable and have some familiarity, even if it is not perfect; however, we will never evolve to live at our maximum potential until we are willing to *Breathe: New Life*. If we are to advance in the possibilities that are before us to seize appropriate opportunities to live in the fullness of our potential, we must be willing to move and transform where we are, *Breathe: New Life*. Energy in our bodies is produced as a result of the **Inhale** of oxygen, which acts as a transformative agent, transforming our food into energy that flows to all of our organs, creating a capacity for function. Therefore, be intentional about your space and place to **Inhale** what will act as agents of transformation, breaking down the stuff of your life, life's circumstances, to equip you with appropriate energy for operating at your maximum capacity to live life and life more abundantly!

## February 19

*But you, Timothy, man of God: Run for your life from all this. Pursue a righteous life—a life of wonder, faith, love, steadiness, courtesy. Run hard and fast in the faith. Seize the eternal life, the life you were called to, the life you so fervently embraced in the presence of so many witnesses.*
I Timothy 6:11-12 (MSG)

Paul's encouragement to Timothy, to run hard and fast in what you believe can and should be, over and over again during their relationship, indicates how much Paul believed that within each of us lies the willpower to win if we would diligently pursue it. Our outcomes are significantly connected to what we put into the game, and as people of faith, we know that with our efforts synergized with God's grace, unmerited favor, we will receive exceedingly, abundantly, more than we can ever ask or think. *Breathe: New Life* is an intentional act of running hard and fast in what we believe, ensuring that we **Inhale** appropriately to be energized to win. As we **Inhale**, we breathe in the atmosphere's material that will help us endure and transform to win, to operate at our maximum capacity. Therefore, we must be intentional about the atmosphere in which we exist, ensuring that it is filled with materials that are of high quality as well as free-flowing toward what can and should be for our life, energizing and strengthening us to transform, overcome whatever may exist to inherit all things.  Create your space, your atmosphere to support your running hard and fast in what you believe can and should be for your life, therefore *Breathe: New Life* for it is critical to achieving your maximum potential as God has ordained, your life and life more abundantly!

## February 20

*And Jabez was more honourable than his brethren: and his mother called his name Jabez, saying Because I bare him with sorrow. And Jabez called on the God of Israel, saying, Oh that thou wouldest bless me indeed, and enlarge my coast, and that thine hand might be with me, and that thou wouldest keep me from evil, that it may not grieve me! And God granted him that which he requested.*
I Chronicles 4:9-10

Life is unpredictable and challenges one's ability to maintain control; some challenges are of your choosing, and others are a result of someone else's choices.  Nevertheless, you and I must take life by the horns and not allow the challenges to drive.  To live at your full potential, you must inhale what fosters it. *Breathe: New Life* is required to live at your maximum potential and is dependent upon the makeup of your atmosphere, the space in which you exist.   Be intentionally creative with your space to ensure you are fueled with the right materials to empower you, expand your lungs, and drive the challenges you

face to your maximum potential.  Please understand that if you ever have a new life and it is abundant, it will not simply be because of a lack of challenges or even the reparations made for and in your challenges; it will be because you chose to intentionally and strategically drive your narrative.  Jabez, labeled a child of sorrow, refused to accept that as his life's narrative; he was of the lineage of Judah, a praiser, a worshipper, and thus he chose to transform his life toward his destiny, not his challenge. Jabez reclaimed his truth and required more of himself, asking God to bless "him," his life for that which would lead to his abundance, to be owned and operated by and through him.
*Breathe: New Life* today by ensuring the space you operate in spurs your sense of destiny, independence of any labels, and freedom to settle in a space beyond repair; a space in which you press forward to your higher calling, the maximum level of potential!

## February 21

*The sons of Joseph spoke to Joshua, saying, "Why have you given us only one lot and one portion as an inheritance, when we are a numerous people whom the Lord has so far blessed?" Then Joshua replied, "If you are a numerous people, go up to the forest and clear ground for yourselves there in the land of the Perizzites and the Rephaim, since the hill country of Ephraim is too narrow for you." The sons of Joseph said, "The hill country is not enough for us, and all the Canaanites who live in the valley have iron chariots, both those who are in Beth-shean and its towns and those in the Valley of Jezreel." Joshua said to the house of Joseph, to Ephraim and to Manasseh, "You are numerous people and have great*

*power; you shall not have only one lot, but the hill country shall be yours. For though it is a forest, you shall clear it and possess it to its farthest borders; for you shall drive out the Canaanites, even though they have iron chariots and though they are strong."*
Joshua 17:14-18 (AMP)

As we *Breathe: New Life,* it is critical that the atmosphere, our space, is conducive to building and developing confidence and courage to engage our circumstances, especially our fears. The power of fear over our lives and circumstances often prevents us from taking on the challenges that stand in our way; we give up before we even try. Therefore, we need to **Inhale** material that pushes and motivates us to resist the fear of the unknown. We will never be able to achieve the new from a position of comfort and convenience; new, by definition, is unknown, and we must be willing to conquer the fear of the unknown to seize the promises of what can and should be for our lives. Remember, we are a great people; we have not been given the spirit of fear but of power, love, and a sound mind. *Breathe: New Life* and **Inhale** your spirit of power, confidence, and courage to overcome what appears impossible, discovering options and/or strategies that allow you to leverage your strengths over weaknesses and opportunities over threats. Thus, we must be intentional about creating an atmosphere, a space that builds and cultivates our power, confidence, and courage, to overcome our fears, producing energy and strength to seize and possess our new life, the what can and should be!

**February 22**

*The blessing of the LORD, it maketh rich,*
*and he addeth no sorrow with it.*
Proverbs 10:22


**Breathe: New Life** into your circumstances by how you define the relationship between yourself and your circumstances. The primary factor in overcoming your circumstances is how you approach them. If you view your circumstances as the driving force behind your narrative, they will define you, the relationship, and the outcome. However, if you refuse to be determined by your circumstances and reclaim your truth in the circumstance, you become the driver and definer of your outcome. The truth of your situation is that you are blessed, and even though the circumstances appear not to confirm it, you are. **Inhale** and seek your blessing, taking the authority God has given to you to live, overcoming and inheriting all things. To successfully take back the reins of your circumstances, you must be both confident and courageous, acting with boldness to exercise your God-given authority to drive your own narrative. The confidence and courage required must be cultivated and fed; therefore, you must be intentional about creating your atmosphere, a space that is conducive to nurturing and feeding you to achieve that which you believe can and should be. Seek to fill your atmosphere with people, places, and things that strengthen, stretch, and mature you in that which can and should be for your life, thus, fueling your confidence and courage because you choose to **Inhale** and **Breathe: New Life**.


**February 23**

*The God of your father—may he help you!*
*And may The Strong God—may he give you his blessings,*
*Blessings tumbling out of the skies,*
*blessings bursting up from the Earth—*
*blessings of breasts and womb.*
*May the blessings of your father*
*exceed the blessings of the ancient mountains,*
*surpass the delights of the eternal hills;*
*May they rest on the head of Joseph,*
*on the brow of the one consecrated among his brothers.*
Genesis 49:25-26 (MSG)

If we choose to **Breathe: New Life**, God has prepared everything we need to fill our atmosphere, to **Inhale** the fuel necessary to empower us to operate at our maximum capacity. Operating at our maximum capacity means we must be energized and strengthened to withstand the wiles of evil and darkness that would separate us from what can and should be, as promised by God. Remember, we wrestle not against flesh and blood but against spiritual wickedness in high places, the spirit of the unknown, such as fear, unworthiness, lack of self-esteem, depression, etc., as we seek to live in the life and life more abundantly promised. Therefore, we must constantly fuel and refuel our engines to withstand and overcome the things that are destined to distract, deter, and downright kill our progress. **Inhale** from your atmosphere the very spirit of overcoming that makes you more than a conqueror in all things. If you thirst, diligently pursue that which God has ordained for your life, what can and should be, God will not only quench your thirst but also empower you to overcome and inherit all things. **Inhale** and *Breathe: New Life*!

## February 24

*The Lord has greatly blessed my master, and he has become great (wealthy, powerful); He has given him flocks and herds, and silver and gold, and servants and maids, and camels and donkeys.*
Genesis 24:35 (AMP)

Without question, as we **Inhale** the appropriate materials to support our living in what can and should be for our lives, we will be empowered to seize and walk into the abundance of our life and life more abundantly. The life God has declared and prepared for us is much greater than we can conceive, and that greater is waiting on our choice to live in it. Therefore, be very intentional to *Breathe: New Life* by creating an atmosphere, a space, in which you have a wealth of materials fueling your energy and strength to take on your circumstances and leverage them for your good. Your abundance is waiting for you. God has already richly blessed you; it is just up to you to become everything God intends, and with it, you will live in the overflow of life and life more abundantly!

## February 25

*Then Isaac planted [seed] in that land [as a farmer] and reaped in the same year a hundred times [as much as he had planted], and*

*the Lord blessed and favored him.  And the man [Isaac] became*
*great and gained more and more until he became very wealthy*
*and extremely distinguished; he owned flocks and herds and a*
*great household [with a number of servants], and the Philistines*
*envied him.*
Genesis 26:12-14 (AMP)


**Breathe: New Life** is made possible as we are intent on **inhaling** from an atmosphere filled with materials that build and develop our energy and strength to combat our challenges, enabling us to live to our maximum potential.  The power of the material that we **Inhale** is not enough; we must put that material to work, working our field to meet and overcome whatever may exist that separates us from living at our maximum potential and seizing that which can and should be for our lives.  Remember, faith without works is dead; thus, if we believe and possess the confidence that we can do something but never put it to the test, it is dead and useless. Get up and work your field, you have ensured that the atmosphere in which you exist is filled with the appropriate material to give you the energy to work out all things for the good in partnership with Christ, the blood penetrating all things on your behalf.  As you **Inhale** the appropriate amount of oxygen, it goes into your bloodstream, breaking down food and transforming it into energy, which feeds your organs and your body to function at its capacity.  The blood is working on your behalf, feed it with the right materials and work your field, you have already overcome to inherit all things, the very what can and should be for your life, *Breathe: New Life*!


**February 26**

*Remember that God, your God, gave you the strength to produce*
*all this wealth to confirm the covenant that he promised to your*
*ancestors—as it is today.*
Deuteronomy 8:18 MSG

The intentionality of creating an atmosphere that fuels your energy and strength to combat the challenges in your life yields an abundant, overflowing harvest. God's intention for all of our lives is that we would live life and live it more abundantly; we would not need anything and can just simply enjoy the fullness of life and bask in His glory, His revelation to and for us. As we **Inhale** from our atmosphere, we produce the necessary agents of transformation that align our lives with what can and should be, giving us the energy and strength to engage all things for our good, overcoming and inheriting the very abundant promises of God. Remember, God desires for you to be fruitful and multiply, to produce all the wealth and more according to His riches. Go ahead and *Breathe: New Life* into and for your circumstances. **Inhale** the resources God has for your life and live life and life more abundantly!

## February 27

*Riches and honour are with me;*
*yea, durable riches and righteousness.*
*My fruit is better than gold,*
*yea, than fine gold; and my revenue than choice silver.*
*I lead in the way of righteousness,*

*in the midst of the paths of judgment:*
*That I may cause those that love me to inherit substance;*
*and I will fill their treasures.*
Proverbs 8:18-21

Among my favorite videos on TikTok are those with the opening line "Excuse me, let me boast" because it reflects a choice that is made, in the midst of it all, to celebrate what you do have, and as a result, you realize that you are rich beyond measure. The confidence and assurance that you are blessed beyond what you deserve are clear indications of both your humility and your reliance on the Creator of all things, who sheds His grace and favor on your life. Your life is not determined by people, places, or things, but instead by your choice to believe in God, His Word for your life. God, His Word for you is inseparable from one another, and thus, when you choose to believe Him and His Word, you realize you are blessed and rich, possessing what you need to live abundantly and/or overcome to inherit all things. ***Breathe: New Life*** because you have a right to transform any and all things for the good in collaboration with God, His Word for your life. ***Breathe: New Life*** so that you might expand your lungs, enlarge your territory, receive the exceedingly, abundantly more than. ***Breathe: New Life*** because you have chosen to be blessed, and thus, you create a space and mindset that causes you to operate from a place of being blessed with riches and honor. As God and His Word pour out on you, you, in turn, pour out into your space, and thus **Inhale,** creating a cycle of blessings that makes you rich!

## February 28

*Wealth and riches are in his house,*
*And his righteousness endures forever.*
Psalm 112:3 (AMP)

The power of discernment allows us to evaluate the quality and free-flowing nature of the materials in our atmosphere to determine what value they bring to our lives and to our outcomes, destination, the place of what can and should be for our lives. Our exercising discernment allows us to be intentional and specific in our preparation to handle the circumstances of our lives, synergizing with God so that whatever we engage in, we would transform and overcome for our good. As you ***Breathe: New Life***, maximize your potential for your desired outcomes so that you **Inhale** from a wealthy space, an atmosphere that is broad, diverse, abundant, and sustainable. The intrinsic value of your atmosphere will equip you for the required transformation and fuel your energy and strength for what can and should be in your life. God, who is inseparable from His Word, is your very present help in focusing and guiding you, identifying what will empower you to transform your circumstances into new life and maximize your potential for life and life more abundantly!

# *EXHALE*

## MARCH

## March 1

*Long life is in her right hand;*
*in her left hand are riches and honor.*
*Her ways are pleasant ways,*
*and all her paths are peaceful.*
*She is a tree of life to those who take hold of her;*
*those who hold her fast will be blessed.*
Proverbs 3:16-18 (NIV)

**Breathe: New Life** is an intentional act that accesses the atmosphere to expand life to its maximum potential in time and eternity.  Therefore, what we choose, discern to access from our space, the atmosphere is critical for the quality of life we will have both in our here and now as well as in the future.  The choices we make to cultivate and nurture the spaces that will bring us energy and strength over our lifetimes are paramount to our establishing and running our race for both short-and long-term benefit.  Choose today to create, cultivate, and sustain your space with that which will bring about peace, harmony, with God's Word for your life, out of the vast resources around you of people, places, and things.  As you seek the peace of that which is around you, you will find peace, and it will take hold of you and your life, causing you to **Exhale** and *Breathe: New Life*!

## March 2

*So above all, constantly seek God's kingdom and his righteousness, then all these less important things will be given to you abundantly. Refuse to worry about tomorrow, but deal with each challenge that comes your way, one day at a time. Tomorrow will take care of itself.*
Matthew 6:33-34 (TPT)

Critical to transforming your circumstances into a new life, your life and life more abundantly, is releasing yourself from excessive baggage. It is very difficult to press forward in your life, carrying unnecessary weight. Excess weight holds you back from exercising at your maximum potential. Anything worth having is worth the work it takes to get it done, and therefore, to lessen your stress, stretch, **Exhale**, release the toxicity in your life, and press forward. God is inseparable from His Word of truth for your life; therefore, focus on your Word, and if anything is unlike or hinders the realization of the Word of truth for you, **Exhale,** loose it, and let go. By no means do I suggest that you ignore the challenges of your life; I do suggest that you discern the excess baggage. Is it worth facing head-on, or is it better to starve it of your attention to focus on pressing forward? Seek God and His Word, the rightness of His promise for your life, and let the other stuff go. Tomorrow will take care of itself. ***Breathe: New Life,*** and the new life and energy in your lighter position will make everything different as you go forward!

## March 3

*As wisdom increases, a great treasure is imparted, greater than many bars of refined gold.*
Proverbs 3:14 (TPT)


To **Breathe: New Life** brings in the new, materials necessary to build, cultivate, and energize you to live in the fulfillment of your life and life more abundantly,  assisting you to take on a spirit of overcoming.  However, for the intake of the Spirit that transforms and overcomes your circumstances, the way must be cleared for the Spirit to take up residence in our lungs, thus maximizing our capacity to **Exhale**.  **Exhale** releases the toxicity, the excess baggage we are carrying that stands in the way of our ability to overcome and transform our lives and circumstances into that which can and should be, live in our maximum potential.  Wisdom is the power of our experiences working together for our good, resting in our ability to make out of our experiences that which promotes maximum potential, creating a cache of lived experiences, wisdom.  Therefore, as opportunities to receive wisdom increase toward the outcome for our life and life more abundantly, God's Word for our lives is revealed as truth, and the untruths of our lives with their toxicity and excess baggage are released.  Thus, **Breathe: New Life**, and as we **Exhale**, we make room for lived experiences to transform and overcome our circumstances, pressing and building our way forward to living in God's Word for our lives, living at our maximum potential!



## March 4


*Receive my instruction and not silver;*

*and knowledge rather than choice gold.*
*For wisdom is better than rubies;*
*and all the things that may be desired are not to be compared to*
*it.*
Proverbs 8:10-11


If we are to **Breathe: New Life,** we must choose that which will empower us by converting our circumstances into what fuels our press toward what can and should be for our lives. The more we access that which empowers us to produce the energy and strength required to overcome, the more our lungs and bodies need to process it, causing us to **Exhale** what is unnecessary and/ or a hindrance to our progression. As we breathe in from our atmosphere, which is not pure or perfect, we take in both the good and bad, and as we choose that which empowers us to transform our materials into energy for our good, we must discern and discard that which does not work for our good. **Exhale** the toxicity of your life and make room for the more, which embodies energy and strength, empowering you to overcome and inherit all things and to live in your maximum potential.


## March 5


*The fear of the LORD is clean, enduring forever:*
*the judgments of the LORD are true and righteous altogether.*
*More to be desired are they than gold, yea, than much fine gold:*
*sweeter also than honey and honeycomb.*
*Moreover by them is thy servant warned:*
*and in the keeping of them, there is great reward.*
*Who can understand his errors?*

*cleanse thou me from secret faults.*
*Keep back thy servant also from presumptuous sins;*
*let them not have dominion over me:*
*then shall I be upright,*
*and I shall be innocent from the great transgression.*
*Let the words of my mouth,*
*and the meditation of my heart, be acceptable in thy sight,*
*O LORD, my strength, and my redeemer.*
Psalm 19:9-14

***Breathe: New Life*** is the challenge of constantly cleaning ourselves, refueling, and releasing to press forward with maximum energy and strength to achieve what can and should be in our lives.  The challenge of cleansing demands, first, that we position ourselves to receive more of what will develop and nurture our energy and strength to achieve and live in what can and should be.  Thus, we must be intentional about the atmosphere in which we exist to ensure it provides that which fuels our energy and strength.  In addition, we must be intentional about making room and releasing excessive baggage so we can maximize our intake of appropriate fuel to sustain our energy and strength to overcome our circumstances.  Release, **Exhale,** that which only takes up space and does absolutely nothing but continue to keep you separated (in sin) from living at your maximum potential and allow the meditation of your heart, more of what can and should be, to take up residence.  ***Breathe: New Life*** by cleansing your life to make room for more, fueling your growth, and releasing excessive baggage to help you maximize your potential to overcome and live more abundantly!

# March 6

*Let me feel your tender love, for I am yours.*
*Give me more understanding of your wonderful ways.*
*I need more revelation from your Word*
*to know more about you, for I'm in love with you!*
*Lord, the time has come for you to break through,*
*for evil men keep breaking your laws.*
*Truly, your message of truth means more to me*
*than a vault filled with the purest gold.*
*Every word you speak, every truth revealed, is always right*
*and beautiful to me, for I hate what is phony or false.*
Psalm 119:124-128 (TPT)

Life can be very difficult to navigate, especially when it is filled with complex and difficult circumstances, and we have no understanding of what, when, or how to do what is necessary to live at our full potential. Although we have a promise from God, our Word of truth, however, amid the complexity and difficulty of our circumstances, we appear lost, not just in understanding but also in the sense of defeat. When we are lost, we need to find our way to that place in our circumstances, despite their complexity and difficulty, in which we can live in the fullness of our capacity, to *Breathe: New Life*. The new life is synonymous with us being more than conquerors and taking back the reins of our narrative, despite our circumstances, which gives way to **Exhale** into our living in the revelation of truth, God's Word for our lives. When we allow God's Word, understanding, and revelation of His truth for our lives to take center stage, we can **Exhale**, releasing the untruths and phoniness of our lives, making room for a vault filled with God's Word and revelation. *Breathe: New Life* and **Exhale** the toxicity of what is not the truth for your life and your circumstances, including the facades that come along with the untruth, and fill your space with God's Word and revelation, providing you understanding and direction to live!

## March 7

*Then he taught me, and he said to me, "Take hold of my words with all your heart; keep my commands, and you will live. Get wisdom, get understanding; do not forget my words or turn away from them. Do not forsake wisdom, and she will protect you; love her, and she will watch over you. The beginning of wisdom is this: Get wisdom. Though it cost all you have, get understanding. Cherish her, and she will exalt you; embrace her, and she will honor you. She will give you a garland to grace your head and present you with a glorious crown."*
Proverbs 4:4-9 (NIV)

To receive our crown, our reward for our actions, to **Breathe: New Life,** demands our willingness to engage in the process of our life by both taking in and releasing, committing to **Exhale** the excessive and toxic so we may live at our maximum potential. Whatever we experience is an opportunity to gain wisdom, lessons learned that will empower and equip us to forge ahead in what can and should be for our lives. The wisdom to inhale is that which energizes and strengthens, and to **Exhale** is the release of excess baggage and that which is toxic, hindering, if not preventing, our pressing forward. No matter what is going on in your life, **Breathe: New Life** with an emphasis on your ability to **Exhale**, releasing from your life that which separates, hinders, and dampens your operating at your maximum capacity to live in your promise of life and life more abundantly.  In all, you're getting, get understanding and releasing what is excessive and unnecessary, pressing forward to what can and should be for your life

## March 8

*Wherewithal shall a young man cleanse his way? by taking heed thereto according to thy word. With my whole heart have I sought thee:*
*O let me not wander from thy commandments.  Thy word have I hid in mine heart,*
*that I might not sin against thee.  Blessed art thou, O LORD: teach me thy statutes.  With my lips have I declared*
*all the judgments of thy mouth.  I have rejoiced in the way of thy testimonies,*
*as much as in all riches.  I will meditate in thy precepts, and have respect unto thy ways.  I will delight myself in thy statutes:*
*I will not forget thy word.*
Psalm 119:9-16

The power of our ability to **Breathe: New Life** is manifested in its cleansing value, which helps us to operate at our maximum potential for living life and life more abundantly.  Whenever we are filled with too much stuff, excessive baggage, toxic materials, weights, and labels that are not intended for us, we are weighed down and hampered, hindered in our progress forward, and/or our take off to what can and should be for our lives.  The more we free ourselves of the necessary baggage and toxic materials of our lives, the better equipped we are to face whatever adversary stands in our way or hinders our progress toward our expected end. **Breathe: New Life** and naturally **Exhale** the excessive baggage and toxicity accumulated throughout your life experiences and press toward the higher calling for you! The continuous carrying of excessive baggage and toxicity will cause you to live beneath your potential and distract you from the fulfillment of your truth, the Word of God for your life, causing you to miss opportunities to seize and possess your promises. Cleanse your way by taking deep breaths of new life and allow your new life to **Exhale** the excess that distracts, deters, and downright deviates you from your word of truth, the promise of your life and life more abundantly!

## March 9

*O Lord, truly I am Your servant;*
*I am Your servant, the son of Your handmaid;*
*You have unfastened my chains.*
*I will offer to You the sacrifice of thanksgiving*
*And will call on the name of the Lord.*
*I will pay my vows to the Lord,*
*Yes, in the presence of all His people,*
*In the courts of the Lord's house (temple)—*
*In the midst of you, O Jerusalem.*
*Praise the Lord! (Hallelujah!)*
Psalm 116:16-19 AMP

*Breathe: New Life* allows us to make room for the blessings that are intended for our lives. As we **Exhale**, we make room for the more that will equip and empower us to live to our maximum potential as God intends. God has promised and already prepared exceedingly, abundantly, more than we can ever ask or think; however, it awaits our willingness to work our field, to respond to his call for our lives, and as we do so, we release, trigger the outpour of our abundance. Our trigger for a new life is preparation to receive, and thus to take in that which equips and empowers us to go through life, working out all things for the good and overcoming whatever exists to arrive at our place of destiny, in which we submit our availability to be used of God. Today, **Exhale** whatever is necessary to make room for more, so you are equipped and empowered to receive your abundance. The choice is yours, pay your vows by taking a long, deep breath, *Breathe: New Life*, and **Exhale**!

## March 10

> *My troubles turned out all for the best—*
> *they forced me to learn from your textbook.*
> *Truth from your mouth means more to me*
> *than striking it rich in a gold mine.*
> Psalm 119:71-72 (MSG)

The troubles of our lives have come so that we may **Exhale**, release the unnecessary baggage and toxicity of our lives, therefore, to ensure they do not come to hurt or harm us but instead to prosper us. The troubles may have one intent, but God works them all out for our good, taking our troubles and turning the process into one that will strengthen and empower us to live life and life more abundantly.  The advantage and privilege of our relationship with the Creator-God provide us, through the Spirit, with insight into what God has intended for us, and, through that insight and by synergizing with God, we can receive the best even from our troubles.  The Creator-God uses our troubles as a cleansing process, sifting out what is unhelpful and downright harmful, and, because of our willingness to **Exhale**, it frees us from their detrimental effects and makes room for our new life. *Breathe: New Life* for God has spoken into your circumstances, even your troubles, His Word of truth, and it will prevail.  Do your part, **Exhale** and make room to take on more of the life and life more abundantly promised you!

## March 11

*I have not turned aside from Your ordinances,*
*For You have taught me.*
*How sweet are Your words to my taste,*
*Sweeter than honey to my mouth!*
*From Your precepts I get understanding;*
*Therefore I hate every false way.*
Psalm 119:102-104 (AMP)

Our intentionality to *Breathe: New Life* encompasses our willingness to **Exhale** what is excessive and toxic, empowering us to press forward in our higher calling.  Our breathing includes the ability to **Exhale**, making room for more, including renewed energy to fuel our progression and our operating at our maximum potential. The more we take in the Word of truth for our lives and that which supports our Word being made real, the more we understand how to navigate life and our circumstances, leveraging them for good. Therefore, do not hesitate to **Exhale**, release the old, the baggage, the toxic, the materials that hinder going forward, and take in the new. ***Breathe: New Life,*** and with it, you gain understanding, insight, to navigate life and your circumstances, gaining energy to press toward that which can and should be for your life, your higher calling!

## March 12

*And isn't it true that we respect our earthly fathers even though they corrected and disciplined us? Then we should demonstrate even greater respect for God, our spiritual Father, as we submit to his life-giving discipline. Our parents corrected us for the short time of our childhood as it seemed good to them. But God corrects us throughout our lives for our good, giving us an invitation to share his holiness. Now all discipline seems to be painful at the time, yet later it will produce a transformation of character, bringing a harvest of righteousness and peace to those who yield to it. So be made strong even in your weakness by lifting your tired hands in prayer and worship. And strengthen your weak knees, for as you keep walking forward on God's paths all your stumbling ways will be divinely healed!*
Hebrews 12:9-13 (TPT)

The powerful thing about life is that without trying, it provides us experiences, the good and the bad, that teach us lessons and in ways discipline us so that we might choose a pathway. The pathway we choose is reflective and informed by our lived experiences and the wisdom of our lives. If we choose to leverage those for the good, we find possibilities that lead to opportunities to live to our maximum potential, in the place of our life and life more abundantly. The choice is ours, given to us by God at Creation, which gives us the free will to choose our pathway; remember that life and its circumstances have no power over you unless you give it to them. *Breathe: New Life* and **Exhale**, release excessive baggage and toxicity based on your choice to press forward into your pathway. Choosing to retain excessive baggage and toxicity will bloat you, reducing your ability to take in more of what will assist you, and it will weigh you down, making it more difficult to press forward in what can and should be your life. Receive your life's experiences and their discipline and discern that which is wise for your pressing forward, developing a cache of wisdom that leads and guides you in the pathway for your life and life more abundantly!

## March 13

*In the days when the judges ruled, there was a famine in the land. So a man from Bethlehem in Judah, together with his wife and two sons, went to live for a while in the country of Moab. The man's name was Elimelek, his wife's name was Naomi, and the names of his two sons were Mahlon and Kilion. They were Ephrathites from Bethlehem, Judah. And they went to Moab and lived there. Now Elimelek, Naomi's husband, died, and she was left with her two*

*sons. They married Moabite women, one named Orpah and the*
*other Ruth. After they had lived there about ten years, both*
*Mahlon and Kilion also died, and Naomi was left without her two*
*sons and her husband. When Naomi heard in Moab that the Lord*
*had come to the aid of his people by providing food for them, she*
*and her daughters-in-law prepared to return home from there.*
*With her two daughters-in-law she left the place where she had*
*been living and set out on the road that would take them back to*
*the land of Judah. Then Naomi said to her two daughters-in-law,*
*"Go back, each of you, to your mother's home. May the Lord show*
*you kindness, as you have shown kindness to your dead husbands*
*and me. May the Lord grant that each of you will find rest in the*
*home of another husband." Then she kissed them goodbye and*
*they wept aloud and said to her, "We will go back with you to your*
*people."*
Ruth 1:1-10 (NIV)


**Exhale** means to breathe out, emit, or give off as a vapor. I would
suggest to you that to **Exhale** is to release excess baggage and
toxicity to you and what can and should be for your life, to give
clarity to who you are and who you are becoming. To live at your
maximum potential, your authenticity must prevail as you engage
in your life's experiences; otherwise, they will dictate to you.
Therefore, the kind of projection you give, the sense of confidence
and clarity about your position, your direction, is critical to
keeping yourself in the driver's seat of your life instead of the
experience driving you. Often, we find ourselves waiting to
**Exhale,** looking for some external force to determine our lives
and/or the outcome of our experience; the power is within us. In
your experiences, never feel like you are trapped or that you have
to settle for what is; exercise your power, for you always have

options, and as you seek and discover the option that keeps you in the driver's seat of your life, choose to drive, and your choice will reveal your destination, the outcome as you proceed.  If, in the process, you find you need to adjust, change course without regret.  Remember, the power is within you; you have not been given the spirit of fear but that of power, love, and a sound mind. Use it and press forward to your higher calling, *Breathe: New Life*. The story of Ruth shows us that when you find yourself trapped and without options, you make choices that lead to outcomes that are not aligned with what can and should be for your life; however, you have the power to course-correct.  Course correct and **Exhale** the excessive baggage and toxicity of your life, revealing your authenticity and your choice to live in your life and life more abundantly!

## March 14

*But Naomi said, "Return home, my daughters. Why would you come with me? Am I going to have any more sons, who could become your husbands?  Return home, my daughters; I am too old to have another husband. Even if I thought there was still hope for me—even if I had a husband tonight and then gave birth to sons—would you wait until they grew up? Would you remain unmarried for them? No, my daughters. It is more bitter for me than for you because the Lord's hand has turned against me!"  At this, they wept aloud again. Then Orpah kissed her mother-in-law goodbye, but Ruth clung to her.  "Look," said Naomi, "your sister-in-law is going back to her people and her gods. Go back with her."  But Ruth replied, "Don't urge me to leave you or to turn back from you. Where you go I will go, and where you stay I will stay. Your*

*people will be my people and your God my God. Where you die I will die, and there I will be buried. May the Lord deal with me, be it ever so severely, if even death separates you and me." When Naomi realized that Ruth was determined to go with her, she stopped urging her. So the two women went on until they came to Bethlehem. When they arrived in Bethlehem, the whole town was stirred because of them, and the women exclaimed, "Can this be Naomi?" "Don't call me Naomi," she told them. "Call me Mara,because the Almightyhas made my life very bitter. I went away full, but the Lord has brought me back empty. Why call me Naomi? The Lord has afflicted me; the Almighty has brought misfortune upon me." So Naomi returned from Moab accompanied by Ruth the Moabite, her daughter-in-law, arriving in Bethlehem as the barley harvest was beginning.*
Ruth 1:11-22 (NIV)

Critical to how we engage the external matters of our lives, including the people, places, and things, is our relationship with ourselves and our decisions. If we are not confident about who we are, we will be less confident about the things we engage with and connect with, giving away our power and our ability to drive our own narrative to others. The key to your success and the reward of your life and life more abundantly, generally in life and specifically in your circumstances, is your ability to drive the narrative. Thus, as we inhale that which will support us in living to our maximum potential, we must discern, release, **Exhale** all excess baggage and toxicity that will prevent us from pressing forward, driving our narrative. Therefore, we must be clear about our position; where we are, and where we are going. In doing so, we must be sure of the connections necessary to get us from where we are to our expected destination, including being available.  ***Breathe: New Life*** by your willingness to **Exhale** that which does not support you in motivating your confidence in and around you to be available to press forward in that which can and should be for your living, living in your life and life more abundantly!

## March 15

*Moses and Aaron brought together all the elders of the Israelites, and Aaron told them everything the Lord had said to Moses. He also performed the signs before the people, and they believed. And when they heard that the Lord was concerned about them and had seen their misery, they bowed down and worshiped.*
Exodus 4:29-31 (NIV)

When we are pursuing that which God has declared for our lives, pressing forward in our Word of truth, we need not worry about what we do not have or hold on to what we do not need as compensation; let go and let God.  God is the author and finisher of your faith, of that which you believe can and should be for your life; it is His responsibility to ensure you have everything you need.  Trust God and ***Breathe: New Life***, including being available to **Exhale** that which hinders and/or keeps you in neutral, preventing your pressing forward.  You can live without them; you can make it without that, you do have what you need: your Word of truth, pursue it diligently, and God will reward you with everything necessary to accomplish what He has begun in you. ***Breathe: New Life*** and see the signs of God's revelation, a deliverance that is not tied to any particular person, place, or thing but instead to your diligently pursuing that which He has ordained for your life and life more abundantly!

## March 16

*Blessed be the Lord God of Israel;*
*for he hath visited and redeemed his people,*
Luke 1:68

We can **Exhale** the excess baggage and toxicity of our lives because whatever we think we may need, God will supply. God intends to make available to you, based on your diligently pursuing that which He has ordained for your life, whatever you may need to accomplish what He intends. Never worry or be dismayed by people, places, and things, especially when they make you feel as though they are indispensable; it's a lie, a trick of the enemy, you got your Word, thus you have God. ***Breathe: New Life*** because you are blessed now, for God is with you and has redeemed you. **Exhale** and be released from the baggage and toxicity of life, and live in your life and life more abundantly!

## March 17

*"Now fear the Lord and serve him with all faithfulness. Throw away the gods your ancestors worshiped beyond the Euphrates River and in Egypt, and serve the Lord. But if serving the Lord seems undesirable to you, then choose for yourselves this day whom you will serve, whether the gods your ancestors served*

*beyond the Euphrates or the gods of the Amorites, in whose land you are living. But as for me and my household, we will serve the Lord."*
Joshua 24:14-15 (NIV)

Letting go of our past and whatever is preventing us from moving forward into what can and should be for our lives is easier said than done; however, it can and must be done. We have become accustomed, if not comfortable, to the way things are, even if we know they are no good for us, and prying ourselves away from them is a task that is both difficult and painful. However, we must focus on what can and should be for our lives and make a choice, for we always have options; thus, we can choose to transform for the good or remain the same. The choice for transformation may require more than we want to give, but it will lead to our good. As we make choices over the course of our lives, we will discover whether they lead us to our desired expectations or create the worst atmosphere for us; choices eventually reveal their destinations. The choice you make will reveal itself, and if it does not get you to where you are expecting, change course; you have the right, the privilege given to you by the blood of Jesus, and you need not feel bad. Lessons learned, your lived experiences provide wisdom. ***Breathe: New Life*** as a result of lessons learned, and **Exhale**, get rid of the unnecessary and the burdensome, and be free to live in your life and life more abundantly.

## March 18

*"At that time I told them, "Get rid of all the vile things that you've become addicted to. Don't make yourselves filthy with the*

*Egyptian no-god idols. I alone am God, your God.  But they rebelled against me, wouldn't listen to a word I said. None got rid of the vile things they were addicted to. They held on to the no-gods of Egypt as if for dear life."*
Ezekiel 20:7-8 (MSG)


Holding in too much, especially of that which is toxic, can be deadly to your life and, in particular, to your pressing forward to the higher calling for your life.  **Exhale** and release before you pop; you can live without it and live better than you believe is possible, beyond what your fears permit.  You have permission to live in your life and life more abundantly.  **Exhale** and ***Breathe: New Life***. Christ has delivered you into a space and place in which you can always get up, dust yourself off, and be reconciled to the promise of God for your life; at one with God and thus His Word of truth for you.  Do not allow the excess baggage and toxicity of your life to deceive you and make you think you cannot make it without them.  **Exhale** and ***Breathe: New Life***; get rid of it before you explode and live in your life and life more abundantly!


## March 19


*Rid yourselves of all the offenses you have committed, and get a new heart and a new spirit. Why will you die, people of Israel?  For I take no pleasure in the death of anyone, declares the Sovereign Lord. Repent and live!*
Ezekiel 18:31-32 (NIV)

You have been given the gift of reconciliation through Jesus to the very promise of life and life more abundantly; do not squander it; reconcile yourself to the truth of what can and should be for you and live. In living, you must rid yourself of that which would harm and cause you to die in your abundant life. **Exhale**, and free yourself to the revelation of God's promises. Although you may not believe you can get rid of and/or do without the excess baggage and toxicity in your life, you can; God made a way through the sacrifice of Christ to empower you to change course at any time. ***Breathe: New Life***, which includes your ability to **Exhale**, releasing that which is not working and will not work for you to live in your maximum potential, your abundance. God desires that all of us, no matter what we carry or what we fear, will be delivered, saved; ***Breathe: New Life*** and **Exhale,** and set your course to that which will cause you to live in your higher calling, the life and life more abundantly prepared for you!


## March 20

*While Jesus was in Bethany in the home of Simon the Leper, a woman came to him with an alabaster jar of very expensive perfume, which she poured on his head as he was reclining at the table. When the disciples saw this, they were indignant. "Why this waste?" they asked. "This perfume could have been sold at a high price and the money given to the poor." Aware of this, Jesus said to them, "Why are you bothering this woman? She has done a beautiful thing to me. The poor you will always have with you,[a] but you will not always have me. When she poured this perfume on my body, she did it to prepare me for burial. Truly I tell you, wherever this gospel is preached throughout the world, what she*

*has done will also be told, in memory of her." Then one of the*
*Twelve—the one called Judas Iscariot—went to the chief*
*priests and asked, "What are you willing to give me if I deliver him*
*over to you?" So they counted out for him thirty pieces of silver.*
*From then on Judas watched for an opportunity to hand him over.*
Matthew 26:6-16 (NIV)

The process of **Exhale** is grounded in release: cleansing from what is not useful and making room for what will support living at your maximum potential. The cleansing, the release, does not just benefit you but also your space, including the people, places, and things in it. Without a doubt, when we **Exhale** and *Breathe: New Life*, the newness is just that new and is unknown and uncomfortable; therefore, we cannot allow the fear of the newness to become paralyzing, causing us to wait to **Exhale.** If we keep holding our breath, we will die and/or explode; therefore, we must release - cleanse ourselves. Let go and cleanse yourself and your space, making ready for the new. It is a risk, but that is what faith is: believing and acting now on what can and should be for your life. You will never get to your destiny if you are not willing to take a risk, believing and taking action on that belief to make your Word of truth flesh, real in your life. As you **Exhale**, you take the risk of moving into the unknown, willingly investing in that which will be, being vulnerable, and for this, God will do as He promised and release unto you that which He beforehand has provided. The woman with the alabaster box took her most precious gift and offered it to God, not knowing that it would yield her a place in memorial, more than she could have imagined or asked for. *Breathe: New Life* cleansing, allowing the release of yourself and space to the newness of life that God has promised, and it will yield the exceedingly, abundantly more - take the risk, invest fully, and watch your cup run over!

## March 21

*And as they thus spake, Jesus himself stood in the midst of them, and saith unto them, Peace be unto you. But they were terrified and affrighted, and supposed that they had seen a spirit. And he said unto them, Why are ye troubled? and why do thoughts arise in your hearts? Behold my hands and my feet, that it is I myself: handle me, and see; for a spirit hath not flesh and bones, as ye see me have. And when he had thus spoken, he shewed them his hands and his feet.*
Luke 24:36-40

To receive the greatness, the abundance of life and life more abundantly promised to you by God requires our willingness to **Exhale**; releasing that which hinders and prevents our pressing forward in the higher calling for our life. It is the fear of the unknown, especially when it comes to taking risks to fulfill our promises, which can be debilitating, causing us to live beneath our potential. However, as we inhale the Spirit of power, love, and a sound mind toward the fulfillment of what can and should be, we are rehabilitated and encouraged to go forward. God's proof of His faithfulness has been and is demonstrated every day; therefore, release and cleanse yourself from that which hinders and realize God's faithfulness, thus evoking an outpouring of your gratitude, positioning you to receive the exceedingly, abundantly more than. **Breathe: New Life**, taking the risk and investing your all for in doing so, you **Exhale**, release, and cleanse, making room for the more!

## March 22

*At this, she bowed down with her face to the ground. She asked him, "Why have I found such favor in your eyes that you notice me —a foreigner?" Boaz replied, "I've been told all about what you have done for your mother-in-law since the death of your husband —how you left your father and mother and your homeland and came to live with a people you did not know before. May the Lord repay you for what you have done. May you be richly rewarded by the Lord, the God of Israel, under whose wings you have come to take refuge." "May I continue to find favor in your eyes, my lord," she said. "You have put me at ease by speaking kindly to your servant—though I do not have the standing of one of your servants."*
Ruth 2:10-13 (NIV)

When you know that it is right, **Exhale** the excess and toxic and make room for the more, for the more will be more than you can contain. Do not hesitate to **Exhale**, go ahead, and *Breathe: New Life*, and despite the odds not being in your favor, traditions and customs unkind to your predicament, or just the sheer impossibility your circumstances create, you can and will have new life. God has chosen you and your path, and if you are willing to take the risk to believe, have faith, and act upon that, God will reveal His favor, grace, on and over your life. God has already worked out all things; He is waiting for you to **Exhale**; take the leap of faith, investing your all, and as a result, He releases upon you that which is exceedingly, abundantly, more than.  Ruth, a Moabite widow whose mother-in-law is old and has no future prospects for a son, finds herself gleaning for leftovers. Despite this, she feels her time is right, lets go of all negativity, and comes upon Boaz.  Boaz becomes Ruth's new life, not only providing for her right now's needs but also providing through her womb, the world's greatest gift, Jesus, who in turn provides to all the right to life and life more abundantly!

## March 23

*When we heard that, we and everyone there that day begged Paul not to be stubborn and persist in going to Jerusalem. But Paul wouldn't budge: "Why all this hysteria? Why do you insist on making a scene and making it even harder for me? You're looking at this backward. The issue in Jerusalem is not what they do to me, whether arrest or murder, but what the Master Jesus does through my obedience. Can't you see that?" We saw that we weren't making even a dent in his resolve, and gave up. "It's in God's hands now," we said. "Master, you handle it."*
Acts 21:12-14 (MSG)

When we **Exhale,** we take a risk that what we release will be replaced by that which would enhance our ability to press forward to our higher calling.  Releasing the excess and toxicity of our lives will take us to a new place, and new places are uncomfortable because of their unfamiliarity; however, if we are to *Breathe: New Life*, it demands our willingness to have faith, believe, and act in the unknown as if what we believe can and should be will be. God the Creator has already prepared our life and life more

94

abundantly specifically for us, and if we believe and act, taking the risk that what we believe will be, in doing so God assures us He will reward us, not because we get it right, but instead because we diligently pursue. Go ahead and *Breathe: New Life*. It will come with risk, but have faith. Paul acted in such a way that, whatever the risk may be, he was intentional about trusting God and pressing forward in his belief in a higher calling. Maybe you've been stuck, living beneath your potential because you haven't taken the necessary risks. Take a leap of faith, get out of your boat, launch out into the deep, and cast your nets. God is faithful and will empower you to seize your promises and live abundantly!

## March 24

*Then Job arose, and rent his mantle, and shaved his head, and fell*
*down upon the ground, and worshipped, And said,*
*Naked came I out of my mother's womb,*
*and naked shall I return thither:*
*the LORD gave, and the LORD hath taken away;*
*blessed be the name of the LORD.*
*In all this Job sinned not, nor charged God foolishly.*
Job 1:20-22

*Breathe: New Life* is a perspective in which we see in and through every experience the opportunity to grow, expand, and enlarge the vision of what can and should be for our lives, fueling our ability to take action to live in the abundance of life. New Life in our situations is always possible, for we have been given the power to reconcile wherever we may be and wherever we should be, to live in God's promises. Therefore, we are given permission, if not the right to **Exhale**, to release any and all things that may prevent and/or hinder us from living to our full potential, the life and life more abundantly promised. Everything, all things are subject to God, and thus, we can release, be free from any and all things, for we came into the world naked, and yet, we have been allowed to inherit all things. Go ahead, and *Breathe: New Life* by the privilege given to you to **Exhale**, release, and be free from any and all things that would hinder you from living in God's promises, the blessing that reveals God Himself in all of His power and glory!

## March 25

*Humble yourselves, therefore, under God's mighty hand, that he may lift you up in due time. Cast all your anxiety on him because he cares for you. Be alert and of sober mind. Your enemy the devil prowls around like a roaring lion looking for someone to devour. Resist him, standing firm in the faith, because you know that the family of believers throughout the world is undergoing the same kind of sufferings. And the God of all grace, who called you to his eternal glory in Christ, after you have suffered a little while, will himself restore you and make you strong, firm and steadfast. To him be the power for ever and ever. Amen.*
I Peter 5:6-11 (NIV)

**Exhale** is the cleansing and releasing of yourself to the flow and move of God's intended will for your life. It is hard to know God's thoughts and ways; they are much higher than ours. Therefore, it is incumbent upon us that if we wish to experience the life and life more abundantly promised, we must make ourselves available to

God. Our availability is not linked to the natural or the physical, but to the Spirit, allowing us to transcend the boundaries of the natural and physical and even go through them to achieve what can and should be for our lives. *Breathe: New Life* by submitting yourself to God and allowing the leading and guiding of His Spirit to prepare, position, and pour out for you the pathway to your living at your maximum potential, your life and life more abundantly. You will experience the difficulties of life, but you are already fitted to overcome them. **Exhale** the excess and toxic, embracing the Spirit of God which empowers us to resist the wiles of the devil, darkness, negativity, and receive God's grace, His favor to transform all things for the good, even beyond the existence of natural and physical obstacles.

## March 26

*But thou, O man of God, flee these things; and follow after righteousness, godliness, faith, love, patience, meekness. Fight the good fight of faith, lay hold on eternal life, whereunto thou art also called, and hast professed a good profession before many witnesses.*
I Timothy 6:11-12

*Breathe: New Life* requires that we be intentional about what we desire and what the new life can and should be. Focusing on the higher calling of our lives gives us the impetus to make appropriate choices toward our expected end, and the more we choose to make decisions, the more our outcomes become apparent. Thus, as we *Breathe: New Life,* it informs our choice to **Exhale**, what we release and allow to be cleansed from us so that we are appropriately positioned and strengthened to press our way toward our higher calling, that which can and should be for our lives. What can and should be is the life and life more abundantly promised specifically for you and generally for the world, and as we flee the things of life that hinder and prevent us from living in God's intent, we release and cleanse, prepare our space to walk and exist in the abundance of God's blessings. **Exhale**, cleanse, and release not only yourself but the entirety of your space, your world, to flee from to be free to the abundance of God's intent.

## March 27

*This is what I have observed to be good: that it is appropriate for a person to eat, to drink and to find satisfaction in their toilsome labor under the sun during the few days of life God has given them —for this is their lot. Moreover, when God gives someone wealth and possessions, and the ability to enjoy them, to accept their lot and be happy in their toil—this is a gift of God. They seldom reflect on the days of their life, because God keeps them occupied with gladness of heart.*
Ecclesiastes 5:18-20 (NIV)

Breathing is critical, if not foundational, to living; thus, as we inhale and **Exhale**, we execute the foundational act of declaring and actually living. The Word of God challenges you and me to live in the fullness of God, declaring and acting in such a way that we actually believe, we have faith. We inhale the power from God to accomplish His will for our lives and **Exhale** all that would hinder or prevent the very act to *Breathe: New Life* in and to our life experiences. We have been empowered to declare that we are going to live and not die, and thus, we *Breathe: New Life*, and act in what can and should be for our lives. Our new life is triggered as we **Exhale**, cleansing and releasing excess and toxic materials, freeing us to live fully in God's abundance. God has given us this great gift, celebrate it, and *Breathe: New Life*, your circumstances, and all of creation are waiting on you, release yourself from the excess and toxic, and live, as you do so, so does your space, the world in which we exist.

## March 28

*So my friends, don't be fooled by your own desires! Every gift God*
*freely gives us is good and perfect, streaming down from the*
*Father of lights, who shines from the heavens with no hidden*
*shadow or darkness and is never subject to change. God was*
*delighted to give us birth by the truth of his infallible Word so that*
*we would fulfill his chosen destiny for us and become the favorite*
*ones out of all his creation!*
James 1:16-18 (TPT)

As you **Exhale**, cleansing and releasing yourself to the greater that awaits you, you make room for God to freely and generously pour into you. God gives generously of His gifts, which are good to and for us, and it is His desire, greatest pleasure, to ensure that we enjoy the life and life more abundantly promised. Do not let what appears to be impossible keep you from getting to a place of strength and power. Your past is your past; forget it, and press toward your higher calling. You cannot change what has happened, but you have the power to choose a different future.

Take advantage of your power of choice and choose life and life more abundantly, cleansing and releasing yourself to *Breathe: New Life*. God's gift, His grace, mercy, and peace await your life, and all creation seeks for you to live your best life, which will also release the best in them!

## March 29

*His wife said, "Still holding on to your precious integrity, are you? Curse God and be done with it!" He told her, "You're talking like an empty-headed fool. We take the good days from God—why not also the bad days?" Not once through all this did Job sin. He said nothing against God.*
Job 2:9-10 (MSG)

Our ability to **Exhale** includes our power of discernment; discerning what needs to go and what we should retain. The power of discernment requires a clear, focused intent on what is and should be. Knowing your purpose and being purpose-driven informs your ability to discern what to retain and what to **Exhale**. *Breathe: New Life* by retaining what strengthens and empowers you to operate and live at your maximum potential, even when it does not look like it at the moment. The only way to endure what urges you to free yourself is to know and understand your destination and what it takes to live and operate at your maximum potential. Although spinach may be bad for some, Popeye knew what it would do for him. In the face of all his tragedies, Job understood that holding on to God as he chooses to *Breathe: New Life* would get him to the end of his story where he gets double for his troubles. Be not deceived, God is not mocked, trust Him and retain Him and His gifts, although the revelation may tarry, wait for it, *Breathe: New Life,* and it will come!

## March 30

*Flee the evil desires of youth and pursue righteousness, faith, love and peace, along with those who call on the Lord out of a pure heart. Don't have anything to do with foolish and stupid arguments, because you know they produce quarrels.*
II Timothy 2:22-23 (NIV)

The process to *Breathe: New Life* is not always smooth, and we must be expectant of the bumps in the road, understanding that delays do not mean denial. Our fear of failure is tremendous, and we must be both prepared and strengthened to overcome it in the face of our experiences. Although what you believe can and should be is your Word of truth, the process will tarry, and thus fear is fueled that it will not happen, causing you to confront your fear not with foolishness but instead with your faith, your willingness to take a risk on that which is sure. Remember, faith is the substance of things hoped for, the evidence of things not seen; faith has no tangibility except you, and you must be willing to believe in you, the vessel of your Word of truth, and get out of the boat, launch out into the deep, and cast your nets. **Exhale**, cleansing, and releasing that you may flee what may come naturally in defiance of what can and should be, and continue to press forward and *Breathe: New Life*!

## March 31

*Not as though I had already attained, either were already perfect: but I follow after, if that I may apprehend that for which also I am apprehended of Christ Jesus. Brethren, I count not myself to have apprehended: but this one thing I do, forgetting those things which are behind, and reaching forth unto those things which are before, I press toward the mark for the prize of the high calling of God in Christ Jesus.*
Philippians 3:12-14

Our desire to **Breathe: New Life** is not without its challenges, in particular, the frustrations that our life experiences bring, making our trying to be consistent, very challenging.  Thus, it is important to understand that to **Breathe: New Life** and to **Exhale** is as important as our inhaling.  The process to **Exhale**, cleansing, and releasing, freeing us from the weight of the past, makes room for our future, which is informed by our past experiences but not hindered by them.  Our freedom from our past is to be cleansed and released by it, gleaning wisdom from our lived experience to inform and support our pressing forward in the higher calling of God for our lives.  God does absolutely nothing by happenstance or accident; it is all divinely ordered.  Therefore, every experience in our life has a purpose.  When we discover God's purpose in our experiences, the good and the bad, we find a key that unlocks the situation that allows us to move forward, but as we move forward, we do so with a permanent key in our collection, assisting us in overcoming future obstacles.  Remember, God through Christ has already saved-delivered us, and it is that salvation-deliverance we seek to embrace; we keep pressing forward.  Paul says I have not attained it totally, but I apprehend that which has apprehended me, pressing through the stuff of my life to my higher calling. Paul stresses we must be consistent through life and its experiences, seeking to glean what we need from our experiences and keep pressing forward to our goal, the prize of our life and life more abundantly, which is built upon our lived experiences.

# DELIVERANCE

## APRIL

## April 1

*And he said unto me, My grace is sufficient for thee: for my strength is made perfect in weakness. Most gladly therefore will I rather glory in my infirmities, that the power of Christ may rest upon me.*
II Corinthians 12:9

**Breathe: New Life** is a challenge to move from where you are to a pathway that leads to where you can and should be so you can enjoy your life and life more abundantly. Often we are confused in living that somehow things are just going to happen, especially in the faith world, however, more than likely what can and should be for your life will happen gradually as well as instantaneously because you have chosen to believe what can and should be and begin operating as if it is and then gradually as you engage the process of your life to get to the place of what can and should be - **Deliverance.** Your journey to what can and should be will have obstacles, complexities, and all forms of hindrances; nevertheless, as you are fueled by your faith, belief, and willingness to act, engage in the process of **Deliverance**, receive God's grace, and favor to get through to get to your expectation. God's grace, favor are more than sufficient for you; His power dwells within and through you to overcome all hindrances. However, there must be a willingness on your part to engage your hindrances, inject the fuel of your faith, take appropriate risks, and **Breathe: New Life**.

## April 2

*If I must needs glory, I will glory of the things which concern mine infirmities.*
II Corinthians 11:30

**Deliverance** rests on our desire and subsequent choices to turn from the way we are headed toward a new direction that leads us on the path of our life and life more abundantly. The revelation, if not the recognition of what is broken in your life, leads to the desire to fix it and get it right so you can press forward with your maximum capacity and your abundance. The brokenness of our lives, if carried, will continue to deteriorate and affect the rest, leading us on a slow road of demise. Turn quickly to seek **Deliverance** by choosing to be free from whatever brokenness we carry and free to that which will create new life. Cry out to God, and in your crying out to Him, His light shines on you, including your brokenness, beginning the process of your **Deliverance**. Do not allow the fear and/or shame within you to hinder you from turning the light onto your brokenness, boldly go before the throne of God with your issues, and let the light of God scatter your darkness and bring **Deliverance** to you! Today, ***Breathe: New Life*** by recognizing your brokenness, revealing it to yourself and God, and watch God scatter your darkness with the light of His promise, your Word of truth, your **Deliverance**!

## April 3

*The next day John seeth Jesus coming unto him, and saith, Behold the Lamb of God, which taketh away the sin of the world. This is he of whom I said, After me cometh a man which is preferred before me: for he was before me. And I knew him not: but that he should be made manifest to Israel, therefore am I come baptizing with water. And John bare record, saying, I saw the Spirit descending from heaven like a dove, and it abode upon him. And I knew him not: but he that sent me to baptize with water, the same said unto me, Upon whom thou shalt see the Spirit descending, and remaining on him, the same is he which baptizeth with the Holy Ghost. And I saw, and bare record that this is the Son of God.*
John 1:29-34

One of the things that consumes us is our desire for someone or something to **deliver** us from our circumstances to something better, freeing us from the complications of disagreeableness, and/or the mundanity of our lives - our sense of brokenness.  We are so consumed that we often find and/or attach ourselves to people, places, or things as an agent or vehicle for escape, to numb ourselves and our experiences, and become addicted to that which provides momentary relief and/or escape.   It is our addictions that serve as a substitute for facing our fears and thus, preventing us from repairing the brokenness that our fears have caused.   I suggest that even amid our brokenness, with our addictions, there is the feeling that there is something better that causes us to cry out, reach for, seek after opportunities for transformation, a **Deliverance** to *Breathe: New Life*.   Everyone, no matter their brokenness or addiction, wants for their lives to be transformed for the better, not just temporarily changed, but instead resurrected to live to their maximum potential, the promise of life and life more abundantly.  The gift of Jesus, the sacrificial lamb for all - no matter whether you profess Him or not - has been given as a vehicle of reconciliation to the Word of promise for your abundant life. Pay attention to your circumstances, recognize what is broken, and take advantage of the opportunity of repair, seeking that which reconciles your experience to that which will empower you. Do not allow your brokenness to cause you to hide or run away. Face the brokenness of your life, cry out for help, and God will respond, healing your brokenness and reconciling you to your promise of abundant life! Go ahead and *Breathe: New Life* and receive **Deliverance**, the transformation of you and your experiences in which you overcome and inherit all things!

## April 4

*For I will pass through the land of Egypt this night, and will smite all the firstborn in the land of Egypt, both man and beast; and against all the gods of Egypt I will execute judgment: I am the LORD. And the blood shall be to you for a token upon the houses where ye are: and when I see the blood, I will pass over you, and the plague shall not be upon you to destroy you, when I smite the land of Egypt.*
Exodus 12:12-13

The difficulties, tragedies, and impossibilities of life are real, both to believers and non-believers; however, the difference is the insurance plan one has to weather the storms of one's life. Insurance assures that when difficulties, tragedies, and impossibilities come, we have additional support to help us through, pick up the pieces, and be reconciled to a level that keeps us on the pathway of our life and life more abundantly. As believers, we have assurance as to the things of life that would prevent or stop our flow to life at its maximum potential, in which the brokenness and even death caused by life's challenges will be turned for our good. We can, through the difficulties, tragedies, and impossibilities *Breathe: New Life* and receive **Deliverance** from God, the way of escape, the way to stand up under whatever it is, and yet win. Life may not be fair, but God's favor, His assurance, balances all things out for our good by His **Deliverance** from the storms of life into peace, harmony with His will for our life and life more abundantly. Go ahead and face what you must; you have insurance that you will be **Delivered** and that you will reap the harvest prepared for your due season. Your due season, the fact that as you continue to work your field even though you are broken, and the things around you seem to all fall apart, your victory is assured. *Breathe: New Life* and receive your **Deliverance**!

## April 5

*He was oppressed and He was afflicted,*
*Yet He did not open His mouth [to complain or defend Himself];*
*Like a lamb that is led to the slaughter,*
*And like a sheep that is silent before her shearers,*
*So He did not open His mouth.*
Isaiah 53:7 (AMP)

Our assurance of **Deliverance** is available to us no matter the circumstances that bind us and/or cause us to live beneath our potential. It does not matter the nature of your incarceration in life, be free, accept, and embrace the love of God that seeks to bring you out - establish **Deliverance** to and for your life. God desires that all would be saved, **Delivered**, and as such gave His only begotten Son to stand in the gap on our behalf, taking it all so that we can be free from it all. The symbol of Christ on the cross, not saying a mumbling word, is that we can be free from that which binds us and the fear and shame that comes with it, especially in the aftermath. The aftermath of our **Deliverance** is also covered so that we never have to fear it will be held against us. In truth, it actually becomes the very thing that triggers our ability to *Breathe: New Life* and seize it.

## April 6

*For you know that you were not redeemed from your useless [spiritually unproductive] way of life inherited [by tradition] from your forefathers with perishable things like silver and gold, but [you were actually purchased] with precious blood, like that of a [sacrificial] lamb unblemished and spotless, the priceless blood of Christ.*
I Peter 1:18-19 (AMP)

As difficult as life's challenges may be, you must always remember that you have been **Delivered** through it all, not just by some weak cause but actually one that has been paid and sealed by the blood of Jesus Christ. The blood of Jesus Christ has been given on your behalf to act as a surety that the contract, the promise of God for your life and life more abundantly, cannot be rescinded or broken. God was willing to give His very best, His only begotten Son, as a sacrifice, allowing Him to bleed and die on your behalf so that you would have the right, a secured privilege to your abundant life. God chose to shed His Son's blood so that you would have a sure foundation, an irrevocable promise from Him to you. All you and I need to do to receive and embrace our **Deliverance** is to ***Breathe: New Life***, to be intentional about bringing into our space that which will resurrect us to what is our maximum potential to live in the abundance of God's promises. The choice is yours, choose today to receive and embrace your **Deliverance**, it is not a deceptive or unsure gift; instead, it is one that has an ensured return of overflow for your life.

## April 7

*And I saw a mighty angel proclaiming in a loud voice, "Who is worthy to break the seals and open the scroll?" But no one in heaven or on earth or under the earth could open the scroll or even look inside it. I wept and wept because no one was found who was worthy to open the scroll or look inside. Then one of the elders said to me, "Do not weep! See, the Lion of the tribe of Judah, the Root of David, has triumphed. He is able to open the scroll and its seven seals." Then I saw a Lamb, looking as if it had been slain, standing at the center of the throne, encircled by the four living creatures and the elders. The Lamb had seven horns and seven eyes, which are the seven spirits of God sent out into all the earth. He went and took the scroll from the right hand of him who sat on the throne. And when he had taken it, the four living creatures and the twenty-four elders fell down before the Lamb. Each one had a harp and they were holding golden bowls full of incense, which are the prayers of God's people. And they sang a new song, saying: "You are worthy to take the scroll and to open*

*its seals, because you were slain, and with your blood you*
*purchased for God persons from every tribe and language and*
*people and nation. You have made them to be a kingdom and*
*priests to serve our God, and they will reign[b] on the earth." Then*
*I looked and heard the voice of many angels, numbering*
*thousands upon thousands, and ten thousand times ten thousand.*
*They encircled the throne and the living creatures and the elders.*
*In a loud voice they were saying: "Worthy is the Lamb, who was*
*slain, to receive power and wealth and wisdom and strength and*
*honor and glory and praise!" Then I heard every creature in*
*heaven and on earth and under the earth and on the sea, and all*
*that is in them, saying: "To him who sits on the throne and to the*
*Lamb be praise and honor and glory and power, for ever and*
*ever!" The four living creatures said, "Amen," and the elders fell*
*down and worshiped.*
Revelation 5:2-14 (NIV)

The very things of our lives that seem to be rooted and immovable are the very things God uses to develop us and our relationship with Him and His Word of truth for our lives. What is perceived as sealed, the rooted and immovable in our lives, has been broken by God for eternity through the offering of His Son as a sacrificial lamb, so that what we perceive as impossible is possible if we would believe and act upon our belief. There is absolutely nothing impossible for you to achieve and/or get over because God has paid the price and thus you have **Deliverance** from it all to the very promises of God for your life. Go ahead, and *Breathe: New Life*, what was shall no longer be, but what He has declared should be for your life is available, your package has already been **Delivered**, choose today to receive and embrace, seize and act in your **Deliverance**. Celebrate your **Deliverance** even though it may not appear to be real in the flesh, in the Spirit, God has broken the seal of any and all things that would separate you from living at your maximum potential, your life and life more abundantly, *Breathe: New Life*. Embrace your **Deliverance** and walk into your exceedingly, abundantly, more than harvest!

## April 8

*Out of that terrible travail of soul, he'll see that it's worth it and be glad he did it. Through what he experienced, my righteous one, my servant, will make many "righteous ones," as he himself carries the burden of their sins. Therefore I'll reward him extravagantly— the best of everything, the highest honors— Because he looked death in the face and didn't flinch, because he embraced the company of the lowest. He took on his own shoulders the sin of the many, he took up the cause of all the black sheep.*
Isaiah 53:11-12 (MSG)

Our promise to inherit all things is connected to our ability to overcome whatever is before us. Please understand that your **Deliverance** has already been provided to and for you; the choice is yours to receive it. To receive your **Deliverance**, *Breathe: New Life* into your situation. Taking on the obstacles that keep you from enjoying your life and living more abundantly is the key to receiving **Deliverance** in your life. If you are unwilling to recognize the brokenness and obstacles in your life and engage with them, you will never unearth your innate ability to take on and overcome the gulf that separates you from your promises. Your **Deliverance** is rooted in how bad you want it. If you do, overcome

114

what you must, and receive your **Deliverance**!  Your **Deliverance** is assured and has been paid for with the blood of Jesus.  Do not be afraid, face your obstacles, and *Breathe: New Life*, your **Deliverance** is at hand!

## April 9

*He's the Anointed One who offered himself as the sacrifice for our sins! He has rescued us from this evil world system and set us free, just as our Father God desired.*
Galatians 1:4 (TPT)

Life is not always fair, and it actually sometimes can be evil and evil intent, but do not fret, *Breathe: New Life* and receive your **Deliverance**, a gift of freedom to you from God.  According to the Scriptures, before the world and you existed, Jesus had already been slain. Thus, when God thought of our creation and our lives, He had already created a plan for us to be free, **Delivered** from whatever would bind us in life.  The Anointed One, the One who has been assigned to ensure our **Deliverance**, willingly does so so that you and I would have the right, privilege, to life and life more abundantly.  Do not allow what your life's challenges may be, evil as they seem, to bind you; you have already won. Establish your Word of truth as your goal and press toward it, and all along the way *Breathe: New Life*; walk and act in your prearranged **Deliverance** and receive the exceedingly, abundantly, more than you can ever ask or think by the power of your Word of truth acting out in you!

# April 10

*Then Joseph said to his brothers, "Come close to me." When they had done so, he said, "I am your brother Joseph, the one you sold into Egypt! And now, do not be distressed and do not be angry with yourselves for selling me here, because it was to save lives that God sent me ahead of you. For two years now there has been famine in the land, and for the next five years there will be no plowing and reaping. But God sent me ahead of you to preserve for you a remnant on earth and to save your lives by a great deliverance. "So then, it was not you who sent me here, but God. He made me father to Pharaoh, lord of his entire household and ruler of all Egypt.*
Genesis 45:4-8 (NIV)

Recent news reports indicate there is an increase in cases of positive COVID, after two years of up and down, and thinking we have turned the corner on this deadly virus, we still find ourselves behind the eight ball. Although what we believe to be evil still exists, we have learned from experience; for that reason, it is still frustrating that we have not been able to eradicate COVID. The lesson I believe I learned from this most deadly virus is critical to our understanding of and navigation of life and its challenges, in particular, the challenge that **Deliverance** is both instant and gradually manifested in our lives. Because of the development of successful vaccinations, we have been able to overcome the enormous amount of deaths caused by COVID, with instantaneous **Deliverance**, although we have not been successful in eradicating it. It is because of the vaccination that even though COVID is stubborn and does not want to go anywhere, we have lessened its impact, causing death, allowing us to *Breathe: New Life.* Yet, the struggle continues, and as it goes forth, we learn more about the virus, equipping us to not only eventually conquer it but also be better prepared for future viruses, lessening their impact, especially its deadly impact on humanity, gradual **Deliverance**. I would suggest that the evil of COVID has helped us use COVID, our enemy, as a footstool to learn lessons and be better prepared. In addition, COVID has provided our world, in various segments, a challenge to advance and better equip ourselves for the new era, using this setback as an opportunity for developing and living in a better world, a world in which, despite it all, we are in God's hands.

## April 11

*God's Spirit is on me; he's chosen me to preach the Message of good news to the poor, Sent me to announce pardon to prisoners and recovery of sight to the blind, To set the burdened and battered free, to announce, "This is God's time to shine!"*
Luke 4:18-19 (MSG)

Our **Deliverance** is a process that demands our interactiveness throughout. Jesus, in the opening sermon of His ministry, lays out the requirement for our participation in the **Deliverance** that God has ordained for us beforehand. What we seek to be free of and liberated has already been done and just awaits our active participation in the process of our **Deliverance**. We must see through it all, the obstacles, complexities, difficulties of our lives that we have been chosen, anointed for them, and as we discover our anointing, it destroys whatever there is that binds us. Therefore, do not spend all your energy on the brokenness of your life and circumstances, but press toward the mark of His calling for your life, and as a result, your yokes and burdens will be destroyed. Remember, it is in your going that God is not only with you, but goodness and mercy will follow you, and you will have all the help you need as you press forward in that which can and should be for your life. You can *Breathe: New Life* and be free of the obstacles, complexities, or difficulties, yet fully equipped to co-create with God, the revelation of Him and you, His wonderfully and fearfully created being.

## April 12

*And Judah said unto his brethren, What profit is it if we slay our brother, and conceal his blood? Come, and let us sell him to the Ishmeelites, and let not our hand be upon him; for he is our brother and our flesh. And his brethren were content. Then there passed by Midianites merchantmen; and they drew and lifted up Joseph out of the pit, and sold Joseph to the Ishmeelites for twenty pieces of silver: and they brought Joseph into Egypt.*
Genesis 37:26-28

God always intervenes in our experiences to direct and order our steps toward the fulfillment of His Word of truth for our lives, our **Deliverance**. It can be difficult to detect God's moves, especially the setbacks in our lives, as God's opportunity to set us up to reveal Him, His Word, and us in and through our experiences. This process that eventually leads to our **Deliverance** demands that we *Breathe: New Life* through our experiences as a vehicle to keep us constantly focused on God's revelation, a higher calling for our lives. Judah, which means Worship, is the brother who suggests, as an alternative to killing Joseph, that they sell him into slavery. As a result, Joseph goes to Egypt, and God's plan is unraveled, bringing abundant life to Joseph, his father, and his brothers, as God intends.  It may be difficult to discern which experience is the one, but know they all line up with God's plans to reveal through you, His Word of truth for your abundant life; therefore, **Breathe: New Life** in and through everything, for it is all connected to your **Deliverance**!

## April 13

*Comfort, comfort my people, says your God.  Speak tenderly to Jerusalem, and proclaim to her that her hard service has been completed, that her sin has been paid for, that she has received from the Lord's hand double for all her sins.*
Isaiah 40:1-2 (NIV)

Be assured of your salvation, your **Deliverance** from whatever is already done; the question is whether or not you are positioned to receive it.  Our positioning to overcome and receive our **Deliverance** has everything to do with how we view our circumstances.  In the heat of the circumstances of our lives, we can easily be deceived into believing that we are powerless to control; however, resist that feeling by viewing our circumstances through the lens of our victory.  As we envision our victory, forgetting what is behind us and pressing forward, we open ourselves to possibilities and opportunities that empower us to reclaim our lives and steer our narrative toward victory. **Breathe: New Life** by speaking over your life that which can and should be, inhaling that which will drive your narrative to your place of abundant life and release, exhale the excess and toxicity, freeing you to press to your higher calling, **Deliverance**!

## April 14

*You intended to harm me, but God intended it for good to accomplish what is now being done, the saving of many lives.*
Genesis 50:20 (NIV)

Do not worry about what it looks like; even though it may look like the end, it is not. God has more for you, and know that where you are is your process for your **Deliverance**. God has ordered our steps, and though we may feel that God is nowhere to be found or would not be in the mess we are in, He is present and a very present help. God desires that you and I be saved, **Delivered**; thus, **Deliverance** is already ours; however, we must engage in the process. The process can be a beast, but press your way, you have your anointing - ordered/chosen steps through whatever you are experiencing. Remember, before there was anything, there was God's Word, and the Word was with God and the Word was God, and God/His Word cannot lie, nor can He repent of it; it is Him and He/His Word will not return void. The Word of truth, God's promises for your life, existed before whatever you are experiencing, meaning that it has been established and therefore is available to you. Therefore, *Breathe: New Life*, whatever you're going through, will yield a greater harvest than you can imagine. Press your way through the process and reap your harvest, receive your **Deliverance**, it is waiting for you.

## April 15

*And the LORD turned the captivity of Job, when he prayed for his*
*friends: also the LORD gave Job twice as much as he had before.*
Job 42:10

Often our circumstances will cause us to become captives; the circumstances driving the narrative for our lives and actions, and thus we seek and need **Deliverance**. The **Deliverance** necessary to break the chains of our captivity is available to us and knocking at our door; however, we must be willing to receive and take action for our **Deliverance**, freedom to manifest, to become real in our walking around experiences. Our **Deliverance** emancipates us from the control and dictates of our circumstances, freeing us to live, move, and have our being in our Word of truth, that which can and should be for our lives. Do not allow your circumstances, no matter how good or bad they are, to drive your narrative, receive and act in your Deliverance, breaking the chains of any and all things that would hinder you from pressing forward into your promised destiny, abundant life. *Breathe: New Life* despite how you feel and what your circumstances dictate, God's promise to us is that every round goes higher and higher as we press forward into our life and life more abundantly!

## April 16

*For your shame ye shall have double;*
*and for confusion they shall rejoice in their portion:*
*therefore in their land they shall possess the double:*

*everlasting joy shall be unto them.*
*For I the LORD love judgment,*
*I hate robbery for burnt offering;*
*and I will direct their work in truth,*
*and I will make an everlasting covenant with them.*
*Isaiah 61:7-8*

The process of our **Deliverance** can be demanding and frustrating, however, because our **Deliverance** is assured, we can endure knowing that we shall overcome and, in overcoming, bask in the overflow. The overflow is the reward we receive for enduring, diligently pursuing what we believe can and should be for our lives - **Delivered** to what God has declared for our life and life more abundantly. In every circumstance of our lives, we have the opportunity to engage in the process of **Deliverance,** and over and over again, we receive God's revelation and His direction toward our promises. Be not deceived, God is not mocked, whatsoever you sow, that will you also reap; **Deliverance** is already yours, and it will be in overflow, abundance, double for your trouble but you must be active in enduring and engaging the process, to *Breathe: New Life*.

## April 17

*And the LORD said, I have surely seen the affliction of my people which are in Egypt, and have heard their cry by reason of their taskmasters; for I know their sorrows; And I am come down to deliver them out of the hand of the Egyptians, and to bring them up out of that land unto a good land and a large, unto a land flowing with milk and honey; unto the place of the Canaanites,*

122

*and the Hittites, and the Amorites, and the Perizzites, and the Hivites, and the Jebusites. Now therefore, behold, the cry of the children of Israel is come unto me: and I have also seen the oppression wherewith the Egyptians oppress them.*
Exodus 3:7-9

As we celebrate the season of Resurrection, I am challenged that there must be a deeper meaning for Christ's suffering, death, and resurrection than our release from external oppressions of evil and overcoming our internal struggle with the wiles of the devil. Perhaps that is why I am no longer easily satisfied: I want more. I want to enjoy every promise Jesus's sacrifice paid for. It is no longer acceptable to just be; I want to live and live abundantly, to operate in the manifestation of His signs and wonders. Therefore, it must be something deeper, greater, and more empowering than just getting past that which stands in my way, because if the truth is told, there will always be some obstacles, something attempting to keep me from my promises. I want to be **Delivered**, transported from my what is to what shall be, while what is still going on, to be conscious, engaged, and empowered in and through my oppression to live abundantly, revealing and experiencing God's signs and wonders. Therefore, I believe we are challenged by Christ's resurrection to stretch our faith; believe and act on what can and should be for our lives, despite and in spite of our external and internal oppressions, with an eye toward our being raised through the process to the manifestation of our promises. Just as God heard the Israelites' cry for relief, He hears ours and is attentive to our genuine need, using the process to stretch our faith as He is actively engaged, revealing and experiencing His signs and wonders, while providing an alternative, His promises for our lives. Know that God's alternative is our land flowing with milk and honey; our living abundantly, although at times it may be occupied and cultivated by something and/or someone else, they are just holding our stuff in preparation for us to believe and thus possess. This Resurrection Day season, *Breathe: New Life* by engaging your process of **Deliverance;** believing and acting on what can and should be for your life, and watch God's signs and wonders follow you!

## April 18

*What shall we then say to these things? If God be for us, who can be against us? He that spared not his own Son, but delivered him up for us all, how shall he not with him also freely give us all things? Who shall lay any thing to the charge of God's elect? It is God that justifieth. Who is he that condemneth? It is Christ that died, yea rather, that is risen again, who is even at the right hand of God, who also maketh intercession for us. Who shall separate us from the love of Christ? shall tribulation, or distress, or persecution, or famine, or nakedness, or peril, or sword? As it is written, For thy sake we are killed all the day long; we are accounted as sheep for the slaughter.*
*Nay, in all these things we are more than conquerors through him that loved us.*
Romans 8:31-37

The process of your **Deliverance** is real and demanding, nevertheless rewarding with signs and wonders that are exceedingly, abundantly, more than you can ever ask or imagine by the power working within you.  The power working within you is the very thing that makes the process's reality and demands bearable and fuels your ability to endure; press your way through. Therefore, **Deliverance** comes to you directly as a result of your engagement with God through this process.  It is not enough just to cry for help; you must also be a part of your help, solution, empowering you from within with what is necessary to overcome that which stands in the way of you living in your **Deliverance**.  Go ahead in your demanding and overpowering experiences, *Breathe: New Life*, inhaling your **Deliverance** and exhaling without cost, blame, or loss as a result of Christ paying for, justifying, and restoring you to the fullness of your potential as God has created you so that you would live in His promise of life and life more abundantly.  Do not worry, although the process feels overwhelming, you are more than a conqueror because of Christ's love and sacrifice for you to live in your abundance.

## April 19

*Now may the God who brought us peace by raising from the dead our Lord Jesus Christ so that he would be the Great Shepherd of his flock; and by the power of the blood of the eternal covenant may he work perfection into every part of you giving you all that you need to fulfill your destiny. And may he express through you all that is excellent and pleasing to him through your life-union with Jesus the Anointed One who is to receive all glory forever!*
*Amen!*
Hebrews 13:20-21 (TPT)

The power of our **Deliverance** is made possible as we go through the process of our **Deliverance**. The process for most people is difficult because it demands that we press forward through the difficulties and chaos of our experiences toward what can and should be for our lives. Because of the pressure to press, we often find ourselves making decisions based on our flesh that may not always align with where we are going, but instead only satisfy the urge to press; temporary relief over long-term benefit.

Remember, the devil is a deceiver, deceiving us into thinking that we need not sacrifice; we only need to satisfy our flesh, and it will determine our outcome and thus our abundant life. Not so, for without sacrifice there is no gain and no sustainable victory. Sacrifice is about putting our flesh behind the building of the Spirit within us. Christ's shedding of His blood served as payment so that the Spirit of God residing within all of us would take precedence over the choices of our flesh to reconcile us to God's promises for our lives. Therefore, *Breathe: New Life* and be reconciled to your **Deliverance**, the shedding of Jesus' blood, His sacrifice has made it possible for you to overcome the flesh for the release of the Spirit within that empowers you to overcome and inherit all things.

## April 20

*Their enemies oppressed them and subjected them to their power. Many times he delivered them, but they were bent on rebellion and they wasted away in their sin. Yet he took note of their distress when he heard their cry; for their sake he remembered his covenant and out of his great love he relented. He caused all who held them captive to show them mercy.*

126

God loves you, and there is absolutely nothing you can do about it but increase your love for Him. God chose to make you and me the crown of His glory, His revelation, meaning we were created to reveal God Himself, which is love. We are the manifestation of God's love in the world as living, breathing creatures who have been fearfully and wonderfully made. The world, all of creation, was created for His glory and given to us to care for and to be fruitful and multiply. Therefore, you and I have the opportunity and the privilege to get past our shortcomings, mistakes, and mess-ups to assume our natural and God-given position in His revelation. Get over you and your shortcomings, God knew and yet chose you, press forward. We all make mistakes, wrong choices, and sometimes pursue the desires of our flesh, pushing us in wrong directions; however, God in creation built an avenue for me and you to get back on the right track, **Breathe: New Life** and receive and embrace God's love that will lead and guide you to your **Deliverance**. God's process of **Deliverance** is your built-in adjustment to your pathway for life and life more abundantly. Celebrate your Resurrection, over and over again through your circumstances, and **Breathe: New Life**!

## April 21

*"Therefore, say to the Israelites: 'I am the Lord, and I will bring you out from under the yoke of the Egyptians. I will free you from being slaves to them, and I will redeem you with an outstretched arm and with mighty acts of judgment. I will take you as my own people, and I will be your God. Then you will know that I am the*

*Lord your God, who brought you out from under the yoke of the*
*Egyptians. And I will bring you to the land I swore with uplifted*
*hand to give to Abraham, to Isaac and to Jacob. I will give it to you*
*as a possession. I am the Lord.'"*
Exodus 6:6-8 (NIV)

Our process of **Deliverance** is the vehicle through which God is
revealed to and through us.  As we go through, press our way
through the difficulties of our lives, we come to know God, not
just His Word and what we have heard or believe about who He is,
but we actually get to experience who He is, thus building our
faith and making us His witness, receiving power.  If we did not
have difficulties, especially those in which we cannot see our way,
and we press through them, trusting Him beyond knowing, we
would not realize who God is and experience His power, the Word
becoming flesh.  Although the difficulties may be oppressive and
we are pleading, crying for God to **Deliver** us, know that the
process itself is made easier as we ***Breathe: New Life***, focus on
what the obstacles will bring in the revelation of God, releasing us
to our higher calling and thus our abundant life.  God will bring
you through to your land of flowing with milk and honey, and all
along the way, reveal His awesome power and might and that
which He has given you to sustain you in your land of promise!

## April 22

*For the Lord your God is bringing you into a good land—a land*
*with brooks, streams, and deep springs gushing out into the*
*valleys and hills; a land with wheat and barley, vines and fig trees,*
*pomegranates, olive oil and honey; a land where bread will not be*

128

*scarce and you will lack nothing; a land where the rocks are iron*
*and you can dig copper out of the hills.*
Deuteronomy 8:7-9 (NIV)


The **Deliverance** God has prepared for us, both in general and in each of our circumstances, is a land flowing with milk and honey; generous and abundant to the point that it will cause us to be fruitful and multiply. Therefore, receiving our **Deliverance** may be tedious, but it cannot be compared to what God has prepared and is waiting for us. Thus, we must choose between engaging in and enduring the process of our **Deliverance**, cultivating who we are to become who God has created us to be, rather than the momentary satisfaction of just being. God has declared for you and me life and life more abundantly in general and specifically in each of our circumstances in which we have the potential to overcome, be triumphant, be more than a conqueror to witness, to be evidence of the power and love of God. *Breathe: New Life* in general and in your circumstances, it is already yours, and choose to engage and endure the process of **Deliverance** for God is bringing you into your good land, your abundance, your place to be fruitful and multiply!


## April 23

*But thanks be to God, which giveth us the victory through our Lord*
*Jesus Christ.*
I Corinthians 15:57

Despite the difficulties of your life, you must remember that you have already been **Delivered** to your place of life and life more abundantly.  Our mindset will determine the space and actions that lead us to our place of promise, our abundant life.  You and I have the victory because Jesus died and sacrificed so that whatever we experience, we will endure and overcome, and even if it appears that it is a death, grave, and hell experience, we will rise again to a place of all power.  *Breathe: New Life* and accept your **Deliverance,** although it will involve a process that meanders, you have already won, you are victorious, set your mind and thoughts to that which embraces and manifests your Deliverance.

## April 24

*He has saved us and called us to a holy life—not because of*
*anything we have done but because of his own purpose and grace.*
*This grace was given us in Christ Jesus before the beginning of*
*time, but it has now been revealed through the appearing of our*
*Savior, Christ Jesus, who has destroyed death and has brought life*
*and immortality to light through the gospel.*
II Timothy 1:9-10 (NIV)

I believe there are at least two things common to all of us.  First, our existence indicates that there is some purpose to our being, and second, no matter where we are or what we believe, we have unexpressed possibilities.  Both the purpose and the unexpressed possibilities of our lives are driving forces that we seek **Deliverance from**.  Deliverance means being saved, rescued, and set free. Therefore, if we are to be set free to live our life's purpose and realize our unexpressed possibilities, it requires our openness and availability to identify our purpose and the passions that drive us to be a positive force in the world. We are called to a holy calling, a unique purpose that is found specifically within us, to which we respond by creating spaces that spring forth life in and through us. Our creation of spaces, fueled by our passions within, is in collaboration with God Himself, our Creator, who, because we choose to diligently pursue our holy calling to create life-giving spaces, provides us the opportunities, the grace to do so. God's grace is tilted in our favor because we have chosen to diligently pursue what He created us to be, fulfilling His revelation, glory, and thus our being His witness. Remember, we shall receive power to be His witness once the Holy Spirit of God within us comes over us, our purpose consuming us and our going forward to create life-giving spaces. *Breathe: New Life* and be **Delivered**, set free to your life's purpose, and express all God's possibilities for life and life more abundantly for and through you!

## April 25

*And we know that all things work together for good to them that*
*love God, to them who are the called according to his purpose.*
Romans 8:28

**Deliverance** is a foregone conclusion when we are operating in that for which we have been called. At creation, God had already determined our life and life more abundantly, and thus, no matter what we face, we can choose the pathway of our abundant life by simply responding to His call. God calls us to live in such a way that we are continuously utilizing the gifts He has given us to create spaces for life, and as we do so, God provides us with favor, grace to overcome and compensate for our shortcomings, removing any threat to our ability to create life and live abundantly. *Breathe: New Life* in your circumstances and walk in your prearranged **Deliverance** for all things will work out for your good because you are walking in response to God's call on your life, and you will be His witness, revealing God's power and love!

## April 26

*Now to him that is of power to stablish you according to my gospel, and the preaching of Jesus Christ, according to the revelation of the mystery, which was kept secret since the world began.*
Romans 16:25

We have been given permission to *Breathe: New Life* into our circumstances because we have been established. With God's unique call on our life and our response to His call, we are equipped with the grace, favor of God that allows us, through our circumstances, despite and in spite of us, to reveal God and thus His fulfilled promises through us. God uses us to reveal Himself. God fearfully and wonderfully created you, and He has chosen the life that unfolds before you for you. If you would believe, choose to positively respond to His call, you are set to overcome any and all things; **Deliverance** is yours for the asking. Your **Deliverance** is set, established before the world began, and your journey of life, with all of its twists and turns, ups and downs, will lead you to the revelation of God's promises for your abundant life. Heed God's call for you and *Breathe: New Life* into your circumstances, focused on the fulfillment of His promises in and through you and your circumstances.

## April 27

*I therefore, the prisoner of the Lord, beseech you that ye walk worthy of the vocation wherewith ye are called, With all lowliness and meekness, with longsuffering, forbearing one another in love; Endeavouring to keep the unity of the Spirit in the bond of peace. There is one body, and one Spirit, even as ye are called in one hope of your calling; One Lord, one faith, one baptism, One God and Father of all, who is above all, and through all, and in you all. But unto every one of us is given grace according to the measure of the gift of Christ. Wherefore he saith, When he ascended up on high, he led captivity captive, and gave gifts unto men. (Now that he ascended, what is it but that he also descended first into the lower parts of the earth? He that descended is the same also that ascended up far above all heavens, that he might fill all things.) And he gave some, apostles; and some, prophets; and some, evangelists; and some, pastors and teachers;*
Ephesians 4:1-11

We can rest assured that, whatever the experiences of our lives, we have grace, favor from God to go through them to get to the place of God's blessing on and for our lives. Our steps have been ordered by God and if we choose to walk in response to His call, ordered steps, for our lives God has already supplied the grace required for us to overcome whatever may exist so that we would be victorious, gaining life and life more abundantly. Paul defines Himself as a prisoner to God's call on His life and begs us to do the same for responding to God's call, walking worthy of the vocation for which we are called, we gain everything, the favor necessary to win. **Breathe: New Life** and walk in the full **Deliverance** of God for the life that has been prepared for you. As you walk in response to His call, you are a gift given so that the world would prosper and God would be revealed, as well as the fullness of God's blessings on your life!

## April 28

*According to the eternal purpose which he purposed in Christ Jesus our Lord: In whom we have boldness and access with confidence by the faith of him. Wherefore I desire that ye faint not at my tribulations for you, which is your glory.*
Ephesians 3:11-13

We need not fall apart because of the difficulties we experience; instead, we should take on an air of expectation, for they are the vehicles in which God reveals Himself. Our **Deliverance** is the process of the revelation of God. As we engage our difficulties, we come to know God in a personal way and, as a result, are set free, **Delivered** to move, and have our being in His intent for our life and life more abundantly. The present state of your affairs can never be compared to the glory, revelation of God through your affairs. Go ahead and **Breathe: New Life** in your experiences and watch God reveal Himself, His eternal purpose, call for your life, and give you the power to overcome and be set free in your life and life more abundantly; the promise of **Deliverance**.

## April 29

*Forasmuch as ye know that ye were not redeemed with corruptible things, as silver and gold, from your vain conversation received by tradition from your fathers; But with the precious blood of Christ, as of a lamb without blemish and without spot: Who verily was foreordained before the foundation of the world, but was manifest in these last times for you, Who by him do believe in God, that raised him up from the dead, and gave him glory; that your faith and hope might be in God.*
I Peter 1:18-21

The sacrifice of Christ serves as payment for you and me to have the right to embrace and walk in **Deliverance**; to be set free from any and all things that would prevent us from living in the maximum potential God intends for our lives. Thus, we need not fear or fret because of the difficulties we may experience in the circumstances of our lives; we can *Breathe: New Life* into them by seeing our victory as complete and working our field to produce that which is already ours. **Deliverance** begins in our spirit and then invades our mind, transforming our thoughts, plans, and thus our actions to that which will bring to pass what is the foregone conclusion, our victory. Your life and life more abundantly have been redeemed, paid for, and thus it is up to you to work the field of your circumstances with the intent of creating overcoming experiences that produce your life and life more abundantly, *Breathe: New Life*!

## April 30

*For ye are bought with a price: therefore glorify God in your body,*
*and in your spirit, which are God's.*
I Corinthians 6:20

Living in the fullness of our **Deliverance** demands that we reveal God in and through our lives. Because the ultimate end of God's **Delivering** to us His promises, our **Deliverance**, is to make us His witness, thus the process of our receiving is cluttered with God's opportunity to reveal Himself to us. The process is the phase of receiving and walking in our **Deliverance**, trusting yet not knowing, which none of us wishes or would avoid if we could; however, it is necessary for our **Deliverance**. As we engage in the process, including the twists and turns, ups and downs, and setbacks, God uses them as an opportunity to help us to know Him in a very personal way, collecting our process lived experiences that serve as evidence of our witness. Thus, *Breathe: New Life* in each of your circumstances, for you will overcome by knowing that much more about the fullness of God and thus receive His power to be His witness, walking and living in your **Deliverance**!

# RECEIVE NEW LIFE

## MAY

## May 1

*Now may the God who brought us peace by raising from the dead our Lord Jesus Christ so that he would be the Great Shepherd of his flock; and by the power of the blood of the eternal covenant may he work perfection into every part of you giving you all that you need to fulfill your destiny. And may he express through you all that is excellent and pleasing to him through your life-union with Jesus the Anointed One who is to receive all glory forever! Amen!*
Hebrews 13:20-21 (TPT)

God has already provided us with that which can and should be for our lives through the sacrifice, offering of Christ. It is up to you and me to accept our responsibility as co-creators with God to ensure the manifestation of what He has provided and promised to and for us. Therefore, the new life you want must be received by you and begin with high expectations. **Receive New Life** by raising your level of expectations beyond what is or the norm to that which can and should be for your life. You are as great as you believe you are, and you can become what you believe you can become; the keyword is to believe. Our beliefs will determine our expectations, and our expectations lay the groundwork for our outcomes. Thus, we must take the initiative to *Breathe: New Life* into our circumstances and watch them turn into building blocks for our life and life more abundantly.

## May 2

*And the very God of peace sanctify you wholly; and I pray God your whole spirit and soul and body be preserved blameless unto the coming of our Lord Jesus Christ. Faithful is he that calleth you, who also will do it.*
I Thessalonians 5:23-24

New life is here for you; the only requirement is that you receive it. **Receiving New Life** to your situation is manifested by you taking action on your expectations and, as a result, producing the new life that can and should be yours in your situation as well as in your life generally. Life takes; however, you have been given the power to take back everything that belongs to you and, with God, to co-create in it that which can and should be for your life, the fulfillment of God's promises for your life and life more abundantly. You have the power within to control and shape your narrative, rooted in your expectations, and as you take charge of your life, you take back control and steer it toward what can and should be. You have been set apart for that which God has ordained. Seize your anointing, take back control, and drive your life to the place of your promise. Without question, life will not always cooperate with God's will for your life. Press forward anyway and *Breathe: New Life*, driving your narrative to **Receive New Life** as you believe and act in your expectations, God's promises for you to be fruitful and multiply!

**May 3**

*But God raised him from the dead, freeing him from the agony of death, because it was impossible for death to keep its hold on him.*
Acts 2:24 (NIV)

**Receive New Life** because, despite and in spite of what appears to be the impossibility of your circumstances, you can live and live abundantly. You can overcome whatever may exist in your life to keep you from living at your maximum potential because God raised Jesus from the dead as evidence that He and you will always win together. The impossibility may loom large and seem insurmountable. *Breathe: New Life*, and watch God empower you to take back the controls of your life and drive your narrative to that which He has promised, your life and life more abundantly. Your choice to believe God and His promise is the fuel necessary for you to raise your expectations in your valleys of the shadows of death and be raised, *Breathe: New Life*! Death cannot hold you down; it is only you who can. Choose today to believe, raise your expectations, and work your field to **Receive New Life,** no matter what is going on in your life.

## May 4

*And God has not only raised the Lord [to life], but will also raise us up by His power.*
I Corinthians 6:14 (AMP)

God's intent in raising Jesus from the dead was to provide evidence that there is nothing in our lives that can overcome us or cause our expectations to evaporate, so that He can raise us back to life.  Whatever you face that seeks to prevent you from getting to your place of being fruitful and multiplying as God intends, can and will be defeated.  Remember, no weapon formed against you will prosper.... You are more than a conqueror.  *Breathe: New Life* into whatever appears to be the impossible, the setback, and press forward in what God has declared, and **Receive New Life**.  It may look dead, but you have a record, evidence that what is dead can be raised back to life, resurrected with all power.  I dare you to believe and *Breathe: New Life*!

## May 5

And what we believe is that the One who raised up the Master Jesus will just as certainly raise us up with you, alive.

II Corinthians 4:14

The key to our ability to **Receive New Life** is our willingness to believe.  Believing that what God has promised will be, must also be fused with the belief that you can do it, despite and in spite of life and the challenges life brings.  Believing in your ability to engage and overcome will be the fuel that helps you to be more than a conqueror and seize that which is yours, your life and life more abundantly in your situation.  Your actions, to *Breathe: New Life*, are fueled by your belief, and as the Word says, as you diligently pursue, God rewards you, fulfilling your unexpressed possibilities that produce His promises for your life.  Receive New Life today by believing and acting on that belief.  If you can believe

God raised Jesus from the dead, He certainly can bring to pass His promise for you to be fruitful and multiply in all things!

## May 6

*The thief cometh not, but for to steal, and to kill, and to destroy: I am come that they might have life, and that they might have it more abundantly.*
John 10:10

To **Receive New Life** requires availability, a willingness to see beyond what is to what shall become, and a commitment to ensure it is made real in your life. We must be discerning of the people, places, and things of our lives to determine their viability for you to bring to pass that which can and should be for your life. The more we allow excessive baggage to remain, the less likely we are to press forward in our higher calling. Therefore, place priority on the people, places, and things in your life that contribute to and/or motivate you to become everything God intends. God, as revealed through Christ, the Word made flesh, has come to our lives so that we might access, in and through all things, God's promise of life and life more abundantly. No matter what you face or the fears you have about facing your circumstances, *Breathe: New Life* by your willingness to see, focus on what you and your circumstances can and will be to bring to pass God's promises for your life and life more abundantly.

## May 7

And then, after your brief suffering, the God of all loving grace, who has called you to share in his eternal glory in Christ, will personally and powerfully restore you and make you stronger than ever. Yes, he will set you firmly in place and build you up.
I Peter 5:10 (TPT)

Life takes, and in its taking, it causes us to contract and/or struggle with pain; however, we can endure the contractions and struggles of our lives by the simple act to **Breathe: New Life**. **Breathe: New Life** in and through the circumstances of our lives allows us to refocus our synergy (spirit and energy) from the contractions and struggles of our lives to our purpose and the higher calling for our lives to be fruitful and multiply in all things. Remember that what has come to deter you from what God has promised for your life is deception, and with your synergy, you must resist the devil, deception, and pain, and it will flee. The pain is your indication that you are moving in the direction of giving birth to your new life, to **Receive New Life** as God has ordained in and through every one of your experiences. Do not allow contractions or struggles to detract you. After going through them, you will be restored to what God intends for your life, and it will be exceedingly, abundantly, more than you can ever ask or think, causing you to rise with all power!

## May 8

*And it fell on a day, that Elisha passed to Shunem, where was a great woman; and she constrained him to eat bread. And so it was, that as oft as he passed by, he turned in thither to eat bread.*

*And she said unto her husband, Behold now, I perceive that this is an holy man of God, which passeth by us continually. Let us make a little chamber, I pray thee, on the wall; and let us set for him there a bed, and a table, and a stool, and a candlestick: and it shall be, when he cometh to us, that he shall turn in thither. And it fell on a day, that he came thither, and he turned into the chamber, and lay there. And he said to Gehazi his servant, Call this Shunammite. And when he had called her, she stood before him. And he said unto him, Say now unto her, Behold, thou hast been careful for us with all this care; what is to be done for thee? wouldest thou be spoken for to the king, or to the captain of the host? And she answered, I dwell among mine own people. And he said, What then is to be done for her? And Gehazi answered, Verily she hath no child, and her husband is old. And he said, Call her. And when he had called her, she stood in the door. And he said, About this season, according to the time of life, thou shalt embrace a son. And she said, Nay, my lord, thou man of God, do not lie unto thine handmaid. And the woman conceived, and bare a son at that season that Elisha had said unto her, according to the time of life.*
II Kings 4:8-17

To **Receive New Life** requires preparation for the transformation process necessary to live the new life desired. Our desires, unexpressed opportunities, can only be leveraged for the good, God's purpose for our lives, because we are appropriately equipped to do so. Therefore, we must imagine and cast a vision for what new life should be and then upon that begin to equip ourselves and spaces to bear the newness that will come and exist as we diligently pursue what we believe can and should be for our lives. The vision must be big enough to attract what is necessary

146

for us to live in the new life, and flexible enough to accommodate the process of transformation for the new life. Thus, our ability to **Breathe: New Life** embraces the process of cultivating, adjusting as required to meet the new challenges that are inevitable in new spaces. Our new spaces are God's opportunity to reveal Himself in ways in which you come to know Him better, but also realize more of the treasure that is within you. It is through the process of transformation, the daily dying, that the revelation of God and you are made real, flesh in your life. **Breathe: New Life** by setting the stage of your life to accommodate and adjust for the new, and in so doing, you have set the stage for your desires, unexpressed opportunities, to be made flesh in and through your lived experiences.

## May 9

*And when the child was grown, it fell on a day, that he went out to his father to the reapers. And he said unto his father, My head, my head. And he said to a lad, Carry him to his mother. And when he had taken him, and brought him to his mother, he sat on her knees till noon, and then died. And she went up, and laid him on the bed of the man of God, and shut the door upon him, and went out. And she called unto her husband, and said, Send me, I pray thee, one of the young men, and one of the asses, that I may run to the man of God, and come again. And he said, Wherefore wilt thou go to him to day? it is neither new moon, nor sabbath. And she said, It shall be well. Then she saddled an ass, and said to her servant, Drive, and go forward; slack not thy riding for me, except I bid thee. So she went and came unto the man of God to mount Carmel. And it came to pass, when the man of God saw her afar off, that he said to Gehazi his servant, Behold, yonder is that Shunammite: Run now, I pray thee, to meet her, and say unto her, Is it well with thee? is it well with thy husband? is it well with the child? And she answered, It is well. And when she came to the man of God to the hill, she caught him by the feet: but Gehazi came near to thrust her away. And the man of God said, Let her alone; for her soul is vexed within her: and the LORD hath hid it from me, and hath not told me. Then she said, Did I desire a son of my lord? did I not say, Do not deceive me? Then he said to Gehazi, Gird up thy loins, and take my staff in thine hand, and go thy way: if thou meet any man, salute him not; and if any salute thee, answer him not again: and lay my staff upon the face of the child. And the mother of the child said, As the LORD liveth, and as thy soul liveth, I will not leave thee. And he arose, and followed her. And Gehazi passed on before them, and laid the staff upon the face of the child; but there was neither voice, nor hearing. Wherefore he went again to meet him, and told him, saying, The child is not awaked. And when Elisha was come into the house, behold, the child was dead, and laid upon his bed. He went in therefore, and shut the door upon them twain, and prayed unto the LORD. And he went up, and lay upon the child, and put his mouth upon his mouth, and his eyes upon his eyes, and his hands upon his hands: and he stretched himself upon the child; and the flesh of the child waxed warm. Then he returned, and walked in the house to and fro; and went up, and stretched himself upon him: and the child sneezed seven times, and the child opened his eyes. And he called Gehazi, and said, Call this Shunammite. So he called her. And when she was come in unto him, he said, Take up thy son. Then she went in, and fell at his feet, and bowed herself to the ground, and took up her son, and went out.*

II Kings 4:18-37

Once we have **Received New Life**, the major challenge is how to sustain it and yet grow. God is always bidding us to come higher, to press forward to a higher calling, thus as we **Receive New Life,** we understand that it is an indication of our growing higher and higher. The higher and higher is the fulfillment of God's promise, sealed with the blood of Jesus, that we have life and life more abundantly, not just to live but to live abundantly in a consistent space of overflowing. Thus, we must *Breathe: New Life* constantly by cultivating our space to accommodate the newness, but also contributing to our growth in our new life. Cultivating requires that we build into our experiences an evaluation protocol, a healthy and intimate relationship with God that challenges us to live in the fullness of our promises but also in our abilities to co-create with Him, making His Word flesh in our lives. In our healthy and intimate relationship with God, we *Breathe: New Life* into our present experiences that press us forward into experiences that take us higher and higher, sustaining and growing our new life.

## May 10

*Then one of them said, "I will surely return to you about this time next year, and Sarah your wife will have a son." Now Sarah was listening at the entrance to the tent, which was behind him. Abraham and Sarah were already very old, and Sarah was past the age of childbearing. So Sarah laughed to herself as she thought, "After I am worn out and my lord is old, will I now have this pleasure?" Then the Lord said to Abraham, "Why did Sarah laugh and say, 'Will I really have a child, now that I am old?' Is*

149

*anything too hard for the Lord? I will return to you at the*
*appointed time next year, and Sarah will have a son."*
Genesis 18:10-14 (NIV)


Often, the vicissitudes of life limit us in our ability to conceive the great things God has for our lives, making it seem impossible and whimsical that we would be able to receive the great things of God, **Receive New Life**. However, God's promises to you are exceedingly, abundantly, more than you can ever ask or think by the power working within you. You are the key to your dreams, your promises fulfilled. If you can conceive it, you can achieve it, but only through your ability to believe that it can and should be. Press toward what can and should be for your life, fueled by your belief, faith, not only in God but in your willingness to diligently pursue, and as you do, ***Breathe: New Life*** and receive God's rewards in overflow. Nothing is too hard for God if you would only believe and act on that belief. God is big and bad enough to give you your heart's desires, unexpressed opportunities fulfilled, which gives Him the glory!


## May 11


*And the LORD visited Sarah as he had said, and the LORD did unto Sarah as he had spoken. For Sarah conceived, and bare Abraham a son in his old age, at the set time of which God had spoken to him.*
Genesis 21:1-2


God will do what He said; if He does not, it will not matter, for heaven and earth will be dissolved, and all will be lost. You can

150

walk worthy in that which God has called you because you have an absolute assurance that all things will work together for your good. After all, God has said it and prepared all of His creation to align for it. Please note your victory is absolute, but it does not mean that there will not be trials and tribulations along the way; the contractions and struggles are necessary to force you to *Breathe: New Life*. *Breathe: New Life* is an indication that you are willing to participate, serving as a co-creator with God, to bring to pass His revelation and the revelation of you and His intent for your life. God will never force us to do anything to **Receive New Life**; it will be a choice that you and I voluntarily make and act in conjunction with Him to bring to pass. No matter the impossibilities of your situation, experience God and *Breathe: New Life*, and you will position yourself to **Receive New Life** in the exceedingly, abundantly, more than as God has promised, working in and through you!

## May 12

*If you declare with your mouth, "Jesus is Lord," and believe in your heart that God raised him from the dead, you will be saved. For it is with your heart that you believe and are justified, and it is with your mouth that you profess your faith and are saved.*
Romans 9:9-10 (NIV)

To **Receive New Life** is a matter of the heart. You must believe in your heart what can and should be for your circumstances and life, and as a result, fuel your action toward that which can and should be. Without faith, believing, and acting, we cannot please God; those who come to Him must believe that He is and that He is a rewarder. The heart matter triggers a three-step process: coming to God in your heart, believing that He is, acting on what we say we believe, and God rewarding us not because we get it right, but because we diligently pursue in actions what we believe. *Breathe: New Life* by taking the necessary actions based on what you believe can and should be for your life, as God, His Word has declared; confessing by word and deed. As you *Breathe: New Life,* you set into motion to **Receive New Life**, in and through your circumstances, simply because of your willingness to believe with action toward your promises from God!

## May 13

*And Isaac was forty years old when he married Rebekah daughter of Bethuel the Aramean from Paddan Aram and sister of Laban the Aramean. Isaac prayed to the Lord on behalf of his wife, because she was childless. The Lord answered his prayer, and his wife Rebekah became pregnant.*
Genesis 25:20-21 (NIV)

**Receive New Life** because you desire it and you ask for it. We have not because we ask not! Know that you do not have to live beneath your potential, you have been permitted to live in the fullness of God's promises for you, your life, and life more abundantly; all you need to do is ask. Without a doubt, life and your circumstances will not always cooperate and often will be in direct opposition to your promise, but God is your very present help; call on Him, and He will answer. *Breathe: New Life* by asking for what it is you believe can and should be for your life, and *Receive New Life*, it awaits your request!

## May 14

*And when he prayed to him, the Lord was moved by his entreaty and listened to his plea; so he brought him back to Jerusalem and to his kingdom. Then Manasseh knew that the Lord is God.*
II Chronicles 33:13 (NIV)

God desires the best for you and me, and He awaits your call unto Him, and He will readily move on your behalf. The vicissitudes of life are many and can be overwhelming, but the fight has been fixed on your behalf with the assurance of God's presence to and for your abundant life. Ask, and it shall be given unto you; seek, and ye shall find; knock, and the door will be opened for you. As you **Breathe: New Life**, diligently believing and acting on your belief, your intimate relationship with God will provide you with everything you need when and how you need it. God promises never to leave you or forsake you, always be with you, and with Him is His reward. **Receive New Life** today by just asking out of the depths of your intimate relationship with God, and you can count on Him being moved on your behalf, releasing your life and life more abundantly in and through all things!

## May 15

*So we fasted and petitioned our God about this, and he answered our prayer.*
Ezra 8:23 (NIV)

God's ear is inclined toward us because He loves us and wants the best for us.  Thus, to **Receive New Life,** you need only ask and diligently pursue, and God will grant you your request.  There is no good thing that God our Father will withhold from us.  Trust and lean unto God's guiding and directing, and you will walk into your new life.  Go ahead and *Breathe: New Life* despite and in spite of the obstacles you see or are afraid of.  God is only a prayer, a call, away, and He will come with the fullness of His power, granting unto you exceedingly, abundantly, more than.

## May 16

*And God strengthened Elijah mightily. Pulling up his robe and tying it around his waist, Elijah ran in front of Ahab's chariot until they reached Jezreel.*
I Kings 18:46 (MSG)

Trust God to provide you with whatever you need to **Receive New Life** in and through each circumstance of your life.  Through your experiences of **Receiving New Life** in your circumstances, you build confidence and faith in God and His holy, unique calling on your life.  With your confidence and faith in what He has called you to, you are equipped with a boldness to take on the circumstances of your life as a victor and not a victim.  Thus, as a result, you *Breathe: New Life* into all things, into everything you do.  Your new life awaits you.  Pull yourself up and tighten your belt.  Challenges will come and may appear stronger than you could ever dream, but know you have already won, **Receive New Life**!

## May 17

*You won't need to take anything with you—trust in God alone.
And don't get distracted from my purpose by anyone you might
meet along the way.*
Luke 10:4 (TPT)

Our trusting God is sufficient for us to overcome all obstacles and
**Receive New Life** in and through our life's experiences.  Each life
experience is an opportunity for God to reveal Himself for who He
is, but also to reveal you for whom He created you to be in all of
His glory.  Therefore, as you engage in the experiences of your life,
*Breathe: New Life* for it has already been set up for you, God's
opportunity to reveal who you have been created to be.  **Receive
New Life** because you are focused on God's revelation in and
through your experiences that bring about the springs of life-
giving water flowing in you.  Remember, God said, "Out of your
belly shall flow rivers of life."  You have everything you need; you
have God on your side, thus. *Breathe: New Life* and watch God
spring His intended purpose for your life and life more abundantly
burst forth and through you to **Receive New Life**!

## May 18

*Then the Lord said to Moses, "Why are you crying out to me? Tell
the Israelites to move on.  Raise your staff and stretch out your
hand over the sea to divide the water so that the Israelites can go
through the sea on dry ground.  I will harden the hearts of the*

*Egyptians so that they will go in after them. And I will gain glory through Pharaoh and all his army, through his chariots and his horsemen.  The Egyptians will know that I am the Lord when I gain glory through Pharaoh, his chariots and his horsemen."*
Exodus 14:15-18 (NIV)

**Breathe: New Life** because it is your right and privilege given by God at your creation.  If you believe, then all things would be possible to you, despite and in spite of the challenges and obstacles you face.  God went so far as to send His only begotten Son so that he would show, be a witness, that even death, hell, and the grave could not contain the promise of life and life more abundantly.  Go ahead and use what you got, ***Breathe: New Life*** into your circumstances and watch God do what only he can do: make a way out of no way, making you victorious and triumphant against all foes.  God, at His creation, created you with everything you need, unearth it and stand before the waters of life, including the challenges and obstacles before you, and cast forth your gift, work your field, and reap your harvest.  In your ability to ***Breathe: New Life,*** you declare before all creation the fullness of God's power.  Therefore, the greater the challenge and the more difficult the obstacle you face, the more it will serve as a witness to the power of God.  Let God out of the box and reveal Himself to all creation and you, His chosen ones, with rights and privileges and thereunto pertaining, **Receive New Life**, in and through all things as the crown of His glory!

**May 19**

*God kept releasing a flow of extraordinary miracles through the hands of Paul. Because of this, people took Paul's handkerchiefs and articles of clothing, even pieces of cloth that had touched his skin, laying them on the bodies of the sick, and diseases and demons left them and they were healed.*
Acts 19:11-12 (TPT)

The new life God has in store for you and me is extraordinary and beyond our wildest imaginations if we would only believe. Our belief is solidified because of our actions upon our belief; speaking [acting on] those things that are not as if they were. The more we act out our belief in our lives and our circumstances, the greater the opportunity for God to reveal Himself and do the miraculous. Remember, signs and wonders follow, meaning that as you walk in that which God has called you, He rewards you with the signs and wonders of His miraculous power operating through and for you. The amazing power of God in Peter's life brought new life to others in a miraculous way that blew people's minds, but also lifted Christ and drew people to Him into an intimate, lived-experienced relationship with Jesus. **Receive New Life** and allow the flow of life in you to astonish people, places, and things in your life, and they too will be drawn to the One who does the exceedingly, abundantly, more than one can ever ask or think. Today, ***Breathe: New Life*** into your circumstances and watch the signs and wonders follow you as you **Receive New Life**!

## May 20

*When he had said this, Jesus called in a loud voice, "Lazarus, come out!" The dead man came out, his hands and feet wrapped with strips of linen, and a cloth around his face.*
John 11:43-44 (NIV)

It does not matter what challenges and/or obstacles you face to **Receive New Life**, if God has promised it, He will call it into existence. Spend a majority of your time developing an intimate relationship with God the Creator, and as you "know" Him, you will come to "know" you and the promises of God for your life. As you "know," you can then appropriately respond to God's call on your life and *Breathe: New Life*. God will always call you and your circumstances out of death to live abundantly in His promises for your life. The very things you fear that would hinder and/or prevent you from living in your abundance will not be able to contain you. Just respond to God's unique calling on your life, and you, as well as everything concerning you, will come forth even though you may be bound. Therefore, **Receive New Life** despite your challenges and obstacles by simply responding to God's unique call on your life and seeing God, who has worked out every detail before you began, reveal Him and His abundantly filled purpose and plan for your life - He is the Creator-God.

## May 21

*The Lord heard Elijah's cry, and the boy's life returned to him, and he lived. Elijah picked up the child and carried him down from the room into the house. He gave him to his mother and said, "Look, your son is alive!" Then the woman said to Elijah, "Now I know*

*that you are a man of God and that the word of the Lord from*
*your mouth is the truth."*
I Kings 17:22-24 (NIV)


**Breathe: New Life** into your circumstances despite them appearing to be dead; allow the work of God to intervene, giving you a relevant revelation of the fullness of God's power. God has ordained for you to be saved, delivered into the life and life more abundantly that is yours. It is His intervening work; therefore, all you need to do is diligently pursue it, and you will receive. Our diligent pursuit of the abundant life God has promised us is not hindered or hampered by death, hell, or the grave, because our God is bigger than life itself and is the Creator-God, with the ability to create out of nothing. With the Creator-God at your disposal, you have everything you need to bring life to your circumstances, diligently pursue it, and position yourself to **Receive New Life**!


## May 22


*I am the LORD, your Holy One, the creator of Israel, your King.*
*Thus saith the LORD, which maketh a way in the sea, and a path in*
*the mighty waters;*
*Which bringeth forth the chariot and horse, the army and the*
*power;*
*they shall lie down together, they shall not rise: they are extinct,*
*they are quenched as tow. Remember ye not the former things,*
*neither consider the things of old.*
*Behold, I will do a new thing; now it shall spring forth; shall ye not*
*know it?*

*I will even make a way in the wilderness, and rivers in the desert.*
*The beast of the field shall honour me, the dragons and the owls:*
*because I give waters in the wilderness, and rivers in the desert,*
*to give drink to my people, my chosen.  This people have I formed*
*for myself;*
*they shall shew forth my praise.*
Isaiah 43:15-21

When I was a child, there was a popular toy called Jack-In-The-Box.  The toy consisted of a box with a crank on the side.  Once the box opened while turning the crank to its maximum level, Jack would pop up, surprisingly and looming large.  The surprise and the looming largest of Jack remind me of God's promises for our lives, our required expectations to **Receive New Life**.  As we work our crank, the calling God has placed on our lives, surprisingly and looming large, will be the abundance of life promised. Surprisingly, because Jack, our new life, takes us by surprise, how and when God moves us into our new life, but also looming large because the new life is exceedingly, abundantly, more than we can ever ask or think.  Therefore, when we choose to work our crank, our field, we position ourselves for the revelation that God is bigger than He was; we see that God does not have to come in a certain way or do it as He did it before, we let Him out of the box to operate in His fullness.  As we see God in His fullness, we realize nothing can contain God, not even His own footsteps, we understand that God is moving, and we can chase Him, and in chasing Him, we walk right into revelation after revelation of the fullness of His power operating in our lives. Operating in the fullness of God's power continues to position us to *Breathe: New Life* and in so doing we can continuously burst forth in God's

160

generosity, life and life more abundantly, in and through all of our experiences.

## May 23

*Therefore if any man be in Christ, he is a new creature: old things are passed away; behold, all things are become new.*
II Corinthians 5:17

Once we position ourselves to **Receive New Life,** we must begin to see everything as new. The challenge in seeing all things as new is for us to be strong and courageous to ask of that which exists in our lives and that which we permit to enter our lives, how do they contribute to and/or cultivate the newness we seek for our lives? In addition to questioning everything that exists and that seeks to come into our space, we must also be willing to say no to that which exists and that which tries to enter our lives. Remember, the natural environment in which we permit ourselves to exist is the pool from which we will inhale to live in the fullness of our life and life more abundantly. Therefore, if we are to *Breathe: New Life,* we must be in a position to **Receive New Life**; totally accepting that which will make us new creatures as well as rejecting that which will keep us the same or worse! As we **Receive New Life**, we must be willing to position ourselves to become new in all ways.

## May 24

*And he that sat upon the throne said, Behold, I make all things new. And he said unto me, Write: for these words are true and faithful.*
Revelation 21:5


Although life has its challenges and often they will appear to be the very thing that will cause us to give up and/or settle for less, the Creator-God has beforehand provided for us an out, an opportunity for us to escape death and yet be triumphant.  The Creator-God is established, and He is in full control over everything.  God sits on the throne of life and thus rules over life with the dictates of His Word.  God's Word is Himself and thus is inseparable from one another, and as Creator-God, He gives us the ability to co-create with Him what He has established by His Word.  **Breathe: New Life** by taking heed to God's Word, it will be the lamp unto your feet and a light unto your pathway, your way to **Receive New Life** in and through each and every experience of your life!


## May 25


*He led you through the vast and dreadful wilderness, that thirsty and waterless land, with its venomous snakes and scorpions. He brought you water out of hard rock.  He gave you manna to eat in the wilderness, something your ancestors had never known, to humble and test you so that in the end it might go well with you. You may say to yourself, "My power and the strength of my hands have produced this wealth for me."  But remember the Lord your God, for it is he who gives you the ability to produce wealth, and so confirms his covenant, which he swore to your ancestors, as it is today.*

Deuteronomy 8:15-18 (NIV)

When we declare that we will live and not die, that things cannot stay the same, and that we want the new, we need not fear the new; we must consciously and subconsciously position ourselves to embrace it. Let's be honest, whatever is new is different and by definition is something we have never experienced before, although we desire and are thirsty for the new, and on the surface are clearly welcoming the new, there is the subconscious of our lives that rattles because of the new's uncertainty, unknowableness, and difference. However, we do not have to fear, the One who has made the new resurrection possible is also the One who will give us the ability to live and experience the abundance in the new, including overcoming our fears. God has and is faithful to and for you. ***Breathe: New Life*** and allow the breath of God's intent and desire for your fullness of life to take control, empowering you to engage whatever may exist and do so as the victor and overcomer. Position yourself to **Receive New Life** by walking in the confidence that the very Creator-God, who knows and has supplied your every need, thus has and will supply your every need, giving you the ability to produce wealth in and through each and every one of your experiences!

## May 26

*Leave Babylon, flee from the Babylonians! Announce this with shouts of joy and proclaim it. Send it out to the ends of the earth; say, "The Lord has redeemed his servant Jacob." They did not*

*thirst when he led them through the deserts; he made water flow*
*for them from the rock; he split the rock and water gushed out.*
Isaiah 48:20-21 (NIV)

**Receive New Life** by moving on from the old. If you continue to give yourself and your space permission to operate the way you always have, you will continue to get what you have always gotten. Therefore, if you are to **Receive New Life,** you must let go of the old; letting go of the old is a challenge that will impact us physically, emotionally, and spiritually. However, it can be met because God has always been faithful, even in our new life. To combat the challenge, we must ***Breathe: New Life***, cultivate our atmosphere, so that it supports the preparations and/or actually living in the new life; inhaling what supports new life and exhaling what does not. The Lord has paid for us, redeemed us, with the sacrifice of Jesus His Son, so that you and I can live in the newness of life, be resurrected from the old, and live in the new. Your new is not just defined as new, but the pathway, the next level, the ordered steps of God for your life and life more abundantly. We cannot expect to continue in Babylon and live in the fullness of what God has promised for our land flowing with milk and honey; we must first let go of Babylon, in our hearts, and thus our minds and spirit will follow. The transformation of our hearts leads to the renewing of our minds, empowering, from within - the Spirit, to act in ways that move us from Babylon to our next level of experiencing our land flowing with milk and honey, our promises!

## May 27

*But now thus saith the LORD that created thee, O Jacob,*

*and he that formed thee, O Israel,*
*Fear not: for I have redeemed thee,*
*I have called thee by thy name; thou art mine.*
*When thou passest through the waters, I will be with thee;*
*and through the rivers, they shall not overflow thee:*
*when thou walkest through the fire, thou shalt not be burned;*
*neither shall the flame kindle upon thee.*
Isaiah 43:1-2

**Breathe: New Life** to and in your circumstances, no matter how impossible and hopeless your circumstances may be, you have the power to transform whatever it is into what should be for your life. Do not fear the unknown or the uncertainty about your ability and/or resources to accomplish what needs to be done. Step forward into the light of what can and should be, and bring you and your space into alignment with what is necessary to bring to pass God's promises for your life. As you make the choice to confront your fears, you trigger the process of alignment of your life and space, and though things rattle, press forward, and all things will fall into place so that you are positioned to **Receive New Life**. The Word of God commands you not to allow fear to reign; you will experience obstacles and difficulties; however, they will not control. God has a calling on your life, and as you respond, He provides all the protection, provision, and power you need! You are an overcomer, and as a reward, you will inherit all things promised to you for your life and life more abundantly!

## May 28

*Praise God, all you peoples. Praise him everywhere and let everyone know you love him! There's no doubt about it: God holds our lives safely in his hands. He's the one who keeps us faithfully following him. O Lord, we have passed through your fire; like precious metal made pure, you've proved us, perfected us, and made us holy. You've captured us, ensnared us in your net. Then, like prisoners, you placed chains around our necks. You've allowed our enemies to prevail against us. We've passed through fire and flood, yet in the end you always bring us out better than we were before, saturated with your goodness.*
Psalm 66:8-12 (TPT)

The positioning of oneself to **Receive New Life** comes with a set of challenges, of which patience and endurance seem to be the more forceful ones; however, do not fret, you still can win. Without a doubt, everything has its challenges, especially if you believe you are walking into that which God has promised; the what can and should be for your life.  Never think just because you got your "Word," God Himself instructing you to walk in your pathway eliminates the challenges; actually, you should look for stronger challenges/demons because they intend to separate and keep you from the fulfillment, revelation, of God's promises. Therefore, you must, with your positioning, strengthen and cultivate your intimate and personal relationship with God, producing and enlarging your faith, the very fuel to produce patience and endurance.  The recent massacres via guns and racism are a great example of the requirement for patience and endurance to **Receive New Life**.  Patience, not with those who support, whether indirectly or directly, and/or through actions or silence, but instead for those who oppose and understand the impact of guns and violence within our community, to be

166

methodical and strategic about our moves for transformation. Our moves toward transformation to a new life require not only short-term thinking but also long-term thinking to develop core values, policies, power, and leverage at the ballot box. We must remember that as we pass through the stuff of our lives to **Receive New Life,** we must ***Breathe: New Life***, taking in to equip and empower so that we might be set anew and release the old, producing the life and life more abundantly promised.

## May 29

*Now, if anyone is enfolded into Christ, he has become an entirely new person. All that is related to the old order has vanished. Behold, everything is fresh and new. And God has made all things new, and reconciled us to himself, and given us the ministry of reconciling others to God. In other words, it was through the Anointed One that God was shepherding the world, not even keeping records of their transgressions, and he has entrusted to us the ministry of opening the door of reconciliation to God. We are ambassadors of the Anointed One who carry the message of Christ to the world, as though God were tenderly pleading with them directly through our lips. So we tenderly plead with you on Christ's behalf, "Turn back to God and be reconciled to him." For God made the only one who did not know sin to become sin for us, so that we might become the righteousness of God through our union with him.*
II Corinthians 5:17-21 (TPT)

We have been allowed to **Receive New Life** not just because we are so good, but instead to bring and make an acceptable new life for others.  God chooses us for the circumstances of our lives because He has equipped us with what we need to overcome; however, we must make that choice, and when we choose to overcome, **Receive New Life,** we accept the mantle of representation for Him, revealing Him in and through our lives. Therefore, as we become one with Him, enfolded in Christ, we become new creatures serving not just ourselves but God in and through humanity.  Never let the devil, darkness, and/or chaos of your life make you think this is all about you.  Yes, God is using you, but for a wider purpose: to bless the space and community in which you exist and to reconcile them to His will.  It is your relationship with God that empowers you to make the choices that lead to the prepared way that God has provided, and in so doing, you represent Him, the living, visible presence of God revealed in the world.  *Breathe: New Life*, creating a revitalization not only in your life but also in your space, your community, bringing new life, new hope to all!

## May 30

*Stand fast therefore in the liberty wherewith Christ hath made us free, and be not entangled again with the yoke of bondage.*
Galatians 5:1

As we are positioned to **Receive New Life**, we must endure; stand fast for what God has promised is true, and if we willingly choose our new life, we will be set free in it.  The old space in which we dwell supports us in holding on to old things; the very things that must be released to walk into our new life. Free yourself by choosing to be open and available to the new; in that way, it becomes easier to walk into your new life. So long as you continue to hold the breath of the old, you will not be able to exhale, making the necessary room for you to *Breathe: New Life*. New life is yours, receive it by letting go; making yourself available to become the new creature, walking in the new life of your liberty; free to be free to your life and life more abundantly!

## May 31

*And ye shall know the truth, and the truth shall make you free.*
John 8:32

*Breathe: New Life* by allowing the truth of God's Word, His promises for your life, to prevail. God desires for you to be free from any and all things that would be in opposition to His promises for your life and life more abundantly. Free yourself by positioning yourself and everything about your life to **Receive New Life**. Clean house by assessing and subsequently releasing the old, non-equipping, and non-empowering aspects of your life and replacing them with that which revitalizes, brings life. Take God at His Word, it is true; you are free to do everything that would empower you to **Receive New Life** and live, live abundantly to declare the works of God!

# *RECONNECT*

## JUNE

## June 1

*And God isn't pleased at being ignored. But if God himself has taken up residence in your life, you can hardly be thinking more of yourself than of him. Anyone, of course, who has not welcomed this invisible but clearly present God, the Spirit of Christ, won't know what we're talking about. But for you who welcome him, in whom he dwells—even though you still experience all the limitations of sin—you yourself experience life on God's terms. It stands to reason, doesn't it, that if the alive-and-present God who raised Jesus from the dead moves into your life, he'll do the same thing in you that he did in Jesus, bringing you alive to himself? When God lives and breathes in you (and he does, as surely as he did in Jesus), you are delivered from that dead life. With his Spirit living in you, your body will be as alive as Christ's!*
Romans 8:8-11 (MSG)

Critical to our ability to *Breathe: New Life* is the value we place on relationships. Relationships provide us the ability to network our way through the circumstances of our lives, empowering us to live in the intent and promises of God. The Creator-God chose you and your path not just for you but for His revelation as seen through you and your connection to others. God created your entire space so that you can achieve that which He intended, and that also included the people, places, and things of your space; thus, as you **Reconnect** to them and God's intent, you are empowered to live in His promises. **Reconnect** to God's intent by developing your relationship with Him and your space, and you will be empowered, you will *Breathe: New Life* in the circumstances that will release your life and life more abundantly!

172

## June 2

*It is the spirit that quickeneth; the flesh profiteth nothing: the*
*words that I speak unto you, they are spirit, and they are life.*
John 6:63

The power of our relationship with God and the Spirit of God
equips us to be sensitive to the move of God and to what is going
on around us.  Without a relationship, the circumstances of our
lives, as complex and difficult as they may be, we are without
discernment of purpose or plan to engage and overcome them.
Relationship by way of the Spirit gives us insight; the ability to
push beyond the surface, the veil of our experiences, so that we
might gain that which will empower as well as provide
discernment for what's next.  Remember, absolutely nothing
happens by accident or happenstance, it is all Divinely ordered.
Thus, you can **Breathe: *New Life*** into and for your circumstances
by the power to **Reconnect**; intentionally developing and
nurturing your relationship with God.

## June 3

*For through him we both have access to the Father by one Spirit.*
*Consequently, you are no longer foreigners and strangers, but*
*fellow citizens with God's people and also members of his*
*household, built on the foundation of the apostles and prophets,*
*with Christ Jesus himself as the chief cornerstone.  In him the*
*whole building is joined together and rises to become a holy*

*temple in the Lord.  And in him you too are being built together to*
*become a dwelling in which God lives by his Spirit.*
Ephesians 2:18-22 (NIV)


The value of our relationship with God lies in our access to the fullness of God, as manifested in His glory, and in the revelation of God in our lives that accrues to our benefit, as well as in God's intent for our space.  God does what He does in our lives so that He would be made real to us and to those around us, the Word becoming flesh.  Therefore, as we are in a relationship with God, we grow in our ability to connect to God as He manifests in and through our spaces, and as a result, we discover God's plan and purpose for our lives in and through the reality of our lives. Remember, God is omnipresent, and as we discover Him in our space, we uncover His plan, causing us to **Reconnect** to that which He has planned for His revelation in and through us.  ***Breathe: New Life*** and **Reconnect** by developing and nurturing a relationship with God that lays the cornerstone for connecting to the people, places, and things of your space, building toward the revelation of God in and through you and your space.


## June 4


*For Christ also suffered once for sins, the righteous for the unrighteous, to bring you to God. He was put to death in the body but made alive in the Spirit.  After being made alive, he went and made proclamation to the imprisoned spirits*
I Peter 3:18-19 (NIV)

When we choose to **Reconnect** to the people, places, and things God has ordained for our lives, we choose to be alive, even though our present reality does not reflect life. Therefore, we cannot allow the difficulty and complexity of developing and nurturing relationships with God and community to become barriers to continuing in dead situations. **Reconnect** to the people, places, and things of your space for which God has called and stir them up as gifts from God and transform you and your space to that which proves the acceptable and perfect will of God. Go ahead and *Breathe: New Life* into your circumstances, drawing on your personal relationship with God and all that He has given around you to bring to pass the saying that death is swallowed up in your victory!

## June 5

*When the people heard this, they were cut to the heart and said to Peter and the other apostles, "Brothers, what shall we do?" Peter replied, "Repent and be baptized, every one of you, in the name of Jesus Christ for the forgiveness of your sins. And you will receive the gift of the Holy Spirit. The promise is for you and your children and for all who are far off—for all whom the Lord our God will call." With many other words he warned them; and he pleaded with them, "Save yourselves from this corrupt generation."*
Acts 2:37-40 (NIV)

As we celebrate Pentecost, we are reminded of **Reconnection** Power that brings about new life, new community, and a new order that produces life and life more abundantly. Pentecost, originally in the Jewish tradition, was the feast of the harvest in which the faithful would gather in Jerusalem from all over the world to give praise to God for His release of abundance in the world.  It was during this gathering that the followers of Jesus were locked in a room for 50 days, giving thanks and prayers for their experiences with Jesus and seeking what was next.  The power of the Holy Ghost was released to them and activated through them, bringing to pass a new present reality.  The activation of the Holy Ghost yielded a boldness and unity among Christ's followers, though His absence was apparent and their situation precarious, that undergirded the Good News of Jesus, pricking the hearts of those without causing them to recognize the offering of new life.  The celebration of Pentecost, the abundance of the power of God operating in lives, offered a fit that some understood was instrumental for them to **Breathe: New Life** and **Reconnect** with God's purpose and plan for them, one another, and for a new order to their lives, which would activate the power of God.

## June 6

*Those who accepted his message were baptized, and about three thousand were added to their number that day.  They devoted themselves to the apostles' teaching and to fellowship, to the breaking of bread and to prayer.  Everyone was filled with awe at the many wonders and signs performed by the apostles.  All the believers were together and had everything in common. They sold property and possessions to give to anyone who had need.  Every day they continued to meet together in the temple courts. They broke bread in their homes and ate together with glad and sincere*

*hearts, praising God and enjoying the favor of all the people. And*
*the Lord added to their number daily those who were being saved.*
Acts 2:41-47 (NIV)

Connecting over and over with the people, places, and things of
your space can be an additional source of power to press through
the veils of darkness to places of promise, yielding abundant life.
Thus, the power of **Reconnection** is available to you; however, you
must accept it to leverage it for your own good. God has worked
out all things for our good, including the people, places, and
things of our lives, but we must be willing to accept them for who
and what they are and according to God's intent. Remember, you
cannot change people; what you can do is influence them by what
and how you do what you do, exercising the power of witnessing
in a world of darkness by turning the light on, and although it may
be a challenge, the sacrifice made will yield you and your space a
harvest. If we have intentionally recognized the importance of
what we allow in our space, everything will work together for our
good, supporting our ability to ***Breathe: New Life***.

## June 7

*Then he called for a light, and sprang in, and came trembling, and*
*fell down before Paul and Silas, And brought them out, and said,*
*Sirs, what must I do to be saved? And they said, Believe on the*
*Lord Jesus Christ, and thou shalt be saved, and thy house.*
Acts 16:29-31

No matter what we are experiencing, we must seek and find the light in our circumstances and **Reconnect** to it to overcome and receive our new life.  God has ordained everything, and your steps are ordered by the Lord, even if you venture out of the pathway of life.  Yet God provides a way of escape.  Thus, when the light appears to you, whether you are on the right path or not, **Reconnect**; it is your way out.  There is absolutely nothing you will experience that will be a surprise to God, even your being bound, God has already provided a way.  **Reconnect** to your Creator God and watch the darkness of your experience scatter for you and your space to *Breathe: New Life*.


## June 8


*Then opened he their understanding, that they might understand the scriptures, And said unto them, Thus it is written, and thus it behoved Christ to suffer, and to rise from the dead the third day: And that repentance and remission of sins should be preached in his name among all nations, beginning at Jerusalem. And ye are witnesses of these things.*
Luke 24:45-48


Life, in particular, often challenges us to a point where we do not understand, nor can we make sense of it, which produces frustration and fear, paralyzing our ability to see beyond what is to what can and should be.  These moments of frustration and fear will make us feel as though we are facing our challenges alone, compounding our lack of understanding and our inability to make sense of our reality, leaving us feeling defeated and hopeless.  However, it is in the challenge of our lives that demands our

178

ability to **Reconnect** to our purpose and plan, thus God and the resources around us, which are God-designed to help us overcome our challenges, equipping us to achieve what can and should be. Our experiences, as we connect with our purpose and plan, our Word becoming flesh (Christ Himself), is the light at the end of our tunnel, opening our eyes, giving understanding, and making us senstive to the resources available, internally and externally, empowering us to leverage those to live in our life and life more abundantly! ***Breathe: New Life*** by opening your understanding to what is from your experiences and **Reconnect,** drawing on your purpose and plan, and the resources of your space to empower you to live and overcome all things!

## June 9

*Repent ye therefore, and be converted, that your sins may be blotted out, when the times of refreshing shall come from the presence of the Lord; And he shall send Jesus Christ, which before was preached unto you: Whom the heaven must receive until the times of restitution of all things, which God hath spoken by the mouth of all his holy prophets since the world began.*
Acts 3:19-21

Repent means an intentional transformation of thinking from what was. The status quo of our lives is what it is as long as we allow it to be; however, when we undergo a radical transformation in our thinking, we position ourselves to seize the opportunity for a new life. As we experience the ups and downs of life, in particular, the challenges we face can cloud our view, distract our efforts, and settle our spirit, keeping us from living to our full potential. Often in the clouding, distraction, and/or settling, we miss opportunities of refreshing that **Reconnect** us to God's purpose, plan, promises for our lives; the exceedingly, abundantly, more than which awaits us. Therefore, the clarion call to repentance is not just about turning from that which separates us, but a deeper and transformational action toward possibilities and opportunities for our life and life more abundantly. *Breathe: New Life* by your willingness to **Reconnect** to God's purpose, plan, promises for your life, and live fully in the greater, the more, the life and life more abundantly which is yours!

## June 10

*And it shall come to pass afterward,*
*that I will pour out my spirit upon all flesh;*
*and your sons and your daughters shall prophesy,*
*your old men shall dream dreams,*
*your young men shall see visions:*
*And also upon the servants and upon the handmaids*
*in those days will I pour out my spirit.*
Joel 2:28-29

The power to **Reconnect** to God's purpose and plan for your life and space is fueled by the Spirit of God operating in and over your life. God willingly releases Himself, His Spirit, to us who are willing to receive, and it provides us the power to live in the fullness of God's promises for our lives. As we press past the veil of our circumstances to see and know God at work in them, we gain insight and sensitivity to what is going on in and around us, so

180

that we may connect the dots for God's intent, revealing God Himself. Thus, as we see and know in our circumstances, God releases His Spirit in and over us, guiding us through our circumstances to the fulfillment of His purpose and plan. *Breathe: New Life* to your circumstances and overcome, positioning yourself to **Reconnect** to God's intentions for your life and life more abundantly under the outpouring of His Spirit.

## June 11

*Ye are the children of the prophets, and of the covenant which God made with our fathers, saying unto Abraham, And in thy seed shall all the kindreds of the earth be blessed. Unto you first God, having raised up his Son Jesus, sent him to bless you, in turning away every one of you from his iniquities.*
Acts 3:25-26

As much as God desires to bless you, He also desires that in blessing you, He would bless your seed, that which is the yield of your harvest. God uses you and me to reach as many and as much as we are willing to connect with, so that our seed may germinate, we might exercise **Reconnect** power, the ability to witness to all of our presence, the purpose and plan of God. Thus, as we engage life, especially its challenges and *Breathe: New Life*, we showcase the ability to connect with God's purpose and plan, His promises for our lives as the way out, and to overcome whatever may be. It is wonderful for us to vocalize what God can and will do, but it is entirely another thing for it to be seen in and through us, both through the process and the end result. Go ahead and exercise **Reconnect** power with God's purpose and plan for your life and showcase for your space the power to live in the promises of God, despite and in spite of life's challenges, by the simple act in which you **Breathe: New Life**.

## June 12

*One day as Jesus was standing by the Lake of Gennesaret, the people were crowding around him and listening to the word of God. He saw at the water's edge two boats, left there by the fishermen, who were washing their nets. He got into one of the boats, the one belonging to Simon, and asked him to put out a little from shore. Then he sat down and taught the people from the boat. When he had finished speaking, he said to Simon, "Put out into deep water, and let down the nets for a catch." Simon answered, "Master, we've worked hard all night and haven't caught anything. But because you say so, I will let down the nets." When they had done so, they caught such a large number of fish that their nets began to break. So they signaled their partners in the other boat to come and help them, and they came and filled both boats so full that they began to sink. When Simon Peter saw this, he fell at Jesus' knees and said, "Go away from me, Lord; I am a sinful man!" For he and all his companions were astonished at the catch of fish they had taken, and so were James and John, the sons of Zebedee, Simon's partners. Then Jesus said to Simon, "Don't be afraid; from now on you will fish for people." So they pulled their boats up on shore, left everything and followed him.*
Luke 5:1-11 (NIV)

One of the amazing things about God in His creation of us is that He has already provided everything we need if we are willing to go and seek to live in His designed purpose and plan for our lives. Relationship with the Creator God and the space in which we exist is foundational to being sensitive to God's purpose and plan. God, when He created everything, and He created everything with everything in mind, thus, whether we know it or not, it is all connected. Fishermen understand that as they take fibrous materials, connective tissue, to create a tool to assist in fishing, it is also symbolic of how God uses each and every one of our experiences for us to cast a net into life and bring in our harvest. The more willing we are to launch out into the deep, intentionally and deeply, to **Breathe: New Life,** the greater the opportunity for us to bring in a haul, all because we understand how connected our experiences are to our reality and our destiny. Cast your nets, your experiences, into the deep of your life and its challenges, and pull in your abundance. Everything about you and your space is at your disposal. **Reconnect** the dots of God's purpose and plan for your life and live in the fullness of His promises.

## June 13

*Afterward Jesus appeared again to his disciples, by the Sea of Galilee. It happened this way: Simon Peter, Thomas (also known as Didymus, Nathanael from Cana in Galilee, the sons of Zebedee, and two other disciples were together. "I'm going out to fish," Simon Peter told them, and they said, "We'll go with you." So they went out and got into the boat, but that night they caught nothing. Early in the morning, Jesus stood on the shore, but the disciples did not realize that it was Jesus. He called out to them,*

*"Friends, haven't you any fish? "No," they answered. He said, "Throw your net on the right side of the boat and you will find some." When they did, they were unable to haul the net in because of the large number of fish. Then the disciple whom Jesus loved said to Peter, "It is the Lord!" As soon as Simon Peter heard him say, "It is the Lord," he wrapped his outer garment around him (for he had taken it off) and jumped into the water. The other disciples followed in the boat, towing the net full of fish, for they were not far from shore, about a hundred yards. When they landed, they saw a fire of burning coals there with fish on it, and some bread. Jesus said to them, "Bring some of the fish you have just caught." So Simon Peter climbed back into the boat and dragged the net ashore. It was full of large fish, 153, but even with so many the net was not torn. Jesus said to them, "Come and have breakfast." None of the disciples dared ask him, "Who are you?" They knew it was the Lord. Jesus came, took the bread and gave it to them, and did the same with the fish. This was now the third time Jesus appeared to his disciples after he was raised from the dead.*
John 21:1-14

We have net-work power because we **Reconnect** to God's purpose and plan for our lives, including our experiences and the people, places, and things of our space. Our power is manifested through the team effort of connecting the dots in our lives and those within them, because of God's intent in our creation; our gifts and their connection to our environment, which God foreknew would be at our disposal. Even when we cannot see God and it appears He is nowhere to be found, He is there. Because of our relationship to Him and our place in Him, we sense His Spirit and thus move according to what leads us to our abundance.  As we *Breathe: New Life* into our circumstances, we do so by our ability to **Reconnect** to everything and everyone in our space as God has ordained.  Thus, as we **Reconnect** we sense and see God, and in our response to Him, we are positioned to receive and accept the fulfillment of His promises for our lives as well as for everything and everyone in our space.

## June 14

*But ye shall receive power, after that the Holy Ghost is come upon you: and ye shall be witnesses unto me both in Jerusalem, and in all Judaea, and in Samaria, and unto the uttermost part of the earth.*
Acts 1:8

Our experiences lay the groundwork for our discovering God's purpose and plan for our lives.  When God created you and me, His intent was complete, meaning everything about who He created us to be was settled and arranged.  Therefore, you and I have the power to choose to live in the life and life more abundantly for which we were created, to **Reconnect** to what God's intent is for our lives.  Each experience is a building block if we seek to connect the dots, and what God intends will be revealed and His power available to you and me.  *Breathe: New Life* and the Spirit of God, His very intent for our lives, will lead and guide us through life to our place of promise; life and life more abundantly, revealing Him, His power, and its availability to and for all.

## June 15

*And when the day of Pentecost was fully come, they were all with one accord in one place.*
Acts 2:1

Critical to our ability to receive the power to accomplish what is required for our life and life more abundantly is our alignment with God's purpose and plan for our lives, including our sensitivity to the environment in which we exist. Remember, God knew and knows exactly where you are and what is going on, and, as a result, created you, built you for it, and, in your experience, deposited the fulfillment of His promises for your life. Although I would dare to say most of us do not want to go through what we must, it is necessary to reach the place of our promise. In the process of fulfilling our promises, we align our lives and environment with them. The day of Pentecost was an annual Jewish celebration. It took on a new life when 120 people chose to see themselves in God's purpose and plan, **Reconnecting** to it and the reality of their environment, and thus, receiving power by taking a deep breath to *Breathe: New Life*!

## June 16

*Be imitators of God in everything you do, for then you will represent your Father as his beloved sons and daughters. And continue to walk surrendered to the extravagant love of Christ, for he surrendered his life as a sacrifice for us. His great love for us*

*was pleasing to God, like an aroma of adoration—a sweet healing*
*fragrance.*
Ephesians 5:1-2 (TPT)

The power of our **Reconnection** with God, His purpose and plan, releases the flow of the fullness of God and His intent for our life and life more abundantly.  The flow of God's intent points us to the ordered steps of our lives that reveal God's Word to us, His Word made flesh.  The more we are willing amid life and its challenges to *Breathe: New Life,* the more we become like God and His intent, triggering the flow of God's blessings in and over our lives, making us His witnesses.  Today, choose to **Reconnect** to God's purpose and plan for your life as well as your environment, be alert and watch along the way of your ordered steps, your blessings, the flow of your life and life more abundantly!

## June 17

*A new commandment I give unto you, That ye love one another;*
*as I have loved you, that ye also love one another. By this shall all*
*men know that ye are my disciples, if ye have love one to another.*
John 13:34-35

The importance of relationships, both with God and with our environment, with one another, and the places and things of our space, was magnified by Christ's establishment of a new command.  Christ commands us that if we are to be imitators of Him, if we are to be in the image of God, His Word becoming flesh, real in our lives, we must do so by **Reconnecting** to God and to that which is our environment.  Remember, God intends that you and I be the crown of His glory, His revelation, and thus, in every experience, we can showcase the fullness of God's love and power at work in life.  Thus, understanding and leveraging the power of your network, your relationship with God, and everything around you, when properly **Reconnected,** allows you to *Breathe: New Life* into your experiences and receive the power to be His witness.  Love is an action verb; therefore, act in your relationship with God, His Word, purpose, and plan, your environment, and showcase, witness God's call and your response to all of His creation, and inherit all things!

## June 18

*Regarding life together and getting along with each other, you don't need me to tell you what to do. You're God-taught in these matters. Just love one another!*
I Thessalonians 4:9 (MSG)

Our power to live in the promises of God lies within us because God has given us the ability to choose; God has set before us life and death, and urges us to choose life.  Thus, *Breathe: New Life* into your situation because you have been permitted by God the Creator to live in the fullness of life, despite and in spite of it all. Choose that which connects you, **Reconnect** to God's purpose and plan for you as seen in your present reality, and in doing so, you make the obvious choice of living in and through whatever your experience may be to the fullness of life and life more abundantly. There may be difficulties and complex relationships within your sphere, but choose life over death in those relationships by loving your way through, being led by God to a life of abundance.  God is love, and as you **Reconnect** with Him, His purpose and plan, you flow in love, bringing to every relationship of your life, the God-led and guided choice, producing the fulfillment of God's promises!

## June 19

*Now Moses was tending the flock of Jethro his father-in-law, the priest of Midian, and he led the flock to the far side of the wilderness and came to Horeb, the mountain of God.  There the angel of the Lord appeared to him in flames of fire from within a bush. Moses saw that though the bush was on fire it did not burn up.  So Moses thought, "I will go over and see this strange sight—why the bush does not burn up."  When the Lord saw that he had gone over to look, God called to him from within the bush, "Moses! Moses!"  And Moses said, "Here I am."  "Do not come any closer," God said. "Take off your sandals, for the place where you are standing is holy ground."  Then he said, "I am the God of your father, the God of Abraham, the God of Isaac and the God of Jacob." At this, Moses hid his face, because he was afraid to look at God.*
Exodus 3:1-6 (NIV)

The challenge in each of life's experiences is to **Reconnect** to God's purpose and plan for our lives, as well as for our environment, and it is met only when we discover our holy ground, our place of communion with God.  Our holy ground is the sacred space where we have the opportunity to directly engage with and encounter God Himself, His Word made flesh in our lives.  On our holy ground, we can see past what is to what can and should be for our lives and receive the necessary fuel to propel us to the very promises of God.  It is our holy ground where we see the viability of our choosing to **Reconnect** with what God is up to in our lives and all around us in such a way that we bask in the revelation of God and the fullness of His power, causing us to be in awe.  It is your experience in and on your holy ground that provides the impetus for you to *Breathe: New Life*, therefore, **Reconnect** to your holy ground, take on your life's challenges, and be empowered to soar to your life and life more abundantly!

## June 20

*And then this, while Joshua was there near Jericho: He looked up and saw right in front of him a man standing, holding his drawn sword. Joshua stepped up to him and said, "Whose side are you on —ours or our enemies'?"  He said, "Neither. I'm commander of God's army. I've just arrived." Joshua fell, face to the ground, and worshiped. He asked, "What orders does my Master have for his servant?"  God's army commander ordered Joshua, "Take your sandals off your feet. The place you are standing is holy."*
Joshua 5:13-15 (MSG)

The great events of our lives that place us at the crossroads between reality and our faith demand that we retreat to an empowering place, to our holy ground.  It is on the holy ground that we receive the impetus to engage the hard, difficult, complex challenges of our lives and do it from a point of strength. Remember, we are challenged to stir up our gifts for God has not given us the spirit of fear but of power, love, and a sound mind. Life's challenges are intended to intimidate us; thus, we must be intentional about creating and establishing our holy ground so that we might find our backbone to engage with the hard and the impossible, and thrive in the abundance promised. **Reconnect** to your power source by establishing your holy ground, a place where you can *Breathe: New Life*!

## June 21

*David again brought together all the able young men of Israel—thirty thousand. He and all his men went to Baalah in Judah to bring up from there the ark of God, which is called by the Name, the name of the Lord Almighty, who is enthroned between the cherubim on the ark. They set the ark of God on a new cart and brought it from the house of Abinadab, which was on the hill. Uzzah and Ahio, sons of Abinadab, were guiding the new cart with the ark of God on it, and Ahio was walking in front of it. David and all Israel were celebrating with all their might before the Lord, with castanets, harps, lyres, timbrels, sistrums and cymbals. When they came to the threshing floor of Nakon, Uzzah reached out and took hold of the ark of God, because the oxen stumbled. The Lord's anger burned against Uzzah because of his irreverent act; therefore God struck him down, and he died there beside the ark of God. Then David was angry because the Lord's wrath had broken out against Uzzah, and to this day that place is called Perez Uzzah. David was afraid of the Lord that day and said, "How can the ark of the Lord ever come to me?" He was not willing to take the ark of the Lord to be with him in the City of David. Instead, he took it to the house of Obed-Edom the Gittite. The ark of the Lord*

*remained in the house of Obed-Edom the Gittite for three months,*
*and the Lord blessed him and his entire household.*
II Samuel 6:1-11 (NIV)

Your holy ground is the spaces in which you are empowered to overcome life's challenges and inherit your new life, to **Reconnect** to God's purpose and plan for your life and the space in which He has caused you to exist. Your holy ground serves as your fueling station, which gives you the ability to engage the hard, the impossible, the very obstacles to your experiences, yielding the life and life more abundantly as promised, the ability to *Breathe: New Life*. Although life will take on, you and your holy space, remember to reverence and guard it; your holy ground is too important to be treated lightly. The irrelevance of your holy space to you or others can kill the motivation and compulsion to fulfill God's promises in your life. Guard your anointing, your holy ground, as if your life depended on it; be sure of what you let in, for it is in this space that you get the stuff you need to take on, overcome, and inherit your life and life more abundantly.

## June 22

*Now King David was told, "The Lord has blessed the household of Obed-Edom and everything he has, because of the ark of God." So David went to bring up the ark of God from the house of Obed-Edom to the City of David with rejoicing. When those who were carrying the ark of the Lord had taken six steps, he sacrificed a bull and a fattened calf. Wearing a linen ephod, David was dancing before the Lord with all his might, while he and all Israel were bringing up the ark of the Lord with shouts and the sound of*

*trumpets. As the ark of the Lord was entering the City of David,*
*Michal daughter of Saul watched from a window. And when she*
*saw King David leaping and dancing before the Lord, she despised*
*him in her heart. They brought the ark of the Lord and set it in its*
*place inside the tent that David had pitched for it, and David*
*sacrificed burnt offerings and fellowship offerings before the Lord.*
*After he had finished sacrificing the burnt offerings and fellowship*
*offerings, he blessed the people in the name of the Lord Almighty.*
*Then he gave a loaf of bread, a cake of dates and a cake of raisins*
*to each person in the whole crowd of Israelites, both men and*
*women. And all the people went to their homes.*
II Samuel 6:12-19 (NIV)

Our reverence for that which is holy in and for our lives spills over
into the blessings that flow into our lives.  You can not and cannot
allow someone or something else to trample on that which you
believe to be your holy ground, for it will cause a slow diminishing
of your holy ground's impact for you to **Reconnect** and receive the
necessary source of energy.  Without question, it will be required
for you to have a constant source and steady flow of energy to
press past the veil of your obstacles to your place of promise.
Your holy ground must be the very place you receive joy and
energy that positively moves you forward in the impossible and
before the unimaginable of your life.  Your Word becoming flesh
demands you **Reconnection**, over and over, to your power source,
and in so doing, you have the opportunity to *Breathe: New Life*.
To *Breathe: New Life* in your circumstances takes you to a level
you never imagined and causes discomfort in those around you,
as they see the awesomeness of God active in your life, which
challenges their lives to new life.  Remember, after which the

power of the Holy Ghost shall come upon you, you shall receive
power to be His witness!

## June 23

*And thou shalt make a vail of blue, and purple, and scarlet, and*
*fine twined linen of cunning work: with cherubims shall it be*
*made: And thou shalt hang it upon four pillars of shittim wood*
*overlaid with gold: their hooks shall be of gold, upon the four*
*sockets of silver. And thou shalt hang up the vail under the taches,*
*that thou mayest bring in thither within the vail the ark of the*
*testimony: and the vail shall divide unto you between the holy*
*place and the most holy. And thou shalt put the mercy seat upon*
*the ark of the testimony in the most holy place.*
Exodus 26:31-34

God, as He spoke to Moses and the children of Israel about how
the space should be in which He dwelt, indicates the importance
and reverence that our holy ground should have. Our holy ground
is the place for our **Reconnecting** to God, His Word, His promises
for our lives. Years of slavery, wandering in wilderness
experiences, going without, and many other challenges, all of
which will have an impact on you and zap you of the required
energy to continue to press past your veils, obstacles to your place
of promise, thus a place to **Reconnect** is critical. Choose today not
to allow the threats and weaknesses of your life and experiences
to keep you from what is yours, the fulfillment of God's promises
for your life, ***Breathe: New Life***. Therefore, **Reconnect** in a space
where you receive empowerment for God's purpose and plan,
promises for your life, and draw on them and the support of the

environment you and God have created as conducive, and press toward the mark of your higher calling!

## June 24

*And the LORD spake unto Moses after the death of the two sons of Aaron, when they offered before the LORD, and died; And the LORD said unto Moses, Speak unto Aaron thy brother, that he come not at all times into the holy place within the vail before the mercy seat, which is upon the ark; that he die not: for I will appear in the cloud upon the mercy seat.*
Leviticus 16:1-2

The presence of God is the space, holy ground, that becomes our phone booths in which we transform ourselves from Clark Kent, our human self, to Superman, Superheroes in which we are empowered to overcome and receive our abundant life. Wherever your holy ground may be, physical or spiritual space, know that it is the place in which you become the clay, and God the Potter. God seeks, through your lived experiences, not only to reveal Himself to you but also to reveal who He has created you to be, unearthing His Spirit within you and releasing it to accomplish what He intends. Do not allow the fact that your holy ground is transformative and that somehow you will lose, not at all, you gain more of yourself and who God created you to be, the real you as an instrument of God's purpose and plan. ***Breathe: New Life*** in your circumstances for the experience allows the real you, the more of you, God's Word becoming flesh, to come out as you **Reconnect** in your holy ground to God's intended purpose and plan for your life and space!

## June 25

*Now the first covenant had regulations for worship and also an earthly sanctuary.  A tabernacle was set up. In its first room were the lampstand and the table with its consecrated bread; this was called the Holy Place.  Behind the second curtain was a room called the Most Holy Place, which had the golden altar of incense and the gold-covered ark of the covenant. This ark contained the gold jar of manna, Aaron's staff that had budded, and the stone tablets of the covenant.  Above the ark were the cherubim of the Glory, overshadowing the atonement cover.  But we cannot discuss these things in detail now.  When everything had been arranged like this, the priests entered regularly into the outer room to carry on their ministry.  But only the high priest entered the inner room, and that only once a year, and never without blood, which he offered for himself and for the sins the people had committed in ignorance.  The Holy Spirit was showing by this that the way into the Most Holy Place had not yet been disclosed as long as the first tabernacle was still functioning.  This is an illustration for the present time, indicating that the gifts and sacrifices being offered were not able to clear the conscience of the worshiper.  They are only a matter of food and drink and various ceremonial washings —external regulations applying until the time of the new order. But when Christ came as high priest of the good things that are now already here, he went through the greater and more perfect tabernacle that is not made with human hands, that is to say, is not a part of this creation.  He did not enter by means of the blood of goats and calves; but he entered the Most Holy Place once for all by his own blood, thus obtaining eternal redemption.*

Hebrews 9:1-12 (NIV)

Life is about choices, and whether your choice is perceived to be "right" or "wrong," it is your choice, your free will, your God-given right to choose.  What is both empowering and joyous about my Christian faith is that God intends for me to have the right to choose, and if, by chance, I discover my choice is not right for me, He yet provides me a way, through His Son's sacrifice, to be reconciled to His will for my life.  God intentionally places before all of us choices, life and death, blessings and curses, and encourages us to choose life, giving us the free will to choose, and whatever choice we make also provides a way of escape.  Be not deceived: when you take away choice, you take away freedom, and as a result, you oppress, producing outcomes that cannot be contained, leading to eventual, uncontrollable chaos, void, and darkness that cover everything.  God is light that creates and scatters, in that order. When we evoke the presence of God, entering the holy ground of our choices, we receive His eternal light, which leads and guides our creative responses while also scattering our darkness.  Our assignment is not to force people to choose our choices, but to introduce them to the God of all choices, who is more often the God of the dos than a God of the don'ts.  Let God be God.  I am confident that God's light, love, and wisdom will empower them in creating their right response with the assurance of eventually scattering their darkness - God did it for me, and He will do it for them.  In case you did not get it, that's **Reconnecting** to *Breathe: New Life*!

## June 26

*By entering through faith into what God has always wanted to do for us—set us right with him, make us fit for him—we have it all together with God because of our Master Jesus. And that's not all: We throw open our doors to God and discover at the same moment that he has already thrown open his door to us. We find ourselves standing where we always hoped we might stand—out in the wide open spaces of God's grace and glory, standing tall and shouting our praise. There's more to come: We continue to shout our praise even when we're hemmed in with troubles, because we know how troubles can develop passionate patience in us, and how that patience in turn forges the tempered steel of virtue, keeping us alert for whatever God will do next. In alert expectancy such as this, we're never left feeling shortchanged. Quite the contrary—we can't round up enough containers to hold everything God generously pours into our lives through the Holy Spirit! Christ arrives right on time to make this happen. He didn't, and doesn't, wait for us to get ready. He presented himself for this sacrificial death when we were far too weak and rebellious to do anything to get ourselves ready. And even if we hadn't been so weak, we wouldn't have known what to do anyway. We can understand someone dying for a person worth dying for, and we can understand how someone good and noble could inspire us to selfless sacrifice. But God put his love on the line for us by offering his Son in sacrificial death while we were of no use whatever to him. Now that we are set right with God by means of this sacrificial death, the consummate blood sacrifice, there is no longer a question of being at odds with God in any way. If, when we were at our worst, we were put on friendly terms with God by the sacrificial death of his Son, now that we're at our best, just think of how our lives will expand and deepen by means of his resurrection life! Now that we have actually received this amazing*

*friendship with God, we are no longer content to simply say it in*
*plodding prose. We sing and shout our praises to God through*
*Jesus, the Messiah!*
Romans 5:1-11 (MSG)

No one or anything is perfect; therefore, we must always build into our life's journey reflection and/or evaluation of our positions and what is going on around us, and, when necessary, make the changes and/or transformations needed for a new life. We need to believe that what we choose is the right step for us at the time and thus are committed to it; however, do not allow your choice to confine you, but instead be open to unplugging, disconnecting to **Reconnect,** to accomplish what can and should be for your life. Building in reflection and evaluation allows you to rediscover God's purpose and plan for your life through new eyes, through the lived experiences God has intended for your development. Remember, we are the clay, and God is the Potter, and He has allowed the experiences of our lives, even our missteps, to serve as shaping and molding tools so that we are transformed into the likeness of Christ, of Him, His will for our lives. ***Breathe: New Life*** by glorying in your triumphs, but also the process of your life's experiences as tools of rediscovery, we have this privilege through the sacrifice of Christ, to **Reconnect** you to that which can and should be for your life!

## June 27

*So now the case is closed. There remains no accusing voice of*
*condemnation against those who are joined in life-union with*
*Jesus, the Anointed One. For the "law" of the Spirit of life flowing*

*through the anointing of Jesus has liberated us from the "law" of sin and death. For God achieved what the law was unable to accomplish, because the law was limited by the weakness of human nature. Yet God sent us his Son in human form to identify with human weakness. Clothed with humanity, God's Son gave his body to be the sin-offering so that God could once and for all condemn the guilt and power of sin. So now every righteous requirement of the law can be fulfilled through the Anointed One living his life in us. And we are free to live, not according to our flesh, but by the dynamic power of the Holy Spirit!*
Romans 8:1-4 (TPT)

The mistakes and missteps of our lives are not death sentences to our living in the fulfillment of God's promises for our lives. We have been given life, and a life that can and will flow abundantly if we choose. Our choices may not always be the best choices, but because of Christ's sacrifice on our behalf, we have the right and privilege to **Reconnect** to that which is God's purpose and plan for our life and life more abundantly. Remember, no matter what you do or what people think of you, there is no condemnation from God. God readily stands with His arms wide open to receive you, no matter what, and He has proven this unconditional love to you with the sacrifice of His only Son. Stop allowing other people, places, or things, including your own internal feelings of guilt and shame, whether warranted or not, to take up your energy and obscure your pathway to your life and life more abundantly. ***Breathe: New Life***, it is your right and privilege, no matter your circumstances, **Reconnect** and bask in God's love and grace, the favor, to and for your life!

## June 28

*If God didn't hesitate to put everything on the line for us,
embracing our condition and exposing himself to the worst by
sending his own Son, is there anything else he wouldn't gladly and
freely do for us?*
Romans 8:32 (MSG)

**Reconnect** to God's purpose and plan for your life, in spite of and
despite what you have done or how you feel and/or how people
make you feel about what you have done, and be reconciled to
God's intent for your life and life more abundantly. God desires
that you would be delivered from whatever would hinder you
from His promises for your life and be fully whole in your
abundant life. Choices you made or those forced upon you by
people, places, or things cannot withstand more of God's love and
grace awaiting you. Remember, God put everything on the line
for you. He gave His best, His Son, to die in your stead so that you
do not have to die and/or waste away in regrets, missteps, or
downright intentional wrong turns. Go ahead and ***Breathe: New
Life*** and see that God will not withhold any good thing from you,
everything He intended for your life and life more abundantly is
and will be yours, just **Reconnect**!

## June 29

*When everything was hopeless, Abraham believed anyway,
deciding to live not on the basis of what he saw he couldn't do but
on what God said he would do. And so he was made father of a*

*multitude of peoples. God himself said to him, "You're going to have a big family, Abraham!" Abraham didn't focus on his own impotence and say, "It's hopeless. This hundred-year-old body could never father a child." Nor did he survey Sarah's decades of infertility and give up. He didn't tiptoe around God's promise asking cautiously skeptical questions. He plunged into the promise and came up strong, ready for God, sure that God would make good on what he had said. That's why it is said, "Abraham was declared fit before God by trusting God to set him right." But it's not just Abraham; it's also us! The same thing gets said about us when we embrace and believe the One who brought Jesus to life when the conditions were equally hopeless. The sacrificed Jesus made us fit for God, set us right with God.*
Romans 8:18-25 (MSG)

We receive power when we **Reconnect** to God's purpose and plan and to the environment in which we exist, because it is there we receive the motivation and encouragement for whatever we face, even if it appears impossible. The power we receive from God's purpose and plan, as well as from our environment, is necessary and serves as energy to press past our challenges with the confidence that what we believe can and should be will be for our lives. Therefore, your power is a direct result of God's promises for your life being made real, the Word made flesh; the process of you working your field; God's promises for your life in connection to what God is up to with you, and around you. Thus, the importance of ensuring that your environment, space, is filled and conducive for pressing toward the higher calling for your life. By no means will your environment be free of toxicity, but know that even in it, you can receive the necessary incentive to press on. Before Abraham became a father, He was called father by God and all those around him, whether with good intentions or bad, challenging him to live in what was not yet manifested, to work His field to make his Word, the promises of God for his life, flesh. **Breathe: New Life** by going forward in what you cannot even see right now as though it were and be, exist in that which has been promised to you, and press forward to live in your life and life more abundantly!

## June 30

*But he was wounded for our transgressions,*
*he was bruised for our iniquities:*
*the chastisement of our peace was upon him;*
*and with his stripes we are healed.*
*All we like sheep have gone astray;*
*we have turned every one to his own way;*
*and the LORD hath laid on him the iniquity of us all.*
Isaiah 53:5-6

Never forget that you have been given the right to choose whatever path of life you desire. No one or nothing has the right to determine the course of your life. Your free will is foundational to your creation; the right to choose. It was so important that God sent His Son to die for you and me so that we would have the right to choose; He was wounded, bruised, the chastisement of our peace was placed upon Him, and He did it all for you and me. He did it so we would be free. Your choice is yours; however, God pleads with you to choose His purpose and plan and with it the exceedingly, abundantly, more than you can ever ask or think by the power that will work in you. However, if you choose differently, God still provides in whatever direction you take an exit ramp to return, to **Reconnect** to His purpose and plan, your abundance, and with it no condemnation. ***Breathe: New Life***, you cannot lose when you choose the prepaid plan God has made just for you!

# *READJUST*

## July

## July 1

*This is the kind of life you've been invited into, the kind of life Christ lived. He suffered everything that came his way so you would know that it could be done, and also know how to do it, step-by-step. He never did one thing wrong, Not once said anything amiss. They called him every name in the book and he said nothing back. He suffered in silence, content to let God set things right. He used his servant body to carry our sins to the Cross so we could be rid of sin, free to live the right way. His wounds became your healing. You were lost sheep with no idea who you were or where you were going. Now you're named and kept for good by the Shepherd of your souls.*
I Peter 2:21-25 (MSG)

The life of Christ serves as a reminder that you and I possess the power to overcome any and all things, and as an example, He shows us how it can be done. We often do not consider that Christ himself was human, flesh and blood, although He was Divine. Therefore, Christ chose God's assignment. He decided to **Readjust** to God's intent for His life, God's intent to become flesh, to show and bring to our lives deliverance in any and all things. Remember, Christ had already been slain before the world was ever laid, because God knew and knows the plans He has for us, and they are not to hurt or harm us but to prosper us and bring us to our expected end, His will for our lives. Christ's humanity and His willingness to endure in the flesh, to endure His experiences, prove that with God and according to His Purpose and plan for our lives, we can overcome and inherit all things. ***Breathe: New Life*** by overcoming, producing power by your ability to endure life's sufferings with a determination to get to your expected end, the promises of God for your life, with an assurance that the Shepherd of your soul has gone and knows the way.

## July 2

*Let my soul live, and it shall praise thee;*
*and let thy judgments help me.*
*I have gone astray like a lost sheep; seek thy servant;*
*for I do not forget thy commandments.*
Psalm 119:175-176

Turning from a direction that is leading nowhere is necessary if you are going to get on track to your destiny. Your destiny is that which can and should be for your life and is fueled by your willingness to believe. If you believe you should have life and life more abundantly, then it is up to you to constantly examine where you are and whether that is the right direction for you to reach your destiny. Thank God that He has provided us the free will to choose with a trigger to **Readjust** if necessary by the death of Jesus Christ, who covers our mistakes, wrong turns, and even our rebellion, allowing us to self-correct for our life and life more abundantly. Go ahead, wherever you are, and *Breathe: New Life* and **Readjust** as necessary to get what is already yours, awaiting you, your life and life more abundantly!

## July 3

*Test yourselves to make sure you are solid in the faith. Don't drift along taking everything for granted. Give yourselves regular checkups. You need firsthand evidence, not mere hearsay, that Jesus Christ is in you. Test it out. If you fail the test, do something about it. I hope the test won't show that we have failed. But if it comes to that, we'd rather the test showed our failure than yours. We're rooting for the truth to win out in you. We couldn't possibly do otherwise.  We don't just put up with our limitations; we celebrate them, and then go on to celebrate every strength, every triumph of the truth in you. We pray hard that it will all come together in your lives.  And that's about it, friends. Be cheerful. Keep things in good repair. Keep your spirits up. Think in harmony. Be agreeable. Do all that, and the God of love and peace will be with you for sure.*
II Corinthians 13:5-9; 11 (MSG)

Life's challenges seek to separate us from the promise of life and life more abundantly and, as a result, often knock us out of alignment with God's original purpose and plan for our lives.  It is the challenges we face that often lead us to make adjustments in our lives to protect us and/or ease our fears, unintentionally justifying our status quo.  Remember, we have not been given the spirit of fear but of power, love, and a sound mind.  Therefore, we must approach life, as well as its challenges, from a perspective that life and its challenges do not have power over us, nor can they drive the narrative of our lives.  We have been given victory not because of how good or perfect we are, but instead by Jesus as a reward for our diligently seeking to live in God's original purpose and plan for our life and life more abundantly.  Thus, all along life's way, we must examine ourselves, our life, and our journey to determine if the conscious and nonconscious adjustments that are made knock us out of alignment with God's plan, and if so, **Readjust** so as to maintain proper alignment.  The regular checkups with ourselves and our journey must be undergirded with our honest and candid confession about the reality of our feelings and the facts of our reality, the truth, that helps us to develop and execute a plan to address our issues, **Readjust,** and empower us to *Breathe: New Life*!

## July 4

*Whenever you eat this bread and drink this cup, you are retelling the story, proclaiming our Lord's death until he comes.  For this reason, whoever eats the bread or drinks the cup of the Lord in the wrong spirit will be guilty of dishonoring the body and blood of the Lord.  So let each individual first evaluate his own attitude and only then eat the bread and drink the cup.  For continually eating and drinking with a wrong spirit will bring judgment upon yourself by not recognizing the body.  This insensitivity is why many of you are weak, chronically ill, and some even dying.  If we have examined ourselves, we should not be judged.  But when we are judged, it is the Lord's training so that we will not be condemned along with the world.*
I Corinthians 11:26-32 (TPT)

Our dedication to that which can and should be for our lives rests upon our ability to regularly examine ourselves.  Our examination is necessary so that we can ensure we are properly aligned with what is our destiny, the outcome.  The more frequently we take the time to evaluate our steps and direction, the sooner we discover the missteps and distractions that seek to detour and clutter our lives, forcing us off our pathway to life and life more abundantly. As we discover our nonalignment, we must **Readjust** ourselves and journey to properly align with the pathway for our intended destination; otherwise, we spiral downward, farther away from what can and should be, causing death to our dreams or our living beneath our potential. ***Breathe: New Life*** by regular maintenance on your life and actions, and in so doing, you are reminded of your destiny as well as the price paid to get where you are, challenging you to **Readjust,** where necessary, for what can and should be for your life!

## July 5

*But if Christ is in you, then even though your body is subject to death because of sin, the Spirit gives life because of righteousness. And if the Spirit of him who raised Jesus from the dead is living in you, he who raised Christ from the dead will also give life to your mortal bodies because of his Spirit who lives in you. Therefore, brothers and sisters, we have an obligation—but it is not to the flesh, to live according to it. For if you live according to the flesh, you will die; but if by the Spirit you put to death the misdeeds of the body, you will live. For those who are led by the Spirit of God are the children of God. The Spirit you received does not make you slaves, so that you live in fear again; rather, the Spirit you received brought about your adoption to sonship. And by him we cry, "Abba, Father." The Spirit himself testifies with our spirit that we are God's children. Now if we are children, then we are heirs— heirs of God and co-heirs with Christ, if indeed we share in his sufferings in order that we may also share in his glory.*
Romans 8:10-17 (NIV)

Life and its challenges will clutter our thoughts, especially our vision of what can and should be in our lives, leading us to make choices we might not make without life's vicissitudes. As a result of the negative impact of life and its challenges on our thinking, we tend to be swayed toward choices that provide temporary relief, making us comfortable in the here and now. Often, when we choose temporary relief, it may not always align with our long-term interest in what can and should be for our lives. Therefore, as we commit to regular maintenance of our lives, God has provided us the opportunity to reevaluate our position and path for us to **Readjust**, realigning ourselves with His purpose and plan for our abundant life. Jesus' death is God's gift to us, in which we have the right to reconcile our flesh, the reality of our experiences, to the Spirit, which leads and guides us to the fulfillment of God's promises for our lives. ***Breathe: New Life*** and inhale more of the Spirit. Take charge of your life; your choices and decisions will align with God's promises for your life, connecting you to the breath of life within you and living more abundantly!

## July 6

*For though we walk in the flesh, we do not war after the flesh: (For the weapons of our warfare are not carnal, but mighty through God to the pulling down of strong holds;) Casting down imaginations, and every high thing that exalteth itself against the knowledge of God, and bringing into captivity every thought to the obedience of Christ;*
II Corinthians 10:3-5

Although life, including the people, places, and things of our lives, comes against us as we seek to press forward in the fulfillment of God's promises, we can not treat them as they treat us; otherwise, we would be no better than they are. **Readjust** your attitude and actions from the default position of the flesh and allow the Spirit, God's purpose and plan, to flow within you to take control. As we allow ourselves to be fully consumed by the Spirit in and over our lives, we are empowered to resist the natural inclination to fight as others fight and/or to act as others act. Remember, our weapons are not carnal, of the world, but instead are of God and are mighty for the pulling down of any and all strongholds. **Readjust** your life and thinking that does not default to your flesh but instead to the Spirit of God that dwells within you and yearns to consume you and *Breathe: New Life*!

## July 7

*We have different gifts, according to the grace given to each of us. If your gift is prophesying, then prophesy in accordance with your faith; if it is serving, then serve; if it is teaching, then teach; if it is to encourage, then give encouragement; if it is giving, then give generously; if it is to lead, do it diligently; if it is to show mercy, do it cheerfully.*
Romans 12:6-8 (NIV)

Our call to **Readjust** in our lives is to better align ourselves with our life's purpose and plan. It is often very tempting to see someone else and believe that somehow the way they did it is the

212

way for you to do it, and thus to shift all your actions and plans to pattern your life after theirs.  Please note that God really did break the mold when He made you.  You are fearfully and wonderfully made and unique in who you are, your creation, as well as your purpose and plan.  Stand firm in who you are and **Readjust** to align with what can and should be for your life, for it is unique to you, and you are the only one who can do it.  Of course, we can learn and adapt from others' lived experiences, but stick to being you and giving your life all you have, for you have what it takes, go ahead and *Breathe: New Life* for it is yours!

## July 8

*If there be therefore any consolation in Christ, if any comfort of love, if any fellowship of the Spirit, if any bowels and mercies, Fulfil ye my joy, that ye be likeminded, having the same love, being of one accord, of one mind. Let nothing be done through strife or vainglory; but in lowliness of mind let each esteem other better than themselves. Look not every man on his own things, but every man also on the things of others.*
*Let this mind be in you, which was also in Christ Jesus:*
Philippians 2:1-5

Alignment with your vision is critical to achieving what you believe can and should be for your life.  Your alignment brings your life and space into accord with what you seek to achieve.  When your life and space do not and will not agree with where you are going, it will be a constant struggle to achieve; the distractions, detours, and downright bad choices due to nonalignment will cause you to spiral downward and/or wander in darkness.  Turn the light on in your life and allow the vision for your life to guide you, making appropriate adjustments in all aspects of your life toward what can and should be.  **Readjust** for the health and wholeness of your life and space, bringing all things into peace, harmony with the will of God for your life, being on one accord with what can and should be for your life.  Go ahead and appropriately **Readjust**, it will assist you in your ability to *Breathe: New Life* in all of your experiences, the taking on of the mind of Christ, leading to your life and life more abundantly.

## July 9

*Brethren, I count not myself to have apprehended: but this one thing I do, forgetting those things which are behind, and reaching forth unto those things which are before, I press toward the mark for the prize of the high calling of God in Christ Jesus.*
Philippians 3:13-14

To achieve that which can and should be for our lives, our vision requires us to diligently pursue it as though our lives depend upon it.  If you or I cannot commit to persevering through the challenges that arise from pursuing our vision, we cannot expect to reach our expected end.  Remember, God knows the plans He has for you, and they are not to hurt or harm you, but to bring you to your expected end.  The obstacles you face are designed to buffet you and keep you from your promise, but God has a hidden escape route in them that, if you are willing to **Readjust** toward your vision, what was meant for evil will empower you to spring forward in your promise. *Breathe: New Life* by stretching yourself, **Readjust** as appropriate to align with your expected end, and press toward God's higher calling for your life, and it will all work for your good!


## July 10


*Don't fool yourself into thinking that you are a listener when you are anything but, letting the Word go in one ear and out the other. Act on what you hear! Those who hear and don't act are like those who glance in the mirror, walk away, and two minutes later have no idea who they are, what they look like. But whoever catches a glimpse of the revealed counsel of God—the free life!—even out of the corner of his eye, and sticks with it, is no distracted scatterbrain but a man or woman of action. That person will find delight and affirmation in the action.*
James 1:22-25 (MSG)


For anything to be successfully completed, action is required. Life and nothing about it is worth having and/or enjoying if it is not easy. Life demands not only choosing to live in the fullness of life and what can and should be for you, but also investing in what you believe by putting your money where your mouth is. Expect nothing from nothing; what you put in is the least you will get out. The more you decide to take action on what you believe, the more you sow into what can and should be, and therefore, yield your harvest. Your beliefs are only matched and excelled by your actions. As you **Readjust** your life to what you believe can and should be you, act on your belief with the intent to produce the expected end. Your expected end is the direct result of your actions, coupled with God's Spirit, His wind blowing in and through your experiences. ***Breathe: New Life,*** not because you hear it, but also because you intentionally act upon it, sow into your life to produce that which you believe can and should be, and God will send His Spirit to carry your actions farther than you can ever ask or think!

## July 11

*Not every one that saith unto me, Lord, Lord, shall enter into the kingdom of heaven; but he that doeth the will of my Father which is in heaven. Many will say to me in that day, Lord, Lord, have we not prophesied in thy name? and in thy name have cast out devils? and in thy name done many wonderful works? And then will I profess unto them, I never knew you: depart from me, ye that work iniquity. Therefore whosoever heareth these sayings of mine, and doeth them, I will liken him unto a wise man, which built his house upon a rock: And the rain descended, and the floods came, and the winds blew, and beat upon that house; and it fell not: for it was founded upon a rock. And every one that heareth these sayings of mine, and doeth them not, shall be likened unto a foolish man, which built his house upon the sand: And the rain descended, and the floods came, and the winds blew, and beat upon that house; and it fell: and great was the fall of it.*
Matthew 7:21-27

If you and I are to live in the fulfilled promises of God for our lives and life more abundantly, then we must **Readjust** our lives to accommodate the Word of our promises. We cannot expect to speak those things for our lives as if they were without taking the required action to bring our lives into that which can and should be.  God and His promises are a gift to us, and as we choose to live in them, both in word and deed, we realize the already fulfilled promises of God for our lives.  Many want to claim, name, and haul promises, but no one wants to pay the price, to earn them, with the diligence to co-create with God that which can and should be.  **Readjust** yourself and allow the power within you, the Spirit of God, to take control and ***Breathe: New Life***; building your promises with God by walking worthy of your vocation on the rock of your labor to be sustained in your life and life more abundantly!

## July 12

*As Jesus was saying these things, a woman in the crowd called out, "Blessed is the mother who gave you birth and nursed you." He replied, "Blessed rather are those who hear the word of God and obey it."*
Luke 11:27-28 (NIV)

The greatest return to God for His blessing on our lives is for us to stay true and align with His Word.  God loved us so much that He sent His Son to reconcile us to His promises for our life and life more abundantly.  Jesus, the Word, God's promise to us made flesh, challenges us to take His promises for our lives and make them real.  The blessings of God to us are wonderful and amazing gifts; however, the gift has been given for our empowerment to fulfill the promises of God in our lives, the very acts that make us the crown of His glory.  **Readjust** your life to align with the Word of God and receive His blessings in and through all things, empowering you to ***Breathe: New Life***!

## July 13

*For not the hearers of the law are just before God, but the doers of the law shall be justified.*

Romans 2:13

We have a wonderful gift, a blessing from God, life and life more abundantly, that is not attached to how great we are, but instead how great and loving our God is.   No matter how blessed I am, I realize it is not something I deserve but a reflection of God's grace and my gratitude to Him for making all things right for me. Indeed, all things work together for the good, but what is most often forgotten or overlooked is that it is for those who love God and who are called according to His purpose.  Those who love God diligently pursue His purpose and plan for their lives, even though they may not be perfect.  God justifies them; He makes it all right for you.  Diligently pursue what you believe is God's promise for your life and watch God reward you for your willingness to pursue it.  Therefore, **Readjust** your life accordingly to align with God's purpose and plan, and whatever stands in the way, from within or without, He moves and/or covers with His grace.  Remember God's grace is sufficient for you in and through every experience of your life so that you can ***Breathe: New Life***!

## July 14

*Delightfully loved children, don't let anyone divert you from this truth. The person who keeps doing what is right proves that he is*

*righteous before God, even as the Messiah is righteous. But the*
*one who indulges in a sinful life is of the devil, because the devil*
*has been sinning from the beginning. The reason the Son of God*
*was revealed was to undo and destroy the works of the devil.*
I John 3:7-8 (TPT)

There is no need for you to be diverted from the truth of God's Word for your life. God intentionally provided a way of reconciliation for you, if you choose. Before the foundations of the world were ever laid, Christ, God's Son, had already been offered so that you and I might enjoy the abundance of life, the promises of God. Therefore, no matter where you are, what you have done, or how far it appears you are from your promise, **Readjust** your life and space for the desired outcome for your life and life more abundantly. God loves you and has made a way for you. ***Breathe: New Life*** in your circumstances and enjoy the awaiting abundance of promises for you to live life and life more abundantly. No matter what darkness, evil, or demonic forces may exist to keep you, divert you, **Readjust**, and receive the power to overcome and inherit all things!

## July 15

*Dear friends, do you think you'll get anywhere in this if you learn*
*all the right words but never do anything? Does merely talking*
*about faith indicate that a person really has it? For instance, you*
*come upon an old friend dressed in rags and half-starved and say,*
*"Good morning, friend! Be clothed in Christ! Be filled with the Holy*
*Spirit!" and walk off without providing so much as a coat or a cup*

*of soup—where does that get you? Isn't it obvious that God-talk*
*without God-acts is outrageous nonsense?*
James 2:14-17 (MSG)


Action is critical to our ability to live in the promises of our life and life more abundantly.  You cannot expect God to drop things out of the air or name it-claim it, call it-haul it, without you putting in the work required to receive; sowing and reaping; being a doer of the Word.  Your promise from God requires you to believe it, and your belief is manifested in your actions.  Remember, without faith, it is impossible to please God; those who come to Him must believe that He is and that He is a rewarder of those who diligently seek Him.  **Readjust** your life and space to properly align with God's promises for your life, His purpose, and plan as a foundation for taking action on what you believe can and should be.  As you take action, love your Word; promises, life, and space, from which you ***Breathe: New Life*** not only for you but also for one another and all of God's creation.


## July 16


*We can all draw close to him with the veil removed from our faces.*
*And with no veil we all become like mirrors who brightly reflect*
*the glory of the Lord Jesus. We are being transfigured into his very*
*image as we move from one brighter level of glory to another. And*
*this glorious transfiguration comes from the Lord, who is the*
*Spirit.*
II Corinthians 3:18 (TPT)

The process of seizing the life and life more abundantly promised to us demands transformation. Change is not sufficient for what is the abundance of God's promises fulfilled in our lives, but instead to move to a deeper and more meaningful transformation from who we were to whom we can and should become. God created each of us with a specific purpose and plan that is a part of the larger framework of God's work in and through His creation; thus, as we journey through life, with its challenges that seek to separate us from the light of truth, we must be willing to **Readjust**. **Readjust** your life so that the challenges that have left residue, causing you to fall out of alignment with your life's purpose and plan, are pressed past the veil of darkness and chaos to co-create with God His intended heaven and earth for you. When we willingly take up the cause to align ourselves and press past our challenges, we see clearly God's revelation for our lives and the pathway to ***Breathe: New Life***, seize His promises for our life and life more abundantly!

## July 17

*For God so loved the world, that he gave his only begotten Son, that whosoever believeth in him should not perish, but have everlasting life.*
John 3:16

The world we live in today is challenging and can leave us wandering aimlessly and hopeless as we move from one crisis to another in our personal, financial, and social lives. The challenges are many: Anti-Blackness, inflation, war, and violence, and each is real, impacts the others, and spurs them. How does one remain sane and hopeful amid the challenges and the appearance of things getting worse? You must believe! Belief seems too simple and insufficient for the crisis that we face, but in reality, it is the only way to clear our view to discover and execute our purpose and plan to get out, over, and beyond so that we might enjoy what can and should be for our life and life more abundantly. Without question, there is a way; however, we must get in the way and see clearly to the end result, our expected outcome of life and life abundantly. To do so requires us to believe, to see what can and should be, and as a result, act. We cannot expect to reach our chosen destiny if we are not willing to take actions that lead to it and, in so doing, are willing to sacrifice the tangible and intangible aspects of our lives and present reality. **Readjust** our perceptions of one another, use of our resources, means of resolutions, and the way we engage life and its challenges so that we can *Breathe: New Life*. God showed us by sacrificing His best, with the hope that you and I, the world, would transform for the better, for His intended purpose and plan for our lives and for life more abundantly, avoiding states of bewilderment and wandering aimlessly, and instead living with purpose and a plan for abundant living.

## July 18

*Very rarely will anyone die for a righteous person, though for a good person someone might possibly dare to die. But God demonstrates his own love for us in this: While we were still sinners, Christ died for us. Since we have now been justified by his blood, how much more shall we be saved from God's wrath through him! For if, while we were God's enemies, we were*

*reconciled to him through the death of his Son, how much more,*
*having been reconciled, shall we be saved through his life!*
Romans 5:7-10 (NIV)

**Readjustment** is possible, no matter what you or others may think.  God, the Creator of all things, has in His creation created a way for you to escape, to willingly correct your path toward your life and life more abundantly.  Remember it is God's desire that you would be saved, delivered to His very promises for your abundance, and has and will do anything to ensure and assist you in overcoming what you face to be reconciled, one with His Word of truth for your life and life more abundantly.  If God was willing to give His only begotten Son, whom He loved, on the chance that you and I would believe His Word of truth, acting, sacrificing, and expecting the fulfillment of God's promises, what would He not do, move, or empower you to overcome?  God loves you unconditionally; all that is required is that you believe and your willingness to diligently pursue what you believe can and should be for your life, and He will reward you.  ***Breathe New Life*** and inherit what has already been prepared, paid for, and awaits you by believing, acting, sacrificing, and expecting God's Word to become flesh, real in your life!

## July 19

*Greater love has no one than this: to lay down one's life for one's friends.  You are my friends if you do what I command.  I no longer call you servants, because a servant does not know his master's business. Instead, I have called you friends, for everything that I learned from my Father I have made known to you.  You did not*

223

*choose me, but I chose you and appointed you so that you might go and bear fruit—fruit that will last—and so that whatever you ask in my name the Father will give you.*
John 15:13-16 (NIV)

We all desire to be rewarded for our work; it is not unnatural, nor should one be ashamed. In many ways, it is our reward and expectation that drive our work. When we work toward something, we, therefore, expect to receive our reward, the fulfillment of our expectations. Your expectations are critical to your diligently pursuing what you believe can and should be for your life. Therefore, set your expectations high and work, press toward that for which you believe can and should be for your life; you are not alone. God has chosen you for your higher calling, and because you press diligently pursue your higher calling, God rewards you, fulfills your expectations, thus, you can ask what you will, and He will give it to you. **Readjust** your life and space to align with God's purpose and plan for your life; ***Breathe: New Life,*** and as a result, your expectations will fall in line with God's will, and you will be rewarded exceedingly, abundantly, more than you can ever ask or think.

## July 20

*For Christ also suffered once for sins, the righteous for the unrighteous, to bring you to God. He was put to death in the body but made alive in the Spirit.*
I Peter 3:18 (NIV)

**Readjust** your life and space to align with God's purpose and plan because He has given everything so you can live fully in His promises for your life and life more abundantly. Christ sacrificed His position as Divine, willingly taking on flesh to do that which had been prepared and established for Him, and in so doing found His place of refuge, His place of power in the Spirit. Christ is our ultimate example for living in God's purpose and plan by modeling actions in which He **Readjusted** from the comfor of His flesh to the empowerment of God's Spirit in and on His life. *Breathe: New Life* and transition yourself from the containment of your flesh to release in the Spirit of God's intent and power for your life and life more abundantly and live, living to overcome and inherit all things!

## July 21

*This is how we've come to understand and experience love: Christ sacrificed his life for us. This is why we ought to live sacrificially for our fellow believers, and not just be out for ourselves. If you see some brother or sister in need and have the means to do something about it but turn a cold shoulder and do nothing, what happens to God's love? It disappears. And you made it disappear. My dear children, let's not just talk about love; let's practice real love. This is the only way we'll know we're living truly, living in God's reality. It's also the way to shut down debilitating self-criticism, even when there is something to it. For God is greater than our worried hearts and knows more about us than we do ourselves.*
I John 3:16-20 (MSG)

Sacrifice is the required position if one wants to achieve what can and should be their life. You must be willing to put on the line that which you hold dear the most if you want to live in the exceedingly, abundantly, more than of your life. You cannot expect to live in abundance without paying the cost; you are willing to **Readjust** your life and space to support the abundant outcome you desire, and it will most often come with your challenge to willingly sacrifice. It is a misnomer that the promises of God are going to be fulfilled just because or somehow they are free from your willingness to believe, to go, to sacrifice, to **Readjust.** Just as Jesus and Abram were asked to offer up the very promise of God, you will experience the choice of whether you, your life, and even your promise are more important than God the Promiser and His purpose and plan. Go ahead and **Readjust**; *Breathe: New Life.* God knew and knows, and as a result of your willingness to sacrifice for the fulfillment of His purpose and plan for your life, He will reward you, causing your cup of life to run over.

## July 22

*God sacrificed Jesus on the altar of the world to clear that world of sin. Having faith in him sets us in the clear. God decided on this course of action in full view of the public—to set the world in the clear with himself through the sacrifice of Jesus, finally taking care of the sins he had so patiently endured. This is not only clear, but it's now—this is current history! God sets things right. He also makes it possible for us to live in his rightness.*
Romans 3:25-26 (MSG)

You can **Readjust** your life and space, despite and in spite of whose fault it may be that you are where you are, without any blame or guilt, for God paid it all with His Son as a sacrifice for you and me, including our guilt and/or regrets.  Stop allowing people, places, and things, including yourself, to make you feel guilty or so consumed with regret that you are immobile, or you accept what is.  God always offers you a new chance, a new life, one that can and will be greater than before.  God shows us His love, graciousness, and welcoming Spirit by offering His Son as the sacrifice, atonement, which reconciles us from wherever we are and whatever caused us to be there to His original intent for our life and life more abundantly.  **Readjust** your life and space without guilt or regret, and *Breathe: New Life*, God has made it possible not once, twice, but an eternal offer to you if you would dare to believe, act, sacrifice, and expect your life and life more abundantly!

## July 23

*But now in Christ Jesus you who once were far away have been brought near by the blood of Christ.*
Ephesians 2:13 (NIV)

No matter what hand life has dealt you or you caused, near to you is the opportunity to achieve the very promises of God for your life and life more abundantly.  All that is required is for you to **Readjust**.  **Readjust** your life and space to align with what can and should be for your life as God has promised.  The mistakes, detours, distractions, guilt, shame, or whatever seeks to separate you from your life and life more abundantly are not so complex, difficult, hard, or horrific that God can not and will not bridge your separation to His will for your life and life more abundantly.  You are not that far gone, no matter what it looks like; your opportunity is near, closer than you think.  **_Breathe: New Life_** as you **Readjust** for the outcome of your life and life more abundantly for God is with you and stands ready and available to see you through to the place of your promises, the what can and should be for your life!

## July 24

*And he said, A certain man had two sons: And the younger of them said to his father, Father, give me the portion of goods that falleth to me. And he divided unto them his living. And not many days after the younger son gathered all together, and took his journey into a far country, and there wasted his substance with riotous living. And when he had spent all, there arose a mighty famine in that land; and he began to be in want. And he went and joined himself to a citizen of that country; and he sent him into his fields to feed swine. And he would fain have filled his belly with the husks that the swine did eat: and no man gave unto him. And when he came to himself, he said, How many hired servants of my father's have bread enough and to spare, and I perish with hunger! I will arise and go to my father, and will say unto him, Father, I have sinned against heaven, and before thee, And am no more worthy to be called thy son: make me as one of thy hired servants. And he arose, and came to his father. But when he was yet a great way off, his father saw him, and had compassion, and ran, and fell on his neck, and kissed him. And the son said unto him, Father, I have sinned against heaven, and in thy sight, and am no more worthy to be called thy son. But the father said to his servants, Bring forth the best robe, and put it on him; and put a ring on his hand, and shoes on his feet: And bring hither the fatted calf, and kill it; and let us eat, and be merry: For this my son was dead, and is alive again; he was lost, and is found. And they began to be merry.*

Luke 15:11-24

This morning, I arose to yet another story concerning the police's negative engagement with a young Black male in TN for a traffic violation that caused me to be both bewildered and righteously indignant and screaming, "Stop, not again." The critical word is "again," which triggers my bewilderment as well as righteous indignation because when are we going to learn, when will we do a reality check and conclude we cannot continue to ignore the root cause, anti-Blackness! We cannot train our way out of anti-Blackness, creating offices of "equity, diversity, and inclusion" that lack any real substance to defy the "white lies." When will we come to ourselves and realize that we are a racist nation with systems and structures that have been shaped and formed on lies to directly and, more often, indirectly support mindsets and actions that result in the horrific outcomes we are experiencing over and over again? When will we challenge who we are at the core and come to ourselves, aligning life and our spaces to **Readjust**, *Breathe: New Life*, in which we transform hearts and mindsets, rooted in truth, willing to repent of the lies and wrongdoings to build a world of mutual respect? The lesson of the Prodigal Son is that he came to himself; an honest and candid reality check to determine who he was, opening up his potential to live in the fullness of life and life more abundantly!

## July 25

*He came and preached peace to you who were far away and peace to those who were near. For through him we both have access to the Father by one Spirit. Consequently, you are no longer foreigners and strangers, but fellow citizens with God's people and also members of his household,*
Ephesians 2:17-19 (NIV)

When we are out of alignment with what our purpose and plan for our life and life more abundantly, it appears we are just wandering around endlessly in life. The wandering caused by non-alignment does not produce for us that which we expect and becomes extremely frustrating and in some instances makes us feel hopeless that things or our plight will never change; however, **Readjust. Readjust** and set in motion what will meet and exceed your expectations, aligning you with your life and life more abundantly. No matter where you are and how hopeless it may seem, God is a very present help, and right there at your disposal, reach out and seize Him and *Breathe: New Life*. You may think you are in a strange place and foreign to the ideals and expectations of what can and should be for your life, but know you are a part of God and He is a part of you. **Readjust** as required, and receive your new life!

## July 26

*Have mercy on me, O God, according to your unfailing love;*
*according to your great compassion blot out my transgressions.*
*Wash away all my iniquity and cleanse me from my sin.*
*For I know my transgressions, and my sin is always before me.*
Psalm 51:1-3 (NIV)


A crucial component to **Readjust,** to align with the purpose and plan for our life and life more abundantly, is our willingness to be honest with ourselves and turn from what hurts our march toward what can and should be for our lives.  Turning away from negative impacts is what we refer to as repentance.  Please remember that sin is not defined necessarily by a list of don'ts, but instead by anything that would separate you, and keep you from what God's promises for your life and life more abundantly. When we are willing to examine ourselves, honest and candid with ourselves concerning our life, we are in a better position to evaluate what is working and what is not to appropriately **Readjust** so that we can *Breathe: New Life*.  You and I can transform the course of our lives to align with God's intent for our life and life more abundantly by calling on God and pleading for His mercy to wash and cleanse us, align us with His will for our life and life more abundantly, it is your right and God's love for you will respond and accomplish in you His intent.


## July 27


*Wherefore he saith, Awake thou that sleepest, and arise from the*
*dead, and Christ shall give thee light.*
Ephesians 5:14

The challenges of our lives often cloud our view and make us feel as though what can and should be for our lives is not possible; however, we cannot rely totally on what we see in the natural but instead on what we can see in the Spirit. God comes to our lives to give us His intent, including guidance on our purpose and plan. As we align with our purpose and plan, God, His Word of promise, becomes the light that illuminates the pathway to that which will bring about our life and life more abundantly, what can and should be as intended by God as revealed by His Spirit. Do not allow the challenges before you to cloud your view, awake from your sleep, and *Breathe: New Life,* **Readjusting** according to walking in the light of your promises that which is necessary to receive your life and life more abundantly!

## July 28

*Arise, shine; for thy light is come,*
*and the glory of the LORD is risen upon thee.*
Isaiah 60:1

Life does deal us significant blows which cause us to believe that we are out of the game and there is no possible way for us to win; however, **Readjust** and arise, and watch the revelation of God and His confidence in you empower you to overcome. Remember, your belief in your purpose and plan, the what can and should be for your life, is fuel for you to arise from whatever challenges you face to win. You may get knocked down and even knocked unconscious, but do not stay there, stir up the gifts, the Spirit within, and arise, shake the dust from your feet, and press onward and upward. Your faith in the fulfillment of your promises in your here and now will compel, empower you to **Readjust** as necessary and get up. As you **Readjust** you *Breathe: New Life* into your circumstances, the inhaling of God's Word, His promises for your life, and as a result, you see the revelation of God in your circumstance to arise and go forth in your life and life more abundantly!

## July 29

*And that, knowing the time, that now it is high time to awake out of sleep: for now is our salvation nearer than when we believed. The night is far spent, the day is at hand: let us therefore cast off the works of darkness, and let us put on the armour of light. Let us walk honestly, as in the day; not in rioting and drunkenness, not in chambering and wantonness, not in strife and envying. But put ye on the Lord Jesus Christ, and make not provision for the flesh, to fulfil the lusts thereof.*
Romans 13:11-14

You and I have been given free will to choose our destiny. God places before us life and death, blessings and curses, and implores us to choose life. By choosing life, we also receive the power of reconciliation through Christ. Thus, as we exercise our free will, built into it is also our option of reconciliation, realignment to God's promises for our life and life more abundantly, if we choose, resulting in our willingness to **Readjust** our lives and spaces to accommodate God's intent. Resurrection is about our ability to freely choose God's intent, purpose, and plan for our lives, and as we do so, we are empowered to **Readjust** our lives, to arise and awake from the sleep of the toxicity of our lives to enjoy God's promises of our abundance.  Therefore, cast off the darkness, and put on your power of reconciliation, live in the Spirit of God and His intent for your life and life more abundantly, transcending your flesh and the challenges of life to *Breathe: New Life*.

## July 30

*So then, let us not be like others, who are asleep, but let us be*
*awake and sober.  For those who sleep, sleep at night, and those*
*who get drunk, get drunk at night.  But since we belong to the day,*
*let us be sober, putting on faith and love as a breastplate, and the*
*hope of salvation as a helmet.  For God did not appoint us to suffer*
*wrath but to receive salvation through our Lord Jesus Christ.  He*
*died for us so that, whether we are awake or asleep, we may live*
*together with him.*
I Thessalonians 5:6-10 (NIV)

Walking in the light of the day, God's promises for your life, defies the challenges of darkness, and thus, our ability to face our darkness lies in our commitment to the light, the truth of God's promises, His purpose, and plan for our life and life more abundantly.  If we allow life's challenges to overcome us, darkness to cover and cloud our truth, which is the promises of God, we cannot and will not access God's pathway for the fullness of joy He intends for our lives.  Therefore, to access our promises of life and life more abundantly, to turn on the light to our pathway demands that we align ourselves with God's intent and, in so doing **Readjust** our life and space.  **Readjust** for you are a person of the day, the light, and as appropriate, take the steps that move you forward in the promises of God for your life and life more abundantly.  Be sober, clear, about God's intent and believe; act on His leading and guiding you to your place of abundance, and *Breathe: New Life*.  Remember, Christ died so that you would arise to the light of God's truth for your life, despite what appears to be the finality of life's challenges, even that of death, hell, and the grave.

## July 31

*If we claim that we're free of sin, we're only fooling ourselves. A claim like that is errant nonsense. On the other hand, if we admit our sins—simply come clean about them—he won't let us down; he'll be true to himself. He'll forgive our sins and purge us of all wrongdoing. If we claim that we've never sinned, we out-and-out contradict God—make a liar out of him. A claim like that only shows off our ignorance of God.*
I John 1:8-10 (MSG)

The most powerful weapon used against us is our own sense of guilt and shame, which forces us to be and act differently from what can and should be in our lives. Yet we have the power to overcome our guilt and shame by simply forgiving ourselves and moving on.  As we all know, it is very difficult to forgive others therefore, it is almost impossible for us to forgive ourselves, however, when you choose to **Readjust** your life to embrace God's unconditional love for you, you will be persuaded that nothing, including your guilt and shame, can separate you from God's love, His intent for your life and life more abundantly.  God knew and knows that we, all humans, saved and unsaved, believers as well as non-believers will sin - separate yourself from the promises of

God for your life and all God requires is that you come to yourself, make the necessary **Readjustment** and live in the fullness of His promises and He will do exceedingly, abundantly, more than by the power that works within you. God has already forgiven you, paid the price to cleanse you, and stands ready and available to assist you in overcoming and inheriting all things just as He intended, ***Breathe: New Life*** and live!

# *REVELATION*

## August

## August 1

*There's not one totally good person on earth,*
*Not one who is truly pure and sinless.*
Ecclesiastes 7:20 (MSG)

Life has taught me that major life **Revelations** are not in how perfect I am or the perfection of my actions; instead, they come through the purging process during difficult times and/or the failures of my life. I would suggest to you that God, through our chaos and challenges, especially that which separates us from Him and His promises for our life, is purposefully designed for us to trust Him, and He uses our trust in Him as a platform to bring about His **Revelation**, His Word made flesh, real. When we can accept the reality of our imperfections, limitations, and even the struggles before us, we are better positioned to let the strength of God and His calling on our lives be seen in us and through us. God knew and knows, and therefore, He has built into our life's journey our imperfection in which He will be made perfect in and through us; in our weakness, His strength is made perfect, revealing His sufficient grace to and for us. Therefore, go ahead and *Breathe: New Life*, God will be revealed, and you will come into **Revelation** of not only God's power but also His choice of His power operating in and through your life to reveal Him and you together!

## August 2

*I acknowledged my sin unto thee,*

*and mine iniquity have I not hid.*
*I said, I will confess my transgressions unto the LORD;*
*and thou forgavest the iniquity of my sin. Selah.*
Psalm 32:5


It is in acknowledging our shortcomings and weaknesses that we can identify what gives us the power to leverage them against them and overcome them.  If we never take a reality check by being real with ourselves, we can never take the actions required to overcome whatever stands in our way and press past it to our higher calling, our life and life more abundantly.  It is in being real with ourselves that we can be real with God and experience His **Revelation** that produces our plan to *Breathe: New Life* and be more than conquerors in our circumstances.  It is God's intent, His desire that you and I would be saved, be delivered, to His promises for our lives, despite and in spite of us.  Thus, being real with ourselves and God gives us the opportunity to see God and to see Him working in and through us; **Revelation** to produce His intent for our lives and life more abundantly!


## August 3


*He that covereth his sins shall not prosper:*
*but whoso confesseth and forsaketh them shall have mercy.*
Proverbs 28:13


As a core value for your life, you must be willing to confess your faults in order to get past them and leverage your strengths to support your pressing toward the promises for your life.  Be assured that all of us have sinned; we all have things in our lives that prevent or seek to separate us from what can and should be for our lives as promised by God. Because sin is common to us all, God declares that He is faithful to us. If we choose to believe His promises for our lives and for life more abundantly in and through all things, He will show Himself and His **Revelation** to lead and guide us to our promises. *Breathe: New Life* by confessing and communicating all things unto God, and He will show up and scatter the darkness, that which would separate you from what is your life and life more abundantly!

## August 4

*Have mercy upon me, O God, according to thy lovingkindness:*
*according unto the multitude of thy tender mercies blot out my*
*transgressions.*
*Wash me throughly from mine iniquity,*
*and cleanse me from my sin.*
*For I acknowledge my transgressions:*
*and my sin is ever before me.*
Psalm 51:1-3

It is in the cleansing of who we are, in reality checks, that we are positioned to receive **Revelation** and press forward in our lives toward what can and should be for our lives. As we are serious and honest with ourselves about the state of our lives, including the challenges before us, we bring a focus to our circumstances that opens us up to strategies and possibilities that are advantageous to our advancement. When we choose to ignore the reality of our experiences, we shortchange our ability to overcome our circumstances and thus inherit what God has ordained for our lives. **Breathe: New Life** by being real with yourself and allowing the Spirit of God to lead and guide you in pathways that empower you to overcome and inherit your life and life more abundantly in and through your circumstances.

## August 5

*But if we walk in the light, as he is in the light, we have fellowship one with another, and the blood of Jesus Christ his Son cleanseth us from all sin.*
I John 1:7

The light of God, His Word, activated in our lives, releases **Revelation**. **Revelation** is defined as a surprising and previously unknown fact, especially one that is made known dramatically - the Divine or supernatural disclosure to humans of something related to human existence or the world. Thus, the insight required to navigate life and its challenges is a result of our willingness to turn on the light. Light naturally scatters darkness so that one can see, receive, **Revelation**. Life is difficult, and the challenges make it even harder to keep your promise; however, God has declared He will be with you, and He is light. The more you allow Him to reign in you and your space, the greater the insight you have. **Breathe: New Life** by getting insight, **Revelation** of what God is up to in and through your life that is readily available to you as you fellowship, develop, and nurture your intimate relationship with God.

## August 6

*And such were some of you: but ye are washed, but ye are sanctified, but ye are justified in the name of the Lord Jesus, and by the Spirit of our God.*
I Corinthians 6:11

Your right to life and life more abundantly, generally and specifically in your experiences, is not because of how perfect you are, but instead how good and gracious God is to you.  Stop allowing your shortcomings, guilt, shame, or inadequacy to keep you from living in the fullness of your potential.  Work your field and allow God, the Creator of you and everything, to handle the rest.  God desires to be in and through you and every one of your experiences, **Revelation** of not only how great He is but also how much He loves and has chosen you.  The **Revelation** found in your circumstances is that you have been chosen by God, and if you are willing to be sensitive to what is God's purpose in your circumstances, you will find the key, the **Revelation** that unlocks your door and releases you into your fullness of joy.  Instead of worrying and being frustrated in your circumstances, ***Breathe: New Life*** by casting all on God and watch Him reveal Himself and who He has created you to be, one who has been built for your journey!

## August 7

*And I said to him, "Sir, you are the one who knows."  Then he said to me, "These are the ones who died in the great tribulation.  They have washed their robes in the blood of the Lamb and made them*

white. *"That is why they stand in front of God's throne and serve him day and night in his Temple. And he who sits on the throne will give them shelter. They will never again be hungry or thirsty; they will never be scorched by the heat of the sun. For the Lamb on the throne will be their Shepherd. He will lead them to springs of life-giving water. And God will wipe every tear from their eyes."*
Revelation 7:14-17 (NLT)

**Revelation** for our life and life more abundantly is a direct result of engaging the situations of our lives and going through them. As a result, we receive the required insight, direction, and guidance that empowers us to overcome what is necessary and live in the fullness of life. As we struggle, wash our lives, the good and bad, we discover the wholeness and power of God to overcome any and all things, and in so doing, we inherit all things, the fulfillment of God's promises in and for our lives, our **Revelation.** Though the trials and tribulations of life seem hard and downright impossible at times, **Breathe: New Life** for God declares that whatever you are going through, He will wipe it away. Wherever you may be with God, it is a safe, loving, and empowering place, so take your troubles to Him and He will reveal Himself, His power, and His promises to you for your life and life more abundantly!

## August 8

*Come now, and let us reason together, saith the LORD: though your sins be as scarlet, they shall be as white as snow; though they be red like crimson, they shall be as wool.*
Isaiah 1:18

As we seek to **Breathe: New Life** into our experiences, we must be confident that whatever presently exists has not come to hurt or harm us, but to assist us in reaching our expected end: the new life and life more abundantly promised. No matter what or where the source of the difficulty, hardship, or misfortune comes from, God invites you into a relationship with Him in which you both exhale and inhale; exhaling the unnecessary stuff of your life by acting in your purpose as well as inhaling all that is good and perfect will, purpose of God in your experiences for the good. It is through our experiences, the good and the bad, that God reveals Himself, gives the required **Revelation**, so we can move forward in our promises of life and life more abundantly. Receive God's invitations in whatever is going on in your life and come, cast it all on Him, He cares for you and will wash, work it all out, provide **Revelation** for your good, your life and life more abundantly.

## August 9

*Joshua, standing before the angel, was dressed in dirty clothes. The angel spoke to his attendants, "Get him out of those filthy clothes," and then said to Joshua, "Look, I've stripped you of your sin and dressed you up in clean clothes." I spoke up and said, "How about a clean new turban for his head also?" And they did it —put a clean new turban on his head. Then they finished dressing him, with God's Angel looking on.*
Zechariah 3:3-5 (MSG)

God will always provide you with the new; all you have to do is ask. Neither you nor I has to live in hell; in the chaos and confusion of life that prevents us from living in the capacity of our

244

lives and life more abundantly, not just overall, but in and through each experience of our lives. God desires that you and I walk in the fullness of His promises, over and over again, to a degree that it is exceedingly, abundantly, more than we can ask or think; our cups running over, and to that end, ensures we can always be made whole from whatever exists. We tend to pick up dirt and stains just through the ordinary process of life, some from within and some from without, but be of good cheer, Christ has overcome the world so that you and I have the right to be made whole. It is in the processes of our being made whole in which **Revelation** of God and His fullness of power and promises are known to us; therefore, in your circumstances, *Breathe: New Life*; be made whole in and through all things, it is God's will.

## August 10

*How much more, then, will the blood of Christ, who through the eternal Spirit offered himself unblemished to God, cleanse our consciences from acts that lead to death, so that we may serve the living God! For this reason Christ is the mediator of a new covenant, that those who are called may receive the promised eternal inheritance—now that he has died as a ransom to set them free from the sins committed under the first covenant.*
Hebrews 9:14-15 (NIV)

The challenges of our lives serve as an invitation from God to trust Him, to rely on Him, and to allow Him to direct our path. It is in trusting God that we receive **Revelation**; we see clearly who God is and His capabilities to do what He has said, making His Word flesh, real in our lives. It is in **Revelation** after **Revelation** that our trust in God is built, thus the wiles of the devil and darkness lose their power over us, and as a result of the light of God's **Revelation**, our darkness is scattered. When God is revealed, the light is turned on in our situations, cleansing us and setting us on the pathway that leads to our fullness of joy. No matter your circumstances, complex or not, allow the light of Christ, the meditator for the fulfillment of God's promises for your life in, inhale and be cleansed of the darkness, the toxicity that exists, and be set free to *Breathe: New Life*!

## August 11

*And from Jesus Christ the Faithful Witness, the Firstborn from among the dead and the ruling King, who rules over the kings of the earth! Now to the one who constantly loves us and has loosed us from our sins by his own blood.*
Revelation 1:5 (TPT)

The resurrection of Christ from the grave provides the greatest witness of the **Revelation** of God. For God in death conquered death, hell, and the grave, manifesting His power to overcome anything. The finality of death, hell, and the grave serves as a reminder, a witness that nothing is over until God says so. Seek God's **Revelation** for your life and *Breathe: New Life.* There is absolutely nothing too hard or impossible for God. If you can believe God's Word for your life and life more abundantly, you can overcome whatever stands in your way and be victorious; loosed from your fears and anything else that separates you from God's Word made flesh, real in your life!

## August 12

*And I heard a great voice out of heaven saying, Behold, the*
*tabernacle of God is with men, and he will dwell with them, and*
*they shall be his people, and God himself shall be with them, and*
*be their God. And God shall wipe away all tears from their eyes;*
*and there shall be no more death, neither sorrow, nor crying,*
*neither shall there be any more pain: for the former things are*
*passed away.*
*And he that sat upon the throne said, Behold, I make all things*
*new. And he said unto me, Write: for these words are true and*
*faithful.*
*And he said unto me, It is done. I am Alpha and Omega, the*
*beginning and the end. I will give unto him that is athirst of the*
*fountain of the water of life freely. He that overcometh shall*
*inherit all things; and I will be his God, and he shall be my son.*
Revelation 21:3-7

Who we are and who we shall become is connected to our ability
to **Breathe: New Life**, not just in general but in each and every
one of our life experiences.  Whatever we engage in, we must see
it through the lens of new life, a **Revelation** of God being fulfilled
in and through us.  No matter what life's challenges may be, or
where we are in them, God is present with us and available to
dwell with us through them to a place of new life.  God has
already prepared what is the new, and the process we must
endure is necessary for it to be revealed, the **Revelation** of the
newness that God awaits us, but we must go through to get to,
overcome to inherit all things.  **Breathe: New Life** into your

experiences, good and bad, and set in motion the process of **Revelation** of God that empowers you through the process to overcome what was to what can and shall be for your life and life more abundantly!

## August 13

*They shall not hunger nor thirst;*
*neither shall the heat nor sun smite them:*
*for he that hath mercy on them shall lead them,*
*even by the springs of water shall he guide them.*
Isaiah 49:10

We, as a result of our relationship with God, have access to the fullness of God, His Word made flesh, real in our lives. Relationships have their benefits, and as we develop and nurture a relationship with God, the Creator, we gain access to all that is His. Nothing He created belongs to Him. Therefore, as we engage each and every circumstance of our lives, it is an opportunity to experience the **Revelation** of God; God revealed so that we not only know Him, but we also bask in His glory, empowering us to press even higher toward His calling for our lives. Remember, there is absolutely nothing happening in your life by happenstance or accident; it is Divinely ordered. Go ahead and *Breathe: New Life*, receive God's Revelation, producing your life and life more abundantly!

## August 14

*I will lift up mine eyes unto the hills, from whence cometh my help.*
*My help cometh from the LORD, which made heaven and earth.*
*He will not suffer thy foot to be moved: he that keepeth thee will not slumber.*
*Behold, he that keepeth Israel shall neither slumber nor sleep.*
*The LORD is thy keeper: the LORD is thy shade upon thy right hand.*
*The sun shall not smite thee by day, nor the moon by night.*
*The LORD shall preserve thee from all evil: he shall preserve thy soul.*
*The LORD shall preserve thy going out and thy coming in from this time forth, and even for evermore.*
Psalm 121


God has built into our journey for life and life more abundantly. God's **Revelation** is an impetus for us to press forward even higher.  God is near and available to us, and as we move forward in what we believe can and should be, as declared by Him, we see the **Revelation** of His power and His choice of us as His agents revealed in our lives.  The Lord is our help, our keeper, and our preserver; we exist and overcome all things by Him and His power operating in our lives, and as we are willing to go, to take action on His purpose and plan for our lives, we see Him, and He reveals us to be who He has created us to be. ***Breathe: New Life*** in your circumstances, for in it is the opportunity for God to be seen, His **Revelation** made real in and through your life. He is just waiting on you to go, and in your going, you trigger His **Revelation**, His showing up and out in your life!


## August 15

*The LORD is my shepherd; I shall not want.*
*He maketh me to lie down in green pastures:*
*he leadeth me beside the still waters.*
*He restoreth my soul:*
*he leadeth me in the paths of righteousness for his name's sake.*
*Yea, though I walk through the valley of the shadow of death,*
*I will fear no evil: for thou art with me;*
*thy rod and thy staff they comfort me.*
*Thou preparest a table before me in the presence of mine enemies:*
*thou anointest my head with oil; my cup runneth over.*
*Surely goodness and mercy shall follow me all the days of my life:*
*and I will dwell in the house of the LORD for ever.*
Psalm 23

As believers, we have assurance that God is with us, no matter where we are or what is going on, and that goodness and mercy will follow us. God has built into our journey, if we are willing to go, the necessary support and assistance to be revealed. The **Revelation** God has awaiting you is triggered as you are willing to go, take action, and trust God. Trusting God allows us to bring the unknown, uncertainty, and bewilderment of life, along with its challenges, to ***Breathe: New Life*** into our experiences. The Lord is our Shepherd, and as such, we need not want for anything. Whatever arises, He supplies all of our needs and works out everything through the **Revelation** of Himself, us, and His purpose and plan for our lives.

**August 16**

*How excellent is thy lovingkindness, O God!*
*therefore the children of men put their trust under the shadow of*
*thy wings.*
*They shall be abundantly satisfied with the fatness of thy house;*
*and thou shalt make them drink of the river of thy pleasures.*
*For with thee is the fountain of life:*
*in thy light shall we see light.*
Psalm 36:7-9

Basking in God as we seek to live in the fullness of our promises for life and life more abundantly, God not only provides for us, but He does so in abundance. God loves us unconditionally; therefore, we can be assured that whatever we may face or see to engage our space, the lovingkindness of God will provide for us and do so in which we bask in the overflow. God Himself lights up our space, and as He lights up our space, we are better able to see and experience **Revelation**, which empowers us to overcome and be more than conquerors, bask in the exceedingly abundant, more than we can ever ask or think. Do not allow the vicissitudes of life to cause you to be weary; God's lovingkindness is with you. Embrace Him in the light of who He is and His promises, and *Breathe: New Life* and bask in your overflow, get soaking wet!

## August 17

*He will swallow up death in victory;*
*and the Lord GOD will wipe away tears from off all faces;*
*and the rebuke of his people shall he take away from off all the*
*earth:*

*for the LORD hath spoken it.*
*And it shall be said in that day,*
*Lo, this is our God;*
*we have waited for him, and he will save us:*
*this is the LORD; we have waited for him,*
*we will be glad and rejoice in his salvation.*
Isaiah 25:8-9

We come to know the truth of God and the fullness of His power, made real in our lives, through the challenges we face. We are often conditioned to think that everything negative comes from the devil; however, if we view it through the lens of God as Lord and Master over all things, we can conclude that God uses the negative as a vehicle for **Revelation**. God never fails; thus, as we experience life with its negativity through the lens of God, we open ourselves up to that which can and should be according to God's promises for our life and life more abundantly. To be open to God's promises creates a sensitivity within our circumstances, especially those which are negative, to God and His power activated in our lives, and as we seek Him, we find Him, **Revelation** of who He is, and as a bonus, He also reveals who we are in Him. Thus, ***Breathe: New Life*** in whatever you face, the Lord and Master of the Universe welcomes the opportunity to reveal the fullness of Himself and Him in you that you would live and declare His works!

## August 18

*Go ye therefore, and teach all nations, baptizing them in the name of the Father, and of the Son, and of the Holy Ghost: Teaching*

*them to observe all things whatsoever I have commanded you:*
*and, lo, I am with you alway, even unto the end of the world.*
*Amen.*
Matthew 28:19-20


It is our mission to go forth into the promises of God, and in so doing, we bring **Revelation** of God to ourselves as well as to others.  God is made real, flesh as we diligently pursue His promises for our life and life more abundantly; we become the living, visible presence of God in the world.  As we are God's ambassadors, we represent Him and the fullness of His power. God seeks to reveal Himself to us as we pursue His Word for our lives and to all His creation, and as a result, His **Revelation** triggers the outpouring of His reward to, for, and through us.  Go ahead and *Breathe: New Life* as He has promised and watch His **Revelation** consume you and your space, providing the manifestation of the fullness of God and His power in and over life!


## August 19


*And he said unto them, Go ye into all the world, and preach the*
*gospel to every creature. He that believeth and is baptized shall be*
*saved; but he that believeth not shall be damned. And these signs*
*shall follow them that believe; In my name shall they cast out*
*devils; they shall speak with new tongues; They shall take up*
*serpents; and if they drink any deadly thing, it shall not hurt them;*
*they shall lay hands on the sick, and they shall recover.*
Mark 16:15-18

When you choose to act according to your purpose and plan, you set the production of **Revelation** in motion. **Revelation** is the uncovering of that which either confirms or denies what you believe can and should be for your life. By no means do I suggest that, because of your alignment with God's promises, everything will look good; rather, I am saying that it will be good. The command to go forth, flowing in your pathway for life, is filled with God's outpouring to give you direction and guidance. It is in God's **Revelation that,** because of our willingness to go, He reveals Himself in both your good and your bad, providing you with insight into His ability, coupled with your choices and willingness to act, your internal power to overcome whatever exists, and/or work it out all for the good. As you choose to act on that which you believe can and should be for your life, ***Breathe: New Life*** into your circumstances, creating an atmosphere for God's **Revelation**, affirming and confirming your anointing, what can and should be for your life!

## August 20

*Now you must go into all the nations and preach repentance and forgiveness of sins so that they will turn to me. Start right here in Jerusalem, for you are my witnesses and have seen for yourselves all that has transpired.*
Luke 24:47-48 (TPT)

As a part of your willingness to flow in that which is God's intent for your life, you complete a part of God's plan for which all creation is waiting. Whatever God is doing through you impacts others, and as you fulfill that which is your assignment, you bring

254

light to others so they, too, might walk into what can and should be for their lives.  You are a part of God's **Revelation** to the world; you bring the visible living presence of God, bringing life and light. Therefore, when you choose to *Breathe: New Life*, flow in God's intent for your circumstances, you generate life for yourself and your space as a witness that it is possible.  Arise to your promises and lift not only yourself but your entire space, all of God's creation!

## August 21

*So then faith cometh by hearing, and hearing by the word of God.*
Romans 10:17

If we are to receive **Revelation**, insight into our lives, and what can and should be as promised, we must put ourselves in a position to hear from God.  Hearing from God, His Word is paramount to moving and flowing in the pathway that leads to our life and life more abundantly.  It will be extremely difficult to overcome the natural chaos, confusion, and life's challenges if we are not fueled and energized by what we believe; otherwise, we settle for and accept things as they are.  Believe, the exercising of our faith is the necessary fuel for us to get past the difficulties of our lives to what are places of peace, which are not absent of conflict or places of settling, but instead places that bring us in harmony with the fulfillment of God's promises for our lives. *Breathe: New Life* by inhaling God's Word, and as you do, it becomes easier to walk into His **Revelation**, discover peace in and through your experiences with the fuel, the impetus to overcome, and flow in the pathway for the fullness of your joy!

## August 22

*If indeed you continue to advance in faith, assured of a firm foundation to grow upon. Never be shaken from the hope of the gospel you have believed in. And this is the glorious news I preach all over the world.*
Colossians 1:23 (TPT)

Life may offer you challenges that appear too hard and/or impossible for you to overcome, but know that those challenges are your rewards.  The reward God has and is providing to each and every one of us in our life's experiences is to grow in the faith and grace of God, which brings about the exceedingly, abundantly, more than we can ever ask or think by the power working within us.  As we engage our challenges, although they may be difficult and appear more than we can handle, we bring about **Revelation**, not just of God but also of the potential of God's power and gifts operating within us.  And the more we see, have this **Revelation** of God in us, the more confident and bold we become to launch out into the deep of our experiences, casting our nets and bringing in an abundant harvest, a witness of who God is and whom He has called us to be.  ***Breathe: New Life*** for you have the potential in each of your experiences for the **Revelation** of God and His life-giving intent and power springing forth from you!

## August 23

*Only be thou strong and very courageous, that thou mayest observe to do according to all the law, which Moses my servant commanded thee: turn not from it to the right hand or to the left, that thou mayest prosper whithersoever thou goest. This book of the law shall not depart out of thy mouth; but thou shalt meditate therein day and night, that thou mayest observe to do according to all that is written therein: for then thou shalt make thy way prosperous, and then thou shalt have good success.*
Joshua 1:7-8

As a core value to ensure that you stay on the pathway for your life and life more abundantly, and as promised by God, you must stay in and study His Word. Remember, to know God is to have eternal life, and to know God is to know His Word; in the beginning, was the Word, and the Word was with God, and the Word was God. There is no way you can live in what can and should be for your life as spoken by God unless you become one with Him, with His Word of truth for you. Get informed by getting informed about your Word of truth. The more capable you are to bring your life and space into alignment, the more you will experience, over and over again, the **Revelation** of God in the fullness of His power operating in your life. God is with you, whether you can see Him or not, and He is made real. The **Revelation** of Him and the truth of His Word come as a direct result of you staying in and true to His Word for your life. ***Breathe: New Life*** into your experiences by being strong and courageous to stay true to, diligently seeking the **Revelation** of God's Word of truth for your life, and your way will be prosperous, and you will have good success.

## August 24

*All scripture is given by inspiration of God, and is profitable for doctrine, for reproof, for correction, for instruction in righteousness: That the man of God may be perfect, throughly furnished unto all good works.*
II Timothy 3:16-17

Stay true to God's Word by relying on and trusting it to find your way to your place of fullness of joy and receive the required **Revelation** in your circumstances to your promise of life and life more abundantly.  God has spoken to you and over your life, and has given you the ability to use it as fuel to press forward.  There is absolutely nothing you will experience that will be by happenstance or accident; all is Divinely ordered, and God's Word of truth for your life is packed with the necessary power for you to engage whatever there is and be victorious.  ***Breathe: New Life*** because God has breathed His Word into you and over your life, and it is more than enough to thoroughly furnish you with all good works, working out all things for your good.

## August 25

*For thou wilt not leave my soul in hell;*
*neither wilt thou suffer thine Holy One to see corruption.*
*Thou wilt shew me the path of life:*
*in thy presence is fulness of joy;*
*at thy right hand there are pleasures for evermore.*
Psalm 16:10-11

We need not fear the challenges of our lives, even though they are filled with chaos, darkness, and negativity; God will not leave us or forsake us, but will be with us. God in our lives, whether we see Him or not, is a prerequisite to receiving **Revelation**, the insight into the unknown and uncertainty that provides us the ability to navigate through in order to get to God's fulfilled promise of life and life more abundantly in our circumstances. Do not let fear grip and/or paralyze you. God will show you the way, and it brings you closer and closer to Him, the One who is the light, causing our darkness to scatter, and with Him, we receive our reward, God's intended blessings for our lives. Go ahead and **Breathe: New Life,** through the challenges, chaos, darkness, and confusion of your life, and receive the light of God, His **Revelation**, leading and guiding you into your fullness of joy and at His right-hand pleasures forevermore.

## August 26

*And the king said unto Araunah, Nay; but I will surely buy it of thee at a price: neither will I offer burnt offerings unto the LORD my God of that which doth cost me nothing. So David bought the threshingfloor and the oxen for fifty shekels of silver.*
II Samuel 24:24

A core value for you and me to achieve what can and should be for our lives is how much we are willing to invest, in tangible and intangible resources, and in so doing bring **Revelation** to you and your space. Nothing you desire and believe can and should be free; you must be willing to invest, work your field, to bring about your harvest, your **Revelation**. The harvest is plentiful; however, the laborers are few. Those who are willing to give up, sacrifice, whatever is required to achieve their harvest. Note that your willingness to buy into your own destiny serves as evidence, a witness of what you believe can and should be, and will persuade others to join you, take up your cause where they can, and assist you in making your Word of truth flesh, real. *Breathe: New Life* to and in your circumstances by taking the lead to invest your own resources in what you believe can and should be for your life and life more abundantly!

## August 27

*But this I say, He which soweth sparingly shall reap also sparingly; and he which soweth bountifully shall reap also bountifully. Every man according as he purposeth in his heart, so let him give; not grudgingly, or of necessity: for God loveth a cheerful giver. And God is able to make all grace abound toward you; that ye, always having all sufficiency in all things, may abound to every good work:*
II Corinthians 9:6-8

Giving is instrumental to your faith. Without offering evidence for your faith, it is empty and hollow. As we invest in what we believe, we affirm it. Therefore, as you purpose in your heart, so give freely and voluntarily as it speaks to, is the Revelation of your faith. Do not give if you do not believe in what you are giving, for it will not be a return on your investment. Believe, have faith, and **Breathe: New Life** by releasing your offering as evidence of what can and should be for your life.  Remember, you cannot beat God's giving, given, and it shall be given back to you pressed down, shaken together, and running over!

## August 28

*If we confess our sins, he is faithful and just to forgive us our sins, and to cleanse us from all unrighteousness.*
I John 1:9

As a core value, you must always create space where you can be honest with yourself and with God.  It is in these safe spaces of honesty that you can reflect, receive insight, **and** gain Revelation aboutthe next steps, and an understanding of your challenges and life journey.  We need not fear that being honest with God would somehow be weaponized against us, for it is His delight to be our Father, protector, provider, advisor, and confidante.  Remember, God asks that we cast all our cares on Him, including our guilt and shame over our shortcomings and/or wrongdoings.  God works it all out for our good, go ahead and **Breathe: New Life**.  In your confessing and communicating all things to God, God reveals His purpose and plan for whatever you are experiencing to prosper you toward His promises for your life and life more abundantly!

## August 29

*Be careful for nothing; but in every thing by prayer and supplication with thanksgiving let your requests be made known*

*unto God. And the peace of God, which passeth all understanding,*
*shall keep your hearts and minds through Christ Jesus.*
*Philippians 4:6-7*

Critical to our relationship with God is our feeding it via communicating and confessing all things to Him; we receive **Revelatio**n, insight into what God is up to and with us in our lives. God leaves an open door to us, and if we wish to get past the veil of our experiences, no matter what they are, we can exhale the toxicity and heaviness of our lives, and God not only releases us from it but reveals to us with more clarity His purpose and plan and His confidence and deposits within us.  If we never had a problem, we would not know that God can solve it, and that we are able, with God's power and gifts, to endure and overcome it. ***Breathe: New Life*** in your circumstances, as difficult as they may be, God will release Himself and you amid your circumstances to overcome and be at peace, in harmony with His will, for your life and life more abundantly!

## August 30

*And the Lord said, Simon, Simon, behold, Satan hath desired to*
*have you, that he may sift you as wheat: But I have prayed for*
*thee, that thy faith fail not: and when thou art converted,*
*strengthen thy brethren.*
*Luke 22: 31-32*

Important for all of us to remember is that we are not in the game of our life alone if we choose to believe in the presence of a very present God, although people, places, and things may very well let you down and/or disappoint you both with their lack of consistency or capacity to assist you in transforming your circumstances. However, in and through the Revelation of Christ, we have the strength of God's intent for our life and life more abundantly, who is making intercession on our behalf, standing in and with us so that whatever challenges we face, God's power is available to us to work for our good. God displaying His power in our lives is God's **Revelation,** showing up in our experiences on our behalf as we seek to overcome. The challenges of our lives are doing just what they are supposed to do, testing and trying our resolve, we must keep pressing, and as we do, God does what He does, shows up, and is our necessary **Revelation**. *Breathe: New Life* for Christ has prayed for you, and you will not fail. God's **Revelation** in and through you will be evident, and you will be converted, transforming your circumstances as well as turning the light on for others.

## August 31

Wisdom is the principal thing; therefore get wisdom:
and with all thy getting get understanding.
Proverbs 4:7

As you choose to *Breathe: New Life* into your circumstances, do so from the vantage point of being informed. Without question, we cannot know everything; however, it is to our advantage to at least have access to the information we need to make choices for our lives and for life more abundantly in our circumstances. Wisdom is the principal thing; therefore, it is advantageous for us to develop, nurture, and sustain our relationship with the Creator and the One who holds all things in His hand. Feed your relationship with God so that as you choose to live, you have access to His **Revelation** in your life, providing you the necessary light for your pathway and a lamp unto your feet. God, is His Word and His promises activate to serve as agents of **Revelation** of God, of you, and His power operating in, through, and around your life. In all you're getting, get understanding, the Wisdom of the Creator-God active in your life and watch the **Revelation** of God do exceedingly, abundantly, more than you can ask or think through you!

# *NEW ATTITUDE*

## SEPTEMBER

## September 1

*Study to shew thyself approved unto God, a workman that needeth not to be ashamed, rightly dividing the word of truth.*
II Timothy 2:15

To live in the fullness of your capacity, it will depend on your ability to focus and press toward your goal.  The goal you have established becomes the fuel that drives you to press forward despite obstacles.  Therefore, the quality of your fuel rests on the soundness of your goal.  To ensure your goal is sound and that your fuel produces the energy required, you must know what you believe can and should be in your life.  You must be intimate with your purpose and plan for your desired outcome, naked and unashamed in the face of life's challenges and adversities.  Paul admonishes us to study the word of truth, the promise, God's purpose and plan, the higher calling, your goal, and to press forward, taking on a **New Attitude**, equipped to rightly discern your pathway, clearing the way to press toward the mark of your higher calling.  Do not be deceived, your distractions, challenges, adversities are real; however, ***Breathe: New Life***, take on a **New Attitude** borne out of your intimacy with your Word of truth, discern and overcome whatever exists to reach your place of life and life more abundantly!

## September 2

*A new commandment I give unto you, That ye love one another;
as I have loved you, that ye also love one another. By this shall all
men know that ye are my disciples, if ye have love one to another.*
John 13:34-35

When we decide to **Breathe: New Life**, choose to live despite our circumstances, we take on a **New Attitude** that dictates that it is all good. It is all good, no matter the complexity and difficulty of our present reality, because we are not alone and the love of God to us runs through us to the people, places, and things of our lives. Love, the very action we take toward the good, conquers whatever may exist before us, although it may not appear like it initially; love will consume and transform all things for our good. This New Attitude of love in and through all things is the fuel, the witness of who we are and whose we are, thus creating the appropriate and supportive atmosphere for us to **Breathe: New Life**.

## September 3

*The Spirit of the Lord is upon me, because he hath anointed me to
preach the gospel to the poor; he hath sent me to heal the
brokenhearted, to preach deliverance to the captives, and
recovering of sight to the blind, to set at liberty them that are
bruised, To preach the acceptable year of the Lord.*
Luke 4:18-19

Once we take on a **New Attitude**, that whatever we face is all good, we begin the process of disempowering our circumstances over our lives and our outcomes.  As long as we allow the circumstances of our lives to dictate, they will and will drive, get back in the driver's seat, and drive your narrative, allowing the Spirit of God's promises, His Word to control your life to take over. Do not be afraid of the unknown or the how; let the Spirit of God's promises for your life control and consume you, and as a result, operate accordingly.  Your **New Attitude** will deceive and catch off guard the circumstances that wish to hinder you and give you the opening to ***Breathe: New Life***.  This is your year, ***Breathe: New Life***, and receive the acceptable, the very fulfillment of God's promises to and for your life and life more abundantly!

## September 4

*That, however, is not the way of life you learned when you heard about Christ and were taught in him in accordance with the truth that is in Jesus.  You were taught, with regard to your former way of life, to put off your old self, which is being corrupted by its deceitful desires; to be made new in the attitude of your minds; and to put on the new self, created to be like God in true righteousness and holiness.  Therefore each of you must put off falsehood and speak truthfully to your neighbor, for we are all members of one body.  "In your anger do not sin": Do not let the sun go down while you are still angry, and do not give the devil a foothold.  Anyone who has been stealing must steal no longer, but must work, doing something useful with their own hands, that they may have something to share with those in need.  Do not let any unwholesome talk come out of your mouths, but only what is helpful for building others up according to their needs, that it may benefit those who listen.  And do not grieve the Holy Spirit of God,*

*with whom you were sealed for the day of redemption. Get rid of all bitterness, rage and anger, brawling and slander, along with every form of malice. Be kind and compassionate to one another, forgiving each other, just as in Christ God forgave you.*
Ephesians 4:20-32 (NIV)

Your decision to **Breathe: New Life** must not be superficial but instead something that is a product of your thought life that now transfers to your active life. Our thought, our mind, is the control center of our body; thus, what descends from there creates the atmosphere for the actions that follow. Therefore, as you **Breathe: New Life,** it is a direct result of the **New Attitude** for your circumstances that has been formed in your thought life that equips you for action. This **New Attitude** demands a cleansing, if you will, of all the toxicity in your present life to transform it into the new life you desire. Thus, you must decide that certain things, including people, places, and things that do not contribute to and/ or support the new life you desire, are avoided and eliminated. In addition, your **New Attitude** does not see the people, places, and things of your life as against you but instead as opportunities for you, and thus you can give that which leads to your breathing, inhaling, if you will, what is necessary for you to **Breathe: New Life**. Remember all things that produce the action required for your outcome, that which you desire should and can be for your life, begin in your thought life, your mind, transform it, and you transform for your new life!

## September 5

*And because of him, when you who are not Jews heard the revelation of truth, you believed in the wonderful news of salvation. Now we have been stamped with the seal of the promised Holy Spirit. He is given to us like an engagement ring, as the first installment of what's coming! He is our hope-promise of a future inheritance which seals us until we have all of redemption's promises and experience complete freedom—all for the supreme glory and honor of God!*
Ephesians 1:13-14 (TPT)

As you receive the revelation of God's truth, His Word for your life, allow it to release you from what was and is to what shall become. It is your becoming that demands a **New Attitude**. God is not just going to do all the work, but He also invites you, through His Spirit, to be a partaker, co-creator with Him, which should and can be for your life and life more abundantly. The power of the narrative of your life lies not in the hands of people, places, or things, but instead with you. Take on the **New Attitude** of the Word of God, His promises for your life, and act accordingly. Engage your circumstances with this **New Attitude** and *Breathe: New Life*, God is just waiting on you to take up your part to trigger the release of your exceedingly, abundantly, more than you can ever ask or think by the power working within you, your **New Attitude**.

## September 6

*When you came to Christ, you were "circumcised," but not by a physical procedure. Christ performed a spiritual circumcision—the*

270

*cutting away of your sinful nature. For you were buried with Christ when you were baptized. And with him you were raised to new life because you trusted the mighty power of God, who raised Christ from the dead.*
*Colossians 2:11-12 (NLT)*

Your decision to choose God's Word for your life washes you, physically and psychologically, giving you a **New Attitude**. Receive your revelation today and be cleansed and *Breathe: New Life*. Your decision to choose to believe in God and embrace His Word for your life sets you on a flight to live in the fullness of His promises for your life and life more abundantly. Be totally consumed, baptized, and raised, *Breathe: New Life,* not because of you or your power, but instead because of the power and might of God.

## September 7

*And have put on the new self, which is being renewed in knowledge in the image of its Creator.*
*Colossians 3:10 (NIV)*

The **New Attitude** that we take on by choosing to believe and act on God's Word for our lives causes us to be renewed in knowledge. To be renewed in knowledge is to be inquisitive and seek to know more about our promises, the purpose and plan for our lives, to execute appropriately, and *Breathe: New Life*. Most of us want the Word of truth, God's promises for our lives, but we want the new in the old wineskins of our lives and experiences.

To *Breathe: New Life* requires a **New Attitude** that brings about a new perspective and thought for life, one that is informed to be released to the opportunities and possibilities God has prepared for us to live and to live abundantly!

## September 8

*And so I insist—and God backs me up on this—that there be no going along with the crowd, the empty-headed, mindless crowd. They've refused for so long to deal with God that they've lost touch not only with God but with reality itself. They can't think straight anymore.*
Ephesians 4:17-18 (MSG)

The **New Attitude** required to *Breathe: New Life* demands confidence in what God has established for your life and life more abundantly.  Circumstances will come, but your boldness of confidence grounds you so you may bend and yet not break.  It is convenient to go along with what is easy and where the crowd is because there seems to be support, and it leaves you feeling surrounded by others, which gives credence to the idea that what you are doing must be okay.  However, where God wishes to take you and reveal Himself and His purpose and plan for your life have been designed specifically for you, and there may not always be a crowd or chorus cheering you on, nevertheless, you must go.  The going, despite the crowd and/or lack of a chorus, demands a **New Attitude** in your circumstances that keeps you rooted and grounded in God's Word for your life and life more abundantly to *Breathe: New Life*.

## September 9

*And be not conformed to this world: but be ye transformed by the renewing of your mind, that ye may prove what is that good, and acceptable, and perfect, will of God.*
Romans 12:2

You and I must determine that we will be released from our present reality to seek and live in the becoming of what God has promised, what should and can be for our lives. If we are to get over the present reality and live in our becoming, we can not allow the present reality to cause us to conform to what is and/or what was instead, we must believe and act in that which should and can be, renewing our minds with the confidence, releasing us from that which would keep us in our now. The now can cause us to become satisfied and/or maintain, but God has greater plans for you, and it is in knowing, believing, and acting in these greater plans that produce a **New Attitude** toward the world and the things of the world. This **New Attitude** demands that you act in every circumstance, especially those that hinder and maintain the status quo, to ***Breathe: New Life***, proving that which is the good, perfect, and acceptable will of God for your life and life more abundantly!

## September 10

*Put on the whole armour of God, that ye may be able to stand against the wiles of the devil. For we wrestle not against flesh and*

*blood, but against principalities, against powers, against the rulers of the darkness of this world, against spiritual wickedness in high places.*
Ephesians 6:11-12


The power of the reality of our experiences is not fully known or even comprehended by us, because whatever is going on is a war between good and evil, light and darkness, God and His enemies. Therefore, let God arise, and all His enemies be scattered; put on the whole armor of God's Word, promises for your life, and let that control be your **New Attitude**. This **New Attitude** gives you boldness of confidence that whatever may exist in your life, in particular the reality of the difficulties and complexities of your experiences, has no power over you; instead, the controlling factor is God's promises, His Word. Hold to your **New Attitude,** putting on that which empowers you through it all to ***Breathe: New Life*** into your circumstances, equipping you to stand and conquer whatever the wiles of the devil, evil, darkness of your life.


## September 11


*The serpent was clever, more clever than any wild animal God had made. He spoke to the Woman: "Do I understand that God told you not to eat from any tree in the garden?" The Woman said to the serpent, "Not at all. We can eat from the trees in the garden. It's only about the tree in the middle of the garden that God said, 'Don't eat from it; don't even touch it or you'll die.'" The serpent told the Woman, "You won't die. God knows that the moment you eat from that tree, you'll see what's really going on. You'll be just*

274

*like God, knowing everything, ranging all the way from good to evil." When the Woman saw that the tree looked like good eating and realized what she would get out of it—she'd know everything! —she took and ate the fruit and then gave some to her husband, and he ate. Immediately the two of them did "see what's really going on"—saw themselves naked! They sewed fig leaves together as makeshift clothes for themselves.*

Genesis 3:1-7 (MSG)

The greatest weapon wielded against us is our fear, rooted in the unknown. We are afraid because we are not certain of the experience, and we feel a lack of control over it; therefore, in such a time, our mind, if not rooted in our promise, runs away with us with all kinds of scenarios that put us in the passenger seat, allowing our experiences to drive. Today, God has declared that you are not the passenger, front or back, but instead, He has given you the power to be the driver. Do not be deceived by your serpents, your experiences that have been designed to force you to give up your power and the positive aspects of your life for their negative offerings. Conquer your fear by discerning the truth of your experience, good or bad, along with the fear of not being in control, and then all the power of the Holy Ghost within, more than your ability, will drive you and set you up for life, even amid the death of your experiences, yielding your life and life more abundantly. It's a **New Attitude** toward your circumstances that checks your fear with the truth of God's Word and ultimately co-creates with that truth of God's Word, creating the ability for you to *Breathe: New Life* in all of your experiences.

## September 12

*Don't fret or worry. Instead of worrying, pray. Let petitions and praises shape your worries into prayers, letting God know your concerns. Before you know it, a sense of God's wholeness, everything coming together for good, will come and settle you down. It's wonderful what happens when Christ displaces worry at the center of your life. Summing it all up, friends, I'd say you'll do best by filling your minds and meditating on things true, noble, reputable, authentic, compelling, gracious—the best, not the worst; the beautiful, not the ugly; things to praise, not things to curse. Put into practice what you learned from me, what you heard and saw and realized. Do that, and God, who makes everything work together, will work you into his most excellent harmonies.*

Philippians 4:6-9 (MSG)

Always remember you have an option; you can choose to live or die in your experiences. If you choose to live, you must be open; you must have a **New Attitude** to your present reality that not only draws on your strengths but also the strength of the Creator God, your co-creator, for the life and life more abundantly that is yours. Remember, Christ, upon defeating death, hell, and the grave, invites you and me to receive the Holy Ghost, the guidance and power necessary to go into that which is God's promise for your life. Do not believe that you got this by yourself or that you are all alone; call on your co-partner, God, for an abundant life and *Breathe: New Life*. The **New Attitude** will help you to focus on what it is you can do and be released and confident of what your partner, co-creator God, can and will do to bring about His glory, a revelation that also reveals you!

276

## September 13

*And the great dragon was cast out, that old serpent, called the*
*Devil, and Satan, which deceiveth the whole world: he was cast*
*out into the earth, and his angels were cast out with him.*
Revelation 12:9

Our **New Attitude** to support the becoming of what should and
can be for our lives demands that we recognize that chaos,
darkness, and evil lurk about, seeking to keep us from life and life
more abundantly. Chaos, darkness, evil do not always come to us
from external means; it is often internal and rooted in our fears,
and external factors leverage those fears to cause our demise. Be
aware of your fears, and do not let them control you. The
serpent, our experiences of chaos, darkness, evil, will be
intentional to deceive you; it is their proving ground, the only
ground they have, the earthly realm, the reality of your
experiences. Therefore, develop and maintain your spiritual
being, sight, and strength through the Spirit of God and His Word
for your life, to see things for what they are, and ***Breathe: New***
***Life!***

## September 14

*Behold, I send you forth as sheep in the midst of wolves: be ye*
*therefore wise as serpents, and harmless as doves.*
Matthew 10:16

To take command of your narrative and drive it to where it should and can be according to God's promises for your life demands a **New Attitude.** The **New Attitude** must see life through the lens of not what is or was but what is to become, through the Spirit that lifts you above the fray of your present reality, giving you a glimpse, a revelation of what is to become. Living in this realm of what will become demands humility and wisdom. Humility is manifested in the actions of a sheep, who is not moving or operating in the flesh or under their own means, but allowing the Spirit of God to lead and guide them into all truth. Remember, we move and have our being in God, His Word for our lives, which transcends our thoughts, opinions, and ideas for the sake of God. As we walk in humility, God, His Spirit, gives us insight into what He is up to and /or the opportunities and possibilities His Word provides for us in our present realities, opening the way for us to *Breathe: New Life*!

## September 15

*And the LORD God commanded the man, saying, Of every tree of the garden thou mayest freely eat: But of the tree of the knowledge of good and evil, thou shalt not eat of it: for in the day that thou eatest thereof thou shalt surely die.*
Genesis 2:16-17

Often, life and our experiences will lead us to think that the grass is always greener on the other side of our destiny, but know that it is not. As a result, we spend our energy focused on the negative aspects of our lives and allow them to drive us, often to places that cannot and will not provide what we should have for our

278

lives. It is in this misappropriation of our energy and our thoughts toward the negative that we cloud and desensitize ourselves to the qualities and the positive of our lives, our gifts, which are given to us to combat whatever faces us and to do so with an outcome of victory. Thus, we must be conscious of and accentuate the positives of our lives, take on a **New Attitude** in which we utilize our gifts and allow them to make room for us, and *Breathe: New Life.* The serpent overpowered Eve's potential for positive thinking and forced her to focus on what she could not do rather than on all that she could do, feeding her fears and personal desires that led to separation from what could and should be in her life. Be aware that your fears and desires can both be used as weapons against you, forcing you to see and believe the grass is greener on the other side, think positively and leverage your gifts to your present reality, and *Breathe: New Life*!

## September 16

*Before you do anything, put your trust totally in God and not in yourself. Then every plan you make will succeed.*
Proverbs 16:3 (TPT)

The process to *Breathe: New Life* requires being positioned to inhale what is necessary and appropriate to live in what can and should be for your life and experiences. Therefore, preparation is key for anyone to live and/or reach the place of living in their life and live more abundantly. The greatest preparation I have discovered for breathing is exercising your lungs; walking expands your lungs due to movement and activity, and breathing exercises in which you take deep breaths- inhaling and exhaling also build your lungs and expand your breathing capacity. The same must be true for you to *Breathe: New Life* into your everyday experiences, as well as your life in general; therefore, you must take on a **New Attitude** toward everything that demands preparation. Before you do anything, put your trust in God, take risks in your life in which you believe God, and therefore expand your faith so that you will be better positioned to trust God and walk by faith and not by sight as you move forward in your promise of life and life more abundantly. The Bible says that the more you stay in His Word, believing and acting accordingly, the more prosperous and successful you will be, *Breathe: New Life*!

## September 17

*But seek ye first the kingdom of God, and his righteousness; and all these things shall be added unto you. Take therefore no thought for the morrow: for the morrow shall take thought for the things of itself. Sufficient unto the day is the evil thereof.*
Matthew 6:33-34

The **New Attitude** required for us to *Breathe: New Life* demands that we focus, be clear and confident about what can and should be for our lives, and allow the other things and distractions to fall away. We tend to spend so much energy on what we do not have that we neglect the development and nurturing of what we do have, which is critical because in what we do have lies our opportunity to grow and bring about new life. The more we focus on what can and should be, the more we are energized to bring it about, while remaining sensitive to the opportunities around us to fulfill our promises.  Seek, focus on the Kingdom of God, God's Word of truth for your life, and all the distractions and insignificant things in your life will disappear.  Stop using up your energy on that which is not you, your distractions from the fulfillment of your Word of truth, take on a New Attitude that focuses on what can and should be, and *Breathe: New Life*!

## September 18

*Let the word of Christ live in you richly, flooding you with all wisdom. Apply the Scriptures as you teach and instruct one another with the Psalms, and with festive praises, and with prophetic songs given to you spontaneously by the Spirit, so sing to God with all your hearts! Let every activity of your lives and every word that comes from your lips be drenched with the beauty of our Lord Jesus, the Anointed One. And bring your constant praise to God the Father because of what Christ has done for you!*
Colossians 3:16-17 (TPT)

To flow in life and life more abundantly promised to you, you must allow the Word of God, His promises to live in you, causing you to take on a **New Attitude** as you approach life and its challenges. This **New Attitude** brings a new perspective as you engage life and positions you to leverage your strengths for your good and the fulfillment of God's Word in your life.  Within your Word of truth is the source of your strength and joy as you navigate life and its challenges; thus, as you achieve an understanding of your Word, you bring into clarity your pathway as well as your ability to *Breathe: New Life*.  Equipped with an understanding of what can and should be for your life, your Word allows you to apply it, rebuking that which would distract and separate you from your promise, scattering the darkness that lies along your journey. Thus, the power of the application of your Word strengthens the perspective you have on life and its journey; developing your faith and your ability to walk by faith and not by sight, in which you are sold out for the fulfillment of God's promises; His Word made flesh, real in your life!

## September 19

*How can a young person live a clean life? By carefully reading the map of your Word. I'm single-minded in pursuit of you; don't let me miss the road signs you've posted. I've banked your promises in the vault of my heart so I won't sin myself bankrupt. . . . By your words I can see where I'm going; they throw a beam of light on my dark path.*
Psalm 119:9-11, 105 (MSG)

The challenge for each of us to **Breathe: New Life,** especially in the challenges of our lives, is to let our Word, promises of God, live in our lives. Allowing your Word to live demands a **New Attitude** in which your Word reigns; centering your attention and allegiance to its fulfillment, the Word becomes flesh, real in your life. Although our Word may not have fully manifested in the natural in our lives, we must allow it to live in us, thus giving direction to our actions as if it were so; the manifestation of that which can and should be for our lives. As we allow our Word to live in our lives, it cleanses and makes our way plain, including providing us the necessary discipline to bring our lives into alignment with what our promises. Difficult and complex may be your experiences; nevertheless, let your Word reign, and it will light up your pathway leading to the very presence of God, the fulfillment of His Word, where there is the fullness of joy and at His right-hand pleasures forevermore.

## September 20

*Walk in the wisdom of God as you live before the unbelievers, and make it your duty to make him known. Let every word you speak be drenched with grace and tempered with truth and clarity. For then you will be prepared to give a respectful answer to anyone who asks about your faith.*
Colossians 4:5-6 (TPT)

*Breathe: New Life* by living in your Word, your promises from God, not just in their generalities, but also in your everyday walking around experiences. You must take on a **New Attitude** that provokes you in each and every experience of your life to live in that which can and should be. Be not deceived or distracted by your experiences, as if they are not important to your overall focus on living in your promise. Remember, nothing happens by happenstance or accident; it is all Divinely ordered. Get understanding in your experience and apply your Word to it and live, *Breathe: New Life*. You must become totally drenched, soaking wet with your promises, God's Word for your life, directing and guiding you in and through all things that point to the power of God operating in your life and your determination to live in your promises. Your **New Attitude**, approach to life, and all of your experiences will weave together both your anointing and

God's power to ensure that all things will work for your good, and you will overcome and inherit every promise of God for your life!

## September 21

*As ye have therefore received Christ Jesus the Lord, so walk ye in him: Rooted and built up in him, and stablished in the faith, as ye have been taught, abounding therein with thanksgiving.*
Colossians 2:6-7

The **New Attitude** required to receive and live in your life and life more abundantly requires that you walk in that which you believe can and should be. Walking in your Word is acting as if it were even though it may not be right now; breathing exercises that expand your lungs and your capacity. Although life and its challenges often cause us to take time to catch our breath, it is in those times that we must have a **New Attitude**: even though we are resting, we are preparing to live in the fullness of what can and should be. In your ups and downs of life's challenges, nurture your relationship with God, with His Word for your life; be rooted and built up in it, and *Breathe: New Life*; prepare and exercise to walk by faith in what shall be for your life!

## September 22

*By him therefore let us offer the sacrifice of praise to God continually, that is, the fruit of our lips giving thanks to his name.*
Hebrews 13:5

The **New Attitude** toward your new life must include praise; joy expressed in appreciation for and in expectation of your promise of life and life more abundantly.  Praise God from whom all blessings flow, those that look good and those that do not, for God's plan will be revealed despite what things look like and thus deserves our joy for acting in and on our behalf.  As you praise your way through, you confuse the enemy, who expects you to wring your hands and let frustration and depression take the driver's seat in your experience, but instead you break out in exuberant joy.  Your joy triggers the flow of life, your ability to **Breathe: New Life** out of your gratitude for God being your very present help in all things and making the way for your exceedingly, abundantly, more than you can ever ask or think!

## September 23

*God-lovers make the best counselors.  Their words possess wisdom and are right and trustworthy.  The ways of God are in their hearts and they won't swerve from the paths of steadfast righteousness.*
Psalm 37:30-31 (TPT)

The **New Attitude** required to **Breathe: New Life** demands that we exercise discernment about what we inhale; the people, places, and things that provide influence to our lives.  God has ordained everything, and it is up to us to try the Spirit by the spirit of that which comes into our circle of influence.  In our circle, there is some good and some bad, and both are needed, but it is up to us to discern which we listen to and/or which have a positive impact on our lives. Remember, we are admonished to watch, fight, and pray; be harmless as a dove but wise as a serpent to **Breathe:**

*New Life* into our experiences.  Having a **New Attitude** prioritizes your Word of truth and God's promises for your life, giving you sensitivity to discern what is wise from what is false and a distraction from living in the fullness of God's promises for your life and life more abundantly!

## September 24

> For sound advice is a beacon,
> good teaching is a light,
> moral discipline is a life path.
> Proverbs 6:23 (MSG)

The **New Attitude** that brings about new life is rooted in sound wisdom and guidance.  Sound wisdom is the appropriate and focused counsel needed as we seek to live the life and life more abundantly promised.  God, His Word has been given to us for proof, as a sound compass, correction, and instruction so that we may be thoroughly furnished to all good works; guidance for the fulfillment of God's promises for our lives.  We can, therefore, in the midst of the challenges of our lives, *Breathe: New Life* because we equip ourselves with God's wisdom and guidance as made real with His Spirit dwelling and consuming us.  Let the Spirit of God, His promised Word for your life, control and be led and guided into the truth of His Word, your life, and life more abundantly!

## September 25

*And he humbled thee, and suffered thee to hunger, and fed thee with manna, which thou knewest not, neither did thy fathers know; that he might make thee know that man doth not live by bread only, but by every word that proceedeth out of the mouth of the LORD doth man live.*
Deuteronomy 8:3

As we engage in life, especially life's challenges, for us to get to the new life offered through them, we must take on a **New Attitude** that defies the challenge looming large and in control of one in which our promise, our Word, controls. God spoke into our lives that we are to have life and life more abundantly, and if we choose to live in that, that is it, and all things, including chaos, confusion, darkness, and evil, must submit. Speak and live in your Word despite the circumstances of your life, and take on the **New Attitude** that your challenges have not come to hurt or harm you, but instead prosper you. Confuse the enemy by glorying; seeking the revelation in your circumstances for the good, and ***Breathe: New Life!*** Remember, we live, move, and have our being in God, in His Word, it gives us life and life more abundantly!

## September 26

*But what saith it? The word is nigh thee, even in thy mouth, and in thy heart: that is, the word of faith, which we preach; That if thou shalt confess with thy mouth the Lord Jesus, and shalt believe in thine heart that God hath raised him from the dead, thou shalt be saved. For with the heart man believeth unto righteousness; and with the mouth confession is made unto salvation.*

The more we take on the **New Attitude** that allows the Word of God, His promise for our lives, to live in and through us, the more our hearts and minds are transformed to align with our promise. Do not take the power of alignment lightly, especially as it relates to your heart (your passions) and mind (thought life), for it will drive your sensibilities to opportunities for your advancement in what can and should be, as well as supporting actions.  Your sensibilities are heightened because of the **New Attitude** to engage each and every experience of your life as an opportunity to *Breathe: New Life*.  As you believe in your heart, you influence your thought life, which in turn shapes your actions that speak and declare the Word of promise for your life.  There will be impossible, difficult, and complex challenges; however, your ability to *Breathe: New Life* hinges on how passionate you are about the promises of God for your life that bring you and your actions into alignment with God's Word for your life.

## September 27

*Study to shew thyself approved unto God, a workman that needeth not to be ashamed, rightly dividing the word of truth.*
II Timothy 2:15

The **New Attitude** for life and life more abundantly must continuously be nourished.  It is the Word of your promise as it grows and matures in you that you have both insight and strength to seize opportunities to achieve and fulfill that which has been promised for your life  Therefore, live in your Word; meditating and studying so that you may be present in your Word and your Word, living in and through you to *Breathe: New Life*.  The breath of life for you requires your alignment, entanglement with your Word so that you can withstand any and all things that would seek to separate you from the fulfillment of your promises, discerning and acting toward your life and life more abundantly!

## September 28

*The earth and sky will wear out and fade away before one word I speak loses its power or fails to accomplish its purpose.*
Matthew 24:35 (TPT)

You can maintain a **New Attitude** as you approach life's experiences because you allow your Word, God's promises for your life and life more abundantly to live in you.  Making your Word the center of your life and living to fulfill your promises, you express faith and confidence that God's Word is true and that everything else will pass away.  The best attitude for anyone in any situation is the confidence that you already have the victory, and as you do so, you will be sensitive to opportunities and possibilities that will support you to *Breathe: New Life*. Remember, God is His Word and thus can not and will not fail. Before anything was, was God, and His Word was with Him, and His Word was God, and His Word became flesh, real in our lives!

## September 29

*In the beginning was the Word, and the Word was with God, and*
*the Word was God.*
John 1:1

Our **New Attitude** toward the circumstances of our life must entail our ability to be confident about our promises, the Word of God for our lives.  The confidence in our Word trumps the very challenges that life offers, no matter the impossibilities, for it is in our faith that we believe that which can and should be, fueling us to press toward the mark of our Word, our higher calling.  In our pressing, we move forward in our promises, and the very obstacles and impossibilities that exist become things of the past as we live in our Word and allow the Word to live in us, with confidence in the truth of our Word pressing us to overcome and inherit all things.  Living in the Word means living in God Himself and His presence, and when we have Him with us, we are more than conquerors, we have overcome the world, we are well equipped for greater is He that is in us than he that is in the world.  Always remember and remain confident that your Word is God Himself, He is with your Word and your Word is Him, so you cannot lose and no adversary will defeat you; if God be for you, who in the world can be against you, ***Breathe: New Life***!

## September 30

*And the Word was made flesh, and dwelt among us, (and we*
*beheld his glory, the glory as of the only begotten of the Father,)*
*full of grace and truth.*

290

John 1:14

Living in your Word and allowing your Word to live in and through you brings about a **New Attitude** that says to the world and to your experiences that what God has declared for my life, I am intent on making it flesh, real. Your declaration to live in your Word causes the darkness and everything that would keep you from God's promise to be on notice and begin their exit to scatter. At the naming of your promises, you set the stage and reclaim your life from your challenges and command the Spirit of God in you and His Word for your life to control. As the world was stewing in darkness and separation from God, His Word, which He established before the foundations of the world were laid, brought life and peace. Thus, no matter what your circumstances may be through the process of time, God will reveal His Word in the flesh and overcome the flesh to make His Word real with all power. Christ coming and being made flesh and overcoming the flesh to receive all power makes real God's Word, His promises in which we too may overcome and *Breathe: New Life* into our circumstances, receiving all power to live in God's promises.

# NEW OPPORTUNITIES

## OCTOBER

## October 1

*But when the fulness of the time was come, God sent forth his*
*Son, made of a woman, made under the law, To redeem them that*
*were under the law, that we might receive the adoption of sons.*
*And because ye are sons, God hath sent forth the Spirit of his Son*
*into your hearts, crying, Abba, Father.*
Galatians 4:4-6

The key to moving forward toward what can and should be in our
lives is the ability to see and seize **New Opportunities**.  Seeing and
seizing **New Opportunities** requires being open and flexible in
one's perspective, so that one is also keenly aware of what is
happening around one through the people, places, and things of
one's life.  Being open and flexible does not mean you are not
focused; it only means that, while you are focused, you also have
peripheral vision that allows you to see and seize **New
Opportunities**.  God, as He did in bringing His Word into flesh,
Jesus, chose **New Opportunities** that no one was looking for: a
woman who had not known a man, a relatively poor descendant
of King David, to open eyes and spirits to the power of God.  There
is absolutely nothing going on in your life through which God can
not empower you, ***Breathe: New Life*** if you focus on His Word for
your life while utilizing your peripheral vision to see the new
thing, the **New Opportunities** God has for you, and all creation.

## October 2

294

*You'll remember, friends, that when I first came to you to let you in on God's sheer genius, I didn't try to impress you with polished speeches and the latest philosophy. I deliberately kept it plain and simple: first Jesus and who he is; then Jesus and what he did— Jesus crucified. I was unsure of how to go about this, and felt totally inadequate—I was scared to death, if you want the truth of it—and so nothing I said could have impressed you or anyone else. But the Message came through anyway. God's Spirit and God's power did it, which made it clear that your life of faith is a response to God's power, not to some fancy mental or emotional footwork by me or anyone else. We, of course, have plenty of wisdom to pass on to you once you get your feet on firm spiritual ground, but it's not popular wisdom, the fashionable wisdom of high-priced experts that will be out-of-date in a year or so. God's wisdom is something mysterious that goes deep into the interior of his purposes. You don't find it lying around on the surface. It's not the latest message, but more like the oldest—what God determined as the way to bring out his best in us, long before we ever arrived on the scene. The experts of our day haven't a clue about what this eternal plan is. If they had, they wouldn't have killed the Master of the God-designed life on a cross. That's why we have this Scripture text: No one's ever seen or heard anything like this, Never so much as imagined anything quite like it—What God has arranged for those who love him. But you've seen and heard it because God by his Spirit has brought it all out into the open before you. The Spirit, not content to flit around on the surface, dives into the depths of God, and brings out what God planned all along.*
I Corinthians 2:1-10 (MSG)

All around us are opportunities for our advancement in that which can and should be for our lives, but we often miss them. We miss our opportunities usually because we are so consumed with what is now of our circumstances that we cannot see anything else; blinded by life and its challenges. In addition, we can be so focused on getting to our expected end that we can't see past what is; the normal and/or status quo of achieving what we desire and therefore, miss opportunities, **New Opportunities** to *Breathe: New Life* in our experiences. The critical thing we must remember about ourselves and that which we believe can and should be for our lives is that we have both been designed for one another. Therefore, as we allow our Word, our promises, our expected end to live in us, and we live in it; becoming one with our Word, we are not only determined to achieve but also are watchful, sensitive, to what will assist us for our good that may be different from what we are expecting or that of anyone else's experiences, **New Opportunities**. The challenge is that if we are made for our Word, and our Word made for us is for us to be who we are, showing up in our circumstances and leveraging who we are for our good, and thus letting go of the rest for God to move, then we are free. As we let go and let God, we are open and flexible to however the Spirit leads, not constrained but flowing in the Spirit toward our promises, and in so doing, we are positioned in whatever we face to *Breathe: New Life*; overcome and inherit all things!

## October 3

*For when you did awesome things that we did not expect, you came down, and the mountains trembled before you.*

*Since ancient times no one has heard, no ear has perceived,*
*no eye has seen any God besides you, who acts on behalf of those*
*who wait for him.*
Isaiah 64:3-4 (NIV)


We can always live in assurance, knowing that we live in God's Word of promise: God will be present with us and show up in unexpected, mind-blowing ways. God is a jealous God and does not want us to have any other gods before Him; thus, He shows up in ways that reassure us how awesome and powerful He is. You never have to worry that your situation is limited and there are no viable options. God always has a way of introducing **New Opportunities in**to our lives and our witness. The record is clear, eyes have not seen, ears have not heard, nor has it entered into the hearts of humankind the great things that await which God has prepared for our lives, thus, no matter what we face, we can *Breathe: New Life*!


## October 4


*The Lord replied, "Listen, I am making a covenant with you in the*
*presence of all your people. I will perform miracles that have never*
*been performed anywhere in all the earth or in any nation. And all*
*the people around you will see the power of the Lord—the*
*awesome power I will display for you.*
Exodus 34:10 (NLT)


God has chosen you for the assignment that is your life; with it, the fulfillment of His Word and His promise to you is that He will perform it. God will do just what He says He will do, despite how difficult or impossible your experience may be.  God desires to create within your experience **New Opportunities** for Him to be revealed to you and through you to others.  God chose you and desires to operate in and through you as His witness; therefore, make yourself available to God, be sensitive to His move in and through your life, and let Him wow you and all your space.  You have the power to *Breathe: New Life* because God intends and wants to display to and for you His glory, His revelation that always brings about life and life more abundantly!

## October 5

*The earth shook, the heavens also dropped*
*at the presence of God: even Sinai itself was moved*
*at the presence of God, the God of Israel.*
Psalm 68:8

As we allow God's Word for our lives to live in us, we exalt God in and over our lives.  In God's presence, there is absolutely nothing that can stand and/or act contrary to His will.  God's will is for you to live life and life more abundantly, and He has caused His Word for your life to achieve that, to provide you with **New Opportunities** that may not readily appear before you or what would be expected as the norm.  Exalt God, His Word for your life, and you will see God provide opportunities for you to overcome and live in the fullness of His promises for your life.  Do not be afraid of the adversities of your life, face them by exalting God, your Word, and *Breathe: New Life*, and in so doing, everything that is will shake and fall at the exalted and very present God, your Word made flesh, real in your experiences.

## October 6

*Lord, how wonderful you are! You have stored up so many good things for us, like a treasure chest heaped up and spilling over with blessings— all for those who honor and worship you! Everybody knows what you can do for those who turn and hide themselves in you.*
Psalm 31:19 (TPT)

Because we are willing to live by faith in God's Word, we can walk in confidence through our life's experiences toward His higher calling for us and in our lives.  Our faith, confidence are reassured because God, through it all, always provides us a way out, a way of escape, **New Opportunities** that we may stand up under that which seeks to separate us or deter us.  When we allow God's Spirit to lead and guide us through life and its challenges, He speaks and acts in oneness with God and His Word for our lives, and these **New Opportunities** await us along our journey to fulfill God's promises.  Go ahead and *Breathe: New Life* into your life experiences for you, know God to be a way maker, miracle worker, promise keeper, and light in the darkness, that is who He is, and He will give access to anything we need to prosper; to overcome and inherit all things!

## October 7

*He explained, "You've been given the intimate experience of insight into the hidden mysteries of the realm of heaven's*

*kingdom, but they have not.  For everyone who listens with an*
*open heart will receive progressively more revelation.*
Matthew 13:11-12 (TPT)

**New Opportunities** to circumvent the darkness and chaos that seem to challenge our press toward our higher calling are available because of God's grace, favor in our lives.  It is God's favor to, and for us to accomplish that which He intends for our life and life more abundantly, that equips us in life's challenges, allowing us, no matter what adversity we face, to have insight. God has given to you and me, as a tool to advance, despite the odds, His Spirit, which provides not only peripheral vision for our lives but also a vision in which we see what is and what shall become, providing us with a constant flow of **New Opportunities**. The choice to believe what can and should be for your life lies with you; therefore, as you believe, you have the confidence that what you cannot handle, God has already provided whatever is necessary, as long as you are open and flexible to the leading and guiding of His Spirit.  Go ahead and *Breathe: New Life* into your experiences and do so with the assurance that you will have peripheral vision and insight, equipping you with sensitivity to see and seize **New Opportunities** for advancement in your higher calling.

## October 8

*So pay careful attention to your hearts as you listen to my teaching, for to those who have open hearts, even more revelation will be given to them until it overflows. And for those who do not*

*listen with open hearts, what little light they imagine themselves*
*to have will be taken away."*
Luke 8:18 (TPT)

As we seek to live in God's Word of promise and allow our Word to live in and through us, we must be open to **New Opportunities** that advance us and fulfill our promises. Openness is required so that we do not become so rigid and inflexible that we hinder the Spirit of God and His Word, but instead allow it to accomplish what the Spirit has been sent to do: lead and guide us. Thus, the Word admonishes us not to quench, to try and control the Spirit, but instead allow it to be free and flow, and as a result, we flow with God and His intent for our lives. **New Opportunities** are just that, new, never seen or thought of before, appearing for the first time; therefore, we have never experienced them before and are not part of our status quo or someone else's experience. Free yourself by being open to the Spirit to take you to heights and experiences never before imagined, or that you can perceive, and in so doing, you will be well-equipped to *Breathe: New Life*. Be open, available, and flexible to the move of God's Spirit, and the Spirit will accomplish what God intends to bring about in your life and life more abundantly, that which can and should be for your life!

## October 9

*And the angel that talked with me came again, and waked me, as a man that is wakened out of his sleep, And said unto me, What seest thou? And I said, I have looked, and behold a candlestick all of gold, with a bowl upon the top of it, and his seven lamps thereon, and seven pipes to the seven lamps, which are upon the top thereof: And two olive trees by it, one upon the right side of the bowl, and the other upon the left side thereof. So I answered and spake to the angel that talked with me, saying, What are these, my lord? Then the angel that talked with me answered and said unto me, Knowest thou not what these be? And I said, No, my lord. Then he answered and spake unto me, saying, This is the word of the LORD unto Zerubbabel, saying,*

*Not by might, nor by power, but by my spirit, saith the LORD of hosts.*

*Who art thou, O great mountain? before Zerubbabel thou shalt become a plain:*

*and he shall bring forth the headstone thereof with shoutings, crying, Grace, grace unto it. Moreover the word of the LORD came unto me, saying, The hands of Zerubbabel have laid the foundation of this house; his hands shall also finish it; and thou shalt know that the LORD of hosts hath sent me unto you. For who hath despised the day of small things? for they shall rejoice, and shall see the plummet in the hand of Zerubbabel with those seven; they are the eyes of the LORD, which run to and fro through the whole earth. Then answered I, and said unto him, What are these two olive trees upon the right side of the candlestick and upon the left side thereof? And I answered again, and said unto him, What be these two olive branches which through the two golden pipes empty the golden oil out of themselves? And he answered me and said, Knowest thou not what these be? And I said, No, my lord. Then said he, These are the two anointed ones, that stand by the Lord of the whole earth.*

Zechariah 4

Life's challenges often make us want to run away and hide, hoping that when we reappear, all we hoped to escape has somehow vanished; however, life does not work that way. Life and its challenges demand that we face them or risk them expanding and/or escalating due to our neglect and/or fear of confronting them. To overcome them, we must press forward and pass through them. The pressures of our challenges and our pressing way through them create tension that relieves pressure while also releasing the flow of possibilities, offering **New Opportunities** to address them. The flow of **New Opportunities** becomes apparent as we seek to live in our Word of an abundant life from God and allow that Word to live in us, producing God's Spirit, which raises our consciousness of how we overcome challenges. Thus, as we overcome, *Breathe: New Life*, our expectations are raised; we have a heightened sensitivity to **New Opportunities,** which increases our expectations and assurances that God's intent will be fulfilled in our lives —not by might, nor by power, but by God's Spirit.

## October 10

*I John, who also am your brother, and companion in tribulation, and in the kingdom and patience of Jesus Christ, was in the isle that is called Patmos, for the word of God, and for the testimony of Jesus Christ. I was in the Spirit on the Lord's day, and heard behind me a great voice, as of a trumpet,*
Revelation 1:9-10

The power of our determination to live in our Word of promise and to let it live in us makes us sensitive to the moving of God all around us.  The challenges of our lives have distracted and diverted our attention; therefore, we must work hard to counter them and overcome all obstacles.  In nature, we all believe that if we focus our attention on the pressures and challenges of our lives, we will solve them and/or accept and adapt to them; however, such pressure and focus actually hinder the flow of the Spirit of your promise.  Focus on your promise and unstop the flow of the Spirit, and as you engage the Spirit of your Word of promise, you will become sensitive to God, to **New Opportunities** around you to *Breathe: New Life*.  As you *Breathe: New Life,* you take back control and, as a result, overcome your challenges and inherit the fulfillment of God's promises for your life, your Word of promise.

## October 11

*After this I looked, and, behold, a door was opened in heaven: and the first voice which I heard was as it were of a trumpet talking with me; which said, Come up hither, and I will shew thee things which must be hereafter.*
*And immediately I was in the spirit: and, behold, a throne was set in heaven, and one sat on the throne.*
Revelation 4:1-2

Being able to lift oneself above life's pressures allows one to see and seize **New Opportunities**.  The pressures of life hold you down, and to muster the strength to overcome them, you must focus on what can and should be for your life, allowing it to control your thoughts and, thus, your actions.  As you focus and press toward the goal of what can and should be, you reduce the power of the pressures in your life and begin the process of disempowering them, positioning you to *Breathe: New Life*. Once we can rise above the fray of life, we can see open doors and **New Opportunities**, and it will be a direct result of us operating and seeking to live in the Spirit.

## October 12

*But I will have mercy upon the house of Judah, and will save them by the LORD their God, and will not save them by bow, nor by sword, nor by battle, by horses, nor by horsemen.*
Hosea 1:7

As we seek to live in God's Word and allow His Word to live in us, we have an assurance that all will be well and all will work out for our good. Often, we suffer under the illusion that belief in God and/or confidence in what we believe can and should shield us from life's adversities, but not so. However, with the adversities, we are equipped with the assurance that God is with us and will be with us to the end, and the end is the fulfillment of God's promises for our lives. Live and walk into your promises equipped with verifiable insurance, sealed by the sacrifice of Christ that makes **New Opportunities** by God's Spirit that are not worldly or expected, yet are made available for you to win, possessing your promises with all power. You have an assurance from God, and thus, you can *Breathe: New Life* because of God's Spirit, the provider of **New Opportunities** within your experiences, equipping you to overcome and inherit all things.

## October 13

*When you win, we plan to raise the roof and lead the parade with our banners. May all your wishes come true! That clinches it—help's coming, an answer's on the way, everything's going to work out. See those people polishing their chariots, and those others grooming their horses? But we're making garlands for God our God. The chariots will rust, those horses pull up lame—and we'll be on our feet, standing tall. Make the king a winner, God; the day we call, give us your answer.*
Psalm 20:5-9 (MSG)

We can go ahead and celebrate our victory amid our adversities because we have assurance that God will provide a way for us to overcome and prosper, to what can and should be, as promised for our lives. Allow your Word of promise from God to live in you, and you in it, and God will open up **New Opportunities** that you never imagined or conceived so that you win. As difficult as it may appear, as impossible as your odds are, and the possibility of you not having an edge on your adversities, be assured, God is not confined to the norm or the expected. *Breathe: New Life*. Call on God, your Word to live in and through your life and experiences, and whatever comes, you have the power of God intervening, opening doors, **New Opportunities** to win, celebrate, and *Breathe: New Life*!

## October 14

*Watch this: God's eye is on those who respect him, the ones who are looking for his love. He's ready to come to their rescue in bad times; in lean times he keeps body and soul together. We're depending on God; he's everything we need. What's more, our hearts brim with joy since we've taken for our own his holy name. Love us, God, with all you've got—that's what we're depending on.*

Psalm 33:18-22 (MSG)

Critical to our being able to see and seize the **New Opportunities** God has available for us to *Breathe: New Life* is our expectation. We must, amid life's challenges, be alert, watching for **New Opportunities** to live above and beyond our adversities, living in the promises of God for our lives. God's intent is for you and me to have life and life more abundantly, not just in the hereafter but also in our right now and here, and to do so He has given to us His Spirit that allows us to flow, be led, and guided into His intent. As we assume the Spirit of God and His Word of promise for our lives, we are challenged to become sensitive and on alert for opportunities for empowerment in and through our lived experiences. Our sensitivity is fueled by our faith, assurance that God is with us and that He has provided our ways of escape, our very tools to handle and overcome our challenges, and to receive our power as a direct result thereof. *Breathe: New Life* by being on alert, made sensitive by the Spirit to the move of God, seeing and seizing the **New Opportunities** within our challenges He has provided for our life and life more abundantly!

## October 15

*Be strong and courageous, be not afraid nor dismayed for the king of Assyria, nor for all the multitude that is with him: for there be more with us than with him: With him is an arm of flesh; but with us is the LORD our God to help us, and to fight our battles. And the people rested themselves upon the words of Hezekiah king of Judah.*
II Chronicles 32:7-8

You need not worry, as you allow your Word of promise to live in you and you in it, for greater is He that is within you than he that is in the world. You are not alone, and what appears to be a minority in abilities, resources, etc., is more than enough. The complexities of your situation will try to make you believe that the challenges are strong and that they, in numbers, outnumber you, but be not deceived, God has more than enough for you, and there is more with you than you believe. Open your eyes and allow the Spirit of God to lead and guide you to **New Opportunities** that He has created around and within you, exceedingly, abundantly, more than you can ever ask or think. Go ahead and be strong and courageous, ***Breathe: New Life*** amid your complexities, and see and seize your **New Opportunities** to live. God is with you and will fight your battles, giving you victory!

## October 16

*Being confident of this very thing, that he which hath begun a good work in you will perform it until the day of Jesus Christ:*
Philippians 1:6

Every ending produces a new beginning; thus, every beginning brings about an ending. The process of life is caught up in a continuous flow of beginnings to endings; this statement implies that it all begins with the end. Thus, what is important to ensure that the beginning, the new beginning, is greater and produces more of our promises fulfilled than what is our ability to do, is to be led and guided by the Spirit to see and seize **New Opportunities** that position and leverage our journey, our lived experiences, toward the fulfillment of our Word of promise. This demands that we understand that our Word of promises has no beginning or end; it is eternal, and its promises reveal that whatever we thought was there is yet more. The yet more of our lives flow as a result of our being totally consumed by the Spirit of God, His Word of promise for our lives that allows us to flow and **Breathe: New Life** into every experience, knowing that it leads to the exceedingly, abundantly, more than we can ever ask or think by the power that works within us. Be assured that God's anointing, His chosen-ness for your life and life more abundantly, has equipped you with the authority to press your way toward your promises with power, and that power will increase as you move from level to level in your promises. Remember, what God has begun in you, he will perform it until the coming of Christ, the end of time.

## October 17

*Jesus said, "Sign on with the One that God has sent. That kind of a commitment gets you in on God's works."*
John 6:29 (MSG)

When you and I realize that God is for us, it changes how we see things and how open we are to possibilities. God is bigger and greater than anything we know, and with that kind of authority and impartation of power to us, we should be empowered from within to engage and overcome whatever we face. Our empowerment is not something that comes from without, but instead from within; confidence that fuels our boldness to face life and its challenges with an assurance that God will provide **New Opportunities** to advance in our Word, His promises for our life and life more abundantly. The choice is ours, sign on with God and be open to the **New Opportunities** in whatever challenge we face with confidence that we will be able to *Breathe: New Life* and make our Word flesh, real in our lives.

## October 18

*So that you may be able to discern what is best and may be pure and blameless for the day of Christ,*
Philippians 1:10 (NIV)

Living in the Word of God for your life and allowing it to live in you fuels your ability to discern that which is a God idea, a **New Opportunity,** as opposed to just a good idea. Remember that the devil, prince of darkness and evil, seeks to sift you, confuse and deceive you, and thus will also present you with **New Opportunities**; however, it is your Word and the Spirit thereof that will assist you in discerning that which is good for you. Do not be deceived, everything that glitters is not gold, or what appears to be the right path, an opportunity for you, is not always so. Choose that which is inextricably tied to the fulfillment of your

Word of life, and it is revealed to you as a direct result of your intimacy with your Word and the Spirit thereof. Clearly identify your path of life that leads to your fullness of joy. **Breathe: New Life**, the power and Spirit of God, His Word for your life, and discern the pathway designed for you and the fulfillment of God's intent for your life and life more abundantly.

## October 19

*Figure out what will please Christ, and then do it.*
Ephesians 5:10 (MSG)

**New Opportunities** are readily available to you and me because we choose to pursue diligently that which God has declared for our lives. God's Word will not return void, meaning that what He has spoken to and over your life, He will bring to completion. His reputation is at stake. Thus, it is incumbent upon us to discern what God intends for our lives, and we do so by developing and nurturing an intimate relationship with Him. The more we are intertwined with God, the more we are sensitive to His will and His way. As we take on Him, we will take on His Word as the vision for our lives to pursue. It is in our pursuit of what we believe God has intended for our lives that we are rewarded and they are manifested through **New Opportunities** available to us to **Breathe: New Life** into our experiences, pressing us forward in His higher calling, His will for our lives.

## October 20

*Now God himself and our Father, and our Lord Jesus Christ, direct our way unto you.*
I Thessalonians 3:11

The promises for our lives come with an assurance package that guarantees we will walk into what God has declared for us. The assurance package is not that we will not face adversity, but that those adversities will not prevent us from overcoming and inheriting what can and should be for our lives, declared by God. Adversities have a way of interrupting, seeking to distract and detour us and our efforts; however, with each one God has provided a way of escape, **New Opportunities** to achieve and possess that which He has promised. God will not leave you in any state or space in which He will not deliver you; it may not appear to you or even be apparent how or when, however, be assured He will; it is a part of your package. ***Breathe: New Life*** and be anxious for nothing. God will show you your path of life, and in His presence, there is the fullness of joy, and at His right hand pleasures forevermore.

## October 21

*To the end he may stablish your hearts unblameable in holiness before God, even our Father, at the coming of our Lord Jesus Christ with all his saints.*
I Thessaoloians 3:13

God desires for you to live in the fullness of your life and life more abundantly and will do what is necessary for you to do so. Despite life's challenges, God will not go back on His Word. Be alert, for He has and will provide **New Opportunities** for you to achieve that which can and should be for your life. The adversities may be overwhelming, but rest assured, you will overcome them. It may be difficult, but you will win. Set your sights on God's promises, and be sensitive to the **New Opportunities** in your experiences that can *Breathe: New Life.* The choice is yours, choose God's Word, His promises for your life, and press through life and its challenges, and all along the way, God will provide you with **New Opportunities** over and over to be victorious in seizing your life and life more abundantly!

## October 22

*May God himself, the God who makes everything holy and whole, make you holy and whole, put you together—spirit, soul, and body —and keep you fit for the coming of our Master, Jesus Christ. The One who called you is completely dependable. If he said it, he'll do it!*
I Thessalonians 5:23-24 (MSG)

God uses our lives and their challenges to shape and mold us for that which He has intended for our life and life more abundantly. God is committed, faithful to you, that absolutely nothing that comes to and around your life can destroy you; He is committed to it all working for your good. Thus, **New Opportunities** are also wrapped up in the challenges we face; therefore, we must be sensitive to God, His Word, and His Spirit operating in our lives, and we must operate in them to discern the **New Opportunities** God provides. The **New Opportunities** are the very mechanism that provides you the key to unlock and defang your challenges so that they become footstools for your elevation, your press to your higher calling. ***Breathe: New Life*** for God is using every aspect of your life, the good and the bad, to shape and mold you for your life and life more abundantly, and in each God has **New Opportunities** that will elevate you in your press!

## October 23

And the disciples were astonished at his words. But Jesus answereth again, and saith unto them, Children, how hard is it for them that trust in riches to enter into the kingdom of God! It is easier for a camel to go through the eye of a needle, than for a rich man to enter into the kingdom of God. And they were astonished out of measure, saying among themselves, Who then can be saved? And Jesus looking upon them saith, With men it is impossible, but not with God: for with God all things are possible. Then Peter began to say unto him, Lo, we have left all, and have followed thee. And Jesus answered and said, Verily I say unto you, There is no man that hath left house, or brethren, or sisters, or father, or mother, or wife, or children, or lands, for my sake, and the gospel's, But he shall receive an hundredfold now in this time, houses, and brethren, and sisters, and mothers, and children, and lands, with persecutions; and in the world to come eternal life. But many that are first shall be last; and the last first.

Mark 10:24-31

Life and its challenges will place us in situations where we do not know what to do, question whether everything we do is worth it and will work, and even doubt our faith and/or the promises of God. Our questioning, as well as our doubt, is normal for us all; what God is doing and what He will do is greater than we can ask or imagine. Therefore, we must rely on God and His Spirit to lead and guide us according to His purpose and plan, and as we do, **New Opportunities** arise to turn what appears both frustrating and impossible into something at peace and possible. God specializes in doing what you or anything else cannot do by your reliance on His Spirit, for He knows the plans that He has for you, and they are not to hurt or harm you but to prosper you and get you to your expected end, your life and life more abundantly! Go ahead, ***Breathe: New Life,*** all you believe you have done or given up will be returned to you in abundance, more than you can ask or think, by allowing His Spirit to lead and guide you to your **New Opportunities** for your overcoming and inheriting all things. Please note that with life there will be persecution, frustration, and doubt, but stand, hold on, be steadfast, your labor is not in vain, ***Breathe: New Life***!

## October 24

*Ah Lord GOD! behold, thou hast made the heaven and the earth*
*by thy great power and stretched out arm, and there is nothing*
*too hard for thee:*
Jeremiah 32:17

We need not fear the impossibilities of our circumstances, for even in the most difficult, God has **New Opportunities** for us to live in the truth of His Word of promises for our lives. With God, absolutely all things are possible, and God will do what it takes so that you and I are equipped and empowered to see and seize **New Opportunities** for overcoming whatever may exist to separate us from our life and life more abundantly. God is the creator of heaven and earth and all things that exist or will exist; thus, there is nothing He is not fully aware of and/or too hard for Him to resolve. *Breathe: New Life* in each and every one of your experiences, especially what appears to be the impossible, your God, God the Creator-God of all things, will make it possible for you to win, overcoming and inheriting all things.

## October 25

*And the angel said unto her, Fear not, Mary: for thou hast found favour with God. And, behold, thou shalt conceive in thy womb, and bring forth a son, and shalt call his name JESUS. He shall be great, and shall be called the Son of the Highest: and the Lord God shall give unto him the throne of his father David: And he shall reign over the house of Jacob for ever; and of his kingdom there shall be no end. Then said Mary unto the angel, How shall this be, seeing I know not a man? And the angel answered and said unto her, The Holy Ghost shall come upon thee, and the power of the Highest shall overshadow thee: therefore also that holy thing which shall be born of thee shall be called the Son of God. And, behold, thy cousin Elisabeth, she hath also conceived a son in her old age: and this is the sixth month with her, who was called barren. For with God nothing shall be impossible. And Mary said, Behold the handmaid of the Lord; be it unto me according to thy word. And the angel departed from her.*

Luke 1:30-38

God will use the impossible in our lives to confirm His Word. Do not get so bent out of shape because of the vicissitudes of life that are both overwhelming and impossible to resolve; all things are possible with God. God has **New Opportunities** in all the challenges that face you; there is nothing that can come up against you, and God's promises for your life and life more abundantly, which He does not provide you an opportunity to overcome. Though your circumstances appear impossible, remember they are a setup for your God, the God-creator of all things, and thus know that all things are for Him and for His will for your life to be revealed. To achieve life and life more abundantly in your impossibilities will require your flexibility; your willingness to allow the Spirit of God and His Word for your life to lead and guide you, even with upside-down thinking and actions, which is His intent to yield your reward. *Breathe: New Life* to the impossibilities of your life with great expectations for your God, the Creator-God has created **New Opportunities** all along your path of life and life more abundantly for you to win, overcome, and inherit all things!

## October 26

*Is any thing too hard for the LORD? At the time appointed I will return unto thee, according to the time of life, and Sarah shall have a son.*
Genesis 18:14

One of the major factors in our decision-making is timing: we are either impatient and/or unsure when to move forward, stay still, or turn right or left, leaving us bewildered, confused, and frustrated.  It is in the chaos of our indecision that we are more susceptible to the wiles of the devil, making choices that lead to eventual separation, a detour, and/or distraction from the pathway of life that leads to the fulfillment of God's promises for our life and life more abundantly.   However, it is in our indecision that we are often faced with the impossibility of our circumstances and thus, we give up or are so confused we cannot see opportunities God has provided for our overcoming creative pathways to possibilities out of our impossibilities, **New Opportunities**.  The **New Opportunities** may be clouded, but can be visible through our faith, confidence, and assurance that nothing is too hard for God, not even the turning around of natural occurrences and/or obstacles.  God is the Creator-God, and all things are subject to Him; thus, ***Breathe: New Life*** into your experience, for God will move all heaven and earth to ensure His Word of promises for your life are fulfilled.  Be assured, there are **New Opportunities** even in nature.  The normal course of life would say it is impossible, but God's Word will not return void, and God will work it all out for your good.  ***Breathe: New Life*** and live in the fullness of your life and life more abundantly!


## October 27, 2022

*And being fully persuaded that, what he had promised, he was*
*able also to perform.*
Romans 4:21

Each experience of our lives as we seek to live in God's promises for our life and life more abundantly builds upon another to provide a cache of faith, assurance of God's presence with us, and His capability to deliver us. Therefore, as we engage with life and its challenges, we are assured that God is present and has provided **New Opportunities** for us to overcome whatever may arise, making us sensitive to God's move in and around us and in our space. As we are sensitive to God's presence, our expectations must be raised so that we can see and seize the **New Opportunities** in our experiences that He has designed for us to build our muscles, equip us for our promise, and reveal more of Himself and His Word in our lives. Though the challenge may be difficult and/or impossible, go ahead and *Breathe: New Life* for God is using your experience to build you up and lift you to the fulfillment of God's promises for your life, and thus, **New Opportunities** are there. As you have the expectations of opportunities, stand still and see the salvation of the Lord; be determined in your press, and doors will open for you, go and overcome to inherit all things!

## October 28

*Our God is in heaven doing whatever he wants to do.*
Psalm 115:3 (MSG)

In our press toward the fulfillment of God's Word for our lives, our ability to *Breathe: New Life* in whatever our circumstances may be must be from a position that God can and will do whatever He wants to fulfill His purpose and plan for our lives. There is nothing that can hinder or stop God from His Word becoming flesh, real in our lives, and we must take on that attitude as we engage in life and its challenges. Such an attitude that God is in charge and He can do whatever He wishes directs our mind and sight to be sensitive to **New Opportunities** in our experiences in which God is providing our way of escape, our strategy to overcome whatever exists to inherit His promises for our lives. Remember, your Worship, your living and walking around acknowledgment that God is God, the Lord, and Master of all things, and everyone is the very thing that empowers you and everything about you to see and seize the **New Opportunities**, unforeseen and /or thought of avenues, to make God's Word for your living flesh, real!

## October 29

*I, too, give witness to the greatness of God, our Lord, high above all other gods. He does just as he pleases—however, wherever, whenever.*
Psalm 135:5-6 (MSG)

However, wherever, whenever there are things that seek to separate you from overcoming life and its challenges toward your promise of a higher calling, you have God. God, who is the Creator-God, knew and knows about everything, even every secret thing of all things, and thus has the ability as well as the power to resolve whatever the kink may be. The resolution is wrought through us and God's ability to provide us with **New Opportunities** to achieve that which He has intended. We never have to be overly preoccupied with the questions or limited by them of how we can achieve, when we will achieve, or where we can achieve, for God knows and is greater than anything; He is the

Creator-God, and all are subject to Him. Therefore, release the pressure off of yourself trying to resolve your impossibilities and **Breathe: New Life** by making yourself available unto God to show you **New Opportunities**, however, wherever, and whenever, unlimited by what is or is not, He will and does as He pleases. Remember, everything belongs to God; He created it all for His glory, the fulfillment of His intent for your life, and life more abundantly!

## October 30

*And Joshua the son of Nun sent out of Shittim two men to spy secretly, saying, Go view the land, even Jericho. And they went, and came into an harlot's house, named Rahab, and lodged there. And it was told the king of Jericho, saying, Behold, there came men in hither to night of the children of Israel to search out the country. And the king of Jericho sent unto Rahab, saying, Bring forth the men that are come to thee, which are entered into thine house: for they be come to search out all the country. And the woman took the two men, and hid them, and said thus, There came men unto me, but I wist not whence they were: And it came to pass about the time of shutting of the gate, when it was dark, that the men went out: whither the men went I wot not: pursue after them quickly; for ye shall overtake them. But she had brought them up to the roof of the house, and hid them with the stalks of flax, which she had laid in order upon the roof. And the men pursued after them the way to Jordan unto the fords: and as soon as they which pursued after them were gone out, they shut the gate.*

*And before they were laid down, she came up unto them upon the roof; And she said unto the men, I know that the LORD hath given you the land, and that your terror is fallen upon us, and that all the inhabitants of the land faint because of you. For we have heard how the LORD dried up the water of the Red sea for you, when ye came out of Egypt; and what ye did unto the two kings of the Amorites, that were on the other side Jordan, Sihon and Og, whom ye utterly destroyed. And as soon as we had heard these things, our hearts did melt, neither did there remain any more courage in any man, because of you: for the LORD your God, he is God in heaven above, and in earth beneath. Now therefore, I pray you, swear unto me by the LORD, since I have shewed you kindness, that ye will also shew kindness unto my father's house, and give me a true token: And that ye will save alive my father, and my mother, and my brethren, and my sisters, and all that they have, and deliver our lives from death. And the men answered her, Our life for yours, if ye utter not this our business. And it shall be, when the LORD hath given us the land, that we will deal kindly and truly with thee.*
Joshua 2:1-14

The present times seem to point to a period of unprecedented crises; major issues/challenges/things are happening all around us and to us at what appears to be abnormal rates and degrees, seemingly making real God's admonition about the end times. However, I wish to suggest as a person of hope, a believer in the life and life more abundantly promised to us eternally, that what may look like the end is not the end but instead a new beginning. If it is that what we are experiencing is a new beginning the crises must be a wake-up call, an alert to live and live in the fullness of our potential, implying that where we are, we are not where we can and should be and pressures of life, within and without, personally and communally, are signs bidding us to come up higher. The chaos and hell of your life may be a trumpet sounding, bidding you to come higher, to the rooftop of your life and experiences, to see and seize **New Opportunities**. Life is ever-changing and with the transformation, if we are to live at our full potential, we too must transform for the good, not conforming to things as they were or are instead transformed by the renewing of our minds to prove that which is the good, perfect, and acceptable will of God, which demands our getting to the rooftop of our lives and experiences. On the rooftop, we have a panoramic view of life, not just in our pressure cooker but one that encompasses our past, present, and most importantly, our future as promised by God, producing hope. In our hope, we have a safe space to make sense of what is to ensure that we can become what can and should be for our lives; see and seize **New Opportunities,** and as a result, reimagine outcomes causing us to *Breathe: New Life*!

## October 31

*But the midwives feared God, and did not as the king of Egypt commanded them, but saved the men children alive.*
Exodus 1:17

God has a way of fulfilling His intended purposes for our lives that causes people, places, and things to forgo their natural inclinations and participate in what God is up to. God's way and thought life is not like ours; He is not limited to what is or what is natural. God supersedes it all to allow His intent to permeate, take control, and drive the narrative of all things. Thus, as you fully engage your life and its challenges from the position of God's promises, Word for your life, God will move all heaven and earth and everything within them, to accomplish what He has established for your life and life more abundantly. Do not allow the hardships, difficulties, complexities, or impossibilities of your experiences to drive your narrative; minds and hearts will be changed to accomplish God's will, *Breath: New Life,* and see and seize your **New Opportunities** to advance in God's intent for your life and life more abundantly!

# *NEW MERCIES*

## NOVEMBER

## November 1

*Rise ye up, take your journey, and pass over the river Arnon: behold, I have given into thine hand Sihon the Amorite, king of Heshbon, and his land: begin to possess it, and contend with him in battle. This day will I begin to put the dread of thee and the fear of thee upon the nations that are under the whole heaven, who shall hear report of thee, and shall tremble, and be in anguish because of thee.*
Deuteronomy 2:24-25

Go forward in that which God has promised you, for as you choose to go, God provides **New Mercies** to you every step of the way, every morning, so that as you engage, you do so with an advantage. The Spirit of God activated in your life is well aware of the adversities you will face, and each experience is a building block to empower you, but also to cause your adversaries to fear you in advance. Following the Spirit of God, the wandering children of Israel in the wilderness defeated the Amorites, and as a result, their victory not only empowered them to take on the next adversary, such as Jericho, but it also caused the people of Jericho to fear them. The fear and trembling of the children of Israel weakened the subsequent adversaries of Israel, preparing the way for the children of Israel to overcome and possess their promise. God is ever-present in your life, allow His Spirit to lead and guide, and in your following, God reveals **New Mercies** every morning, setting you up to ***Breathe: New Life*** into your experiences, overcoming and possessing your promises!

## November 2

*Every place whereon the soles of your feet shall tread shall be yours: from the wilderness and Lebanon, from the river, the river Euphrates, even unto the uttermost sea shall your coast be. There shall no man be able to stand before you: for the LORD your God shall lay the fear of you and the dread of you upon all the land that ye shall tread upon, as he hath said unto you.*
Deuteronomy 11:24-25

God has promised you and me that if we diligently pursue His Word for our lives, He will reward us, and that reward includes blessings everywhere our feet tread. Note that it is in the diligent pursuit that we are rewarded, not because of perfection; thus, God's blessings are simply tied to His Word for our lives. God chose the children of Israel to manifest His glory and power, and when they were willing to be led and guided by Him, He blessed their every step, and their every step caused fear and trembling in anyone or anything that would come up against them. The blessings of God are available to us, despite and in spite of us; they are **New Mercies,** and those mercies will cause fear and trembling among our adversaries. Take advantage of your **New Mercies** found every day and in every experience, and *Breathe: New Life*, anyone or anything that would come against you will fail, sending forth fear and trembling because of God's visible blessings on your life!

## November 3

*And Moses said unto the people, Fear ye not, stand still, and see the salvation of the LORD, which he will shew to you to day: for the Egyptians whom ye have seen to day, ye shall see them again no more for ever. The LORD shall fight for you, and ye shall hold your peace.*

*And the LORD said unto Moses, Wherefore criest thou unto me? speak unto the children of Israel, that they go forward: But lift thou up thy rod, and stretch out thine hand over the sea, and divide it: and the children of Israel shall go on dry ground through the midst of the sea. And I, behold, I will harden the hearts of the Egyptians, and they shall follow them: and I will get me honour upon Pharaoh, and upon all his host, upon his chariots, and upon his horsemen. And the Egyptians shall know that I am the LORD, when I have gotten me honour upon Pharaoh, upon his chariots, and upon his horsemen.*

*And the angel of God, which went before the camp of Israel, removed and went behind them; and the pillar of the cloud went from before their face, and stood behind them: And it came between the camp of the Egyptians and the camp of Israel; and it was a cloud and darkness to them, but it gave light by night to these: so that the one came not near the other all the night. And Moses stretched out his hand over the sea; and the LORD caused the sea to go back by a strong east wind all that night, and made the sea dry land, and the waters were divided. And the children of Israel went into the midst of the sea upon the dry ground: and the waters were a wall unto them on their right hand, and on their left.*

Exodus 14:13-22

There is absolutely nothing too hard for God, the Creator-God, for all things have been created by Him and for Him and His glory, His revelation in our lives. Thus, as we seek to live in His Word for our lives and allow it to live through us, there is nothing we cannot overcome to live in God's intent for our life and life more abundantly. The required perspective is that we believe all things are subject to God and that we have assurance as we allow Him to lead and guide us; He will provide **New Mercies** every step of the way. We may not deserve to be overcomers, but because we are willing to diligently pursue, get up when knocked down, by our own means or by external forces, and yet press forward to *Breathe: New Life,* God will provide the mercy necessary for us to clear our pathway to victory. The Creator-God has already given us what we all need; all we must do is stretch out with it, and in doing so, He reveals **New Mercies** to us every morning, positioning us to *breathe: New Life*!

## November 4

*For the LORD your God dried up the waters of Jordan from before you, until ye were passed over, as the LORD your God did to the Red sea, which he dried up from before us, until we were gone over: That all the people of the earth might know the hand of the LORD, that it is mighty: that ye might fear the LORD your God for ever.*
Joshua 4:23-24

We have the very presence of God as our help when we choose to press forward to His higher calling for our lives. God provides so that we would be empowered, internally pushed, to be faithful to

His Word for our lives as He is faithful to us.  God desires that you and I would be saved; delivered from what is to His promises for our life and life more abundantly, not just in general but also specifically for each and every experience of our life.  See and seize God's opportunities He has provided and overcome your circumstances to *Breathe: New Life,* not because you deserve it or should get it, but instead because of His continuous provision of opportunities with **New Mercies.**  Guilt and shame are the main culprits from within and which our adversaries will use to convince us to give up, accept things as they are, or spiral down a deep dark hole but God promised He is with you always and thus available to you are **New Mercies**, despite and in spite of your failings or others attempts to prevent and separate you from your promises.  *Breathe: New Life* by remembering what God has already done, which leads to what He will and can do as you choose to press diligently to pursue His higher calling for your life, and He will provide you with **New Mercies** to cross over and possess your promises.

## November 5

*And the LORD said unto Moses, Fear him not: for I have delivered him into thy hand, and all his people, and his land; and thou shalt do to him as thou didst unto Sihon king of the Amorites, which dwelt at Heshbon.*
Numbers 21:34

God is faithful, consistent in His efforts to ensure that you will be able to live in His intended promises for your life.  Because of God's faithfulness, we have not been consumed, and thus, we need not fear our adversities, whether they loom large or appear impossible. God is faithful to ensure that He provides us opportunities, whether we are perfect or not, with **New Mercies** to achieve His purpose and plan for our lives. The challenge for us is to fear not and to act with boldness on God's intent, not allowing anything, even our guilt and shame due to our human frailties, to stand in the way of our pressing forward to His higher calling. God has called us, and thus, we must respond. Although you may be inadequate or unworthy, respond by diligently pressing, pursuing His purpose and plan for your life, acting to *Breathe: New Life*, and God is there, providing opportunities for you to overcome and inherit all things!

## November 6

*The thought of my suffering and homelessness is bitter beyond words. I will never forget this awful time, as I grieve over my loss. Yet I still dare to hope when I remember this: The faithful love of the Lord never ends![ His mercies never cease. Great is his faithfulness; his mercies begin afresh each morning. I say to myself, "The Lord is my inheritance; therefore, I will hope in him!"*
Lamentations 3:19-24 (NLT)

Memory has been defined as the faculty of the mind by which data or information is encoded, stored, and retrieved when needed. Further, memory is defined as the retention of information over time to influence future action. Thus, it is in our memory banks that we can draw to confront new experiences with antidotes and safety measures, empowering us to leverage them against whatever we face and yet be victorious, overcoming and inheriting all things. These memory banks hold pain and suffering from our experiences, but also within them our victories, the ability to get through them, empowering us to live despite and in spite of the experience. In addition, our memory banks hold the revelation of God and His Word, which is active and continuously reveals **New Mercies** in and through our lives, whether we deserve them or not, and/or in opposition to the weight of guilt and shame that may be attached to our experiences. God's revelation and mercy, His compassion, and unending love, when released from our memory, cause an increase in our efforts to press forward, especially in our difficulties, to overcome them and *Breathe: New Life*, simply because we remember.

## November 7

*But Lord, be merciful to us, for we have waited for you.*
*Be our strong arm each day and our salvation in times of trouble.*
Isaiah 33:2 (NLT)

Life will provide challenges that make you want to give up on life and on yourself because it seems you just cannot get things right, be honest, or even be honest most of the time, and we allow the guilt and shame of our failures to control us. It is in the moments when we face life's challenges that we feel inadequate or in a shoulda, coulda, woulda space, where we beat ourselves up, that we must see the mercies of God available to us. God has and will continue to provide **New Mercies** to us every morning, not because of us but instead because of His faithfulness to us to give us every opportunity possible to succeed in that which He has intended for our lives.  Seek to live in God's will for you, praying for its clarity every day in your life, and whatever you face, you can *Breathe: New Life* to your experience due to the availability and willingness of God to provide you with **New Mercies**!

## November 8

*My choice is you, God, first and only.  And now I find I'm your choice! You set me up with a house and yard.  And then you made me your heir! The wise counsel God gives when I'm awake is confirmed by my sleeping heart.  Day and night I'll stick with God; I've got a good thing going and I'm not letting go.*
Psalm 16:5-8 (MSG)

**New Mercies** revealed every day in our lives are our inheritance; however, only if we choose God and with Him comes His abundant love and gifts for us.  As we choose God, we, as part of our benefits package, receive **New Mercies** available to us in every one of our experiences.  There is absolutely nothing you can face, or that will engage you, that God did not know or does not know, and as a result has already prepared that which you need to overcome.  You are God's heir, and everything He has done, is doing, and will do has you in mind to receive His promises for your life and to ensure that you have available to you **New Mercies**, day in and day out.  The **New Mercies** God has built into your life are with Him, and He is ever present with you, and when you choose that which is your inheritance, God Himself, you are empowered through those **New Mercies** to *nbreathe New life* into your experiences.  Stick with God and *Breathe: New Life* in whatever you face or engage with a power that makes you heir to all of God's promises fulfilled in your life!

## November 9

*Yet, in spite of all this, I still belong to you; you hold me by my right hand. You lead me with your secret wisdom. And following you brings me into your brightness and glory! Whom have I in heaven but you? You're all I want! No one on earth means as much to me as you. Lord, so many times I fail; I fall into disgrace. But when I trust in you, I have a strong and glorious presence protecting and anointing me. Forever you're all I need!*
Psalm 73:23-26 (TPT)

Our intimate relationship with Christ yields a harvest of **New Mercies** that always positions us, as needed, to win and overcome whatever may oppose our life and life more abundantly! Despite it all, our shortcomings, the chaos, and the complexity of our circumstances, God shows us **New Mercies**, not once, not twice, but they are new every morning. Therefore, do not hesitate to press your way to your higher calling, although you may not always make the mark or be in the right, God is ever present to lift you and provide for you if you are willing to choose Him, His purpose and plan for your life, your higher calling. ***Breathe: New Life*** for you always has a safety net, a way of escape, not because of how right you are, but instead how compassionate and loving God is, consistently providing you all you need, **New Mercies** every day!

## November 10

*Also at that time, people will say, "Look at what's happened! This is our God! We waited for him and he showed up and saved us! This God, the one we waited for! Let's celebrate, sing the joys of his salvation.*
Isaiah 25:9 (MSG)

Life's challenges seek to position us in a state of depression; depressing our strength by making us believe that there is no way out of our circumstances and an impossibility of us achieving what can and should be for our lives. It is in this state of depression that can make you feel alone, which very well may slip into loneliness unless we declare that God is the strength of our lives and that He, including His Word of promises for our life and life more abundantly, is forever with us. Our celebration of God, His Word, His presence, in our lives raises our hope, expectations, of God intervening, whether we deserve it or not, because of who He is and our desire for Him to be active in our lives. As we desire God, diligently seeking Him, calling to Him, or crying out to Him, God responds by providing us with **New Mercies,** showing His compassion and love to lift us out of depressed states. As we arise from depression, we are positioned to ***Breathe: New Life*** into our experiences and experience joy, the celebration of who God is and what He is doing with and for us!

## November 11

*For David speaketh concerning him, I foresaw the Lord always before my face, for he is on my right hand, that I should not be moved: Therefore did my heart rejoice, and my tongue was glad; moreover also my flesh shall rest in hope: Because thou wilt not leave my soul in hell, neither wilt thou suffer thine Holy One to see corruption. Thou hast made known to me the ways of life; thou shalt make me full of joy with thy countenance.*
Acts 2:25-28

To experience the **New Mercies** of God in the experiences of our life, we must be able to see the light also in our darkness to have hope, expectations, amid life's challenges and impossibilities. Our ability to hope in hopeless situations provides insight into our experiences, allowing us to see God and, in turn, to see ourselves from the perspective of His presence, power, and promises. Because of the tender mercies of the Lord, He causes the sun to come down, scattering our darkness and dispelling the shadows of death, giving us hope to rise out of our despair to a place of power and promises of what can and should be for our life and life more abundantly. It is in **New Mercies** every day that we can and will rise, resurrected, to the fulfillment of God's promise for our lives: to *Breathe: New Life*. See God, the light of God's presence, power, and promise, no matter how dark it may be or how impossible it appears, catch the light of God in and through your experiences, causing the light of God to rise, scattering darkness and death for you to *Breathe: New Life*!

## November 12

*I will lift up mine eyes unto the hills, from whence cometh my help.*

*My help cometh from the LORD, which made heaven and earth.*
*He will not suffer thy foot to be moved: he that keepeth thee will*
*not slumber.*
*Behold, he that keepeth Israel shall neither slumber nor sleep.*
*The LORD is thy keeper: the LORD is thy shade upon thy right hand.*
*The sun shall not smite thee by day, nor the moon by night.*
*The LORD shall preserve thee from all evil: he shall preserve thy*
*soul.*
*The LORD shall preserve thy going out and thy coming in from this*
*time forth, and even for evermore.*
Psalm 121

Amid life and its challenges, we must be willing to seek God's help; His **New Mercies** are revealed to us for us to get past our shortcomings and the difficulty of our circumstances, so God will be revealed. In our diligent pursuit of what we believe is God's purpose for our lives, He intervenes on our behalf, making up for our shortcomings with His presence and power. God's intervention is not based on a possibility or probability, nor on our perfection or the perfection of our circumstances, but on His Word, which declares He is always with us, never slumbering or sleeping. We can *Breathe: New Life* despite and in spite of us and/or our circumstances because of the tender mercies, **New Mercies**, available every morning; in every circumstance, He will keep us and preserve us for His purposes to be fulfilled in our lives!

## November 13

*Thou art my hiding place; thou shalt preserve me from trouble;*

*thou shalt compass me about with songs of deliverance. Selah.*
*I will instruct thee and teach thee in the way which thou shalt go:*
*I will guide thee with mine eye.*
Psalm 32:7-8


When we choose to find ourselves in God and His Word for our lives, despite what we may face or what may come against us, we have shelter, a hiding place in God.  Our hiding place in God is well-equipped with **New Mercies** that will open a way in spite of us and our abilities or capacity to overcome whatever may exist to separate us from our promises of life and life more abundantly, the fulfillment of God's Word for our lives.  God desires that all humanity be saved, delivered, to His expressed intent for life and life more abundantly, and thus God will lead and guide us to that pathway.  The pathway may be dimmed and/or clouded by life and life's challenges; nevertheless, God, by His **New Mercies,** can break through, providing us the space to ***Breathe: New Life*** into our experiences to win, overcome, and inherit all things.  Release yourself from total responsibility for your circumstances by wrapping yourself in the security of God and His Word, letting Him lead and guide you to your promises with **New Mercies** every day, making a way for your abundant living!


## November 14


*Then shall thy light break forth as the morning,*
*and thine health shall spring forth speedily:*
*and thy righteousness shall go before thee;*
*the glory of the LORD shall be thy reward.*

Isaiah 58:8

God rewards us for diligently seeking Him, His Word, His promises, for our lives, and our reward is not contingent upon how perfect we are, but instead how determined we are amid our shortcomings or separations from Him to get back on track. The more determined we are to stay on the pathway God has purposed for our lives, the more open we are to the **New Mercies** He provides as a reward for our willingness to flow in His purpose. Although God desires for us to be saved, delivered, He also understands our lack of capacity and ability as humans to always get it right; thus, He justified us and made things right with His **New Mercies.** Do not worry or fret, God's **New Mercies** are available every morning, in every experience, as you diligently seek to get through the evening of life's challenges to the morning joy of His reward. *Breathe: New Life* and allow the light of God to invade your evening experiences, the darkness of your life, internal as well as external, and He will bring you into His promises, His Word for your life, revealing Him and His fulfilled promises with joy!

## November 15

*My soul yearns, even faints, for the courts of the Lord;*
*my heart and my flesh cry out for the living God.*
Psalm 84:2 (NIV)

Though life and its challenges weigh heavily on us, and we often wear them with both guilt and shame, it is our yearning, crying out for the **New Mercies** of God, that sustains us and gives us hope. Having hope is essential to being able to *Breathe: New Life* into our circumstances, whether or not the death has been created by outside influences or within our own being and actions. Hope overcomes the challenges as well as the guilt and shame of the experiences so that we can *Breathe: New Life*. Do not allow your shortcomings, inadequacies, or lack of capacity to stand in the way of your promises of God, for whatever reason, yearn for, long after, cry out for **New Mercies** to God, and He will provide what you need to overcome, and inherit all things!

## November 16

*Looking for that blessed hope, and the glorious appearing of the great God and our Saviour Jesus Christ;*
Titus 2:13

As we press toward the higher calling of our lives, even beyond the impossibilities of life's challenges and our own weaknesses, we express our expectation and hope for the fulfillment of God's promises, despite and in spite of the opposition we face. The hope for the revelation of God and His Word of promises is made possible not because of how good or great we are, nor how strong we are to overcome our challenges, but instead because of God's generosity of **New Mercies** available to us. God is great not just because of His power but more so because of His continuous compassion and love toward us, His **New Mercies** every day we see, and as a result, we are equipped to *Breathe: New Life* into and for our experiences. You are an overcomer because God shows His mercy toward us, despite and in spite of us, and they are new every morning in every experience; thus, press toward the mark of your higher calling!

## November 17

*For thou wilt not leave my soul in hell;*
*neither wilt thou suffer thine Holy One to see corruption.*
*Thou wilt shew me the path of life:*
*in thy presence is fulness of joy;*
*at thy right hand there are pleasures for evermore.*
Psalm 16:10-11

We have an assurance from God that is inclusive of our promise package, which equips us with whatever we may need to get out of wherever we are, so that we would rise to the fulfillment of God's promises. God's Word is complete in itself with every opportunity for us to succeed and every mercy, **New Mercies** every morning to ensure that we succeed. We cannot lose with God; therefore, *Breathe: New Life*, inhaling God's provisions and reinforced promises for you to live life and live it more abundantly. God will always point you toward the path that leads to His promises, to His very presence in your life, and there you will experience your fullness of joy, positioned to receive the abundance of His promises for your life!

## November 18

*Beloved, now are we the sons of God, and it doth not yet appear what we shall be: but we know that, when he shall appear, we shall be like him; for we shall see him as he is.*
I John 3:2

While pursuing God's Word and promises for your life, wherever you are and whatever is going on, know that it is not the end. Keep pressing forward; God wishes to do exceedingly, abundantly more than you can ever ask or imagine through you. Diligently pursuing God's Word for your life is the mechanism by which God transforms us into what He intends: to be like Him. Therefore, what we are experiencing, the challenges of our lives, God uses to shape and form us into His likeness, and as we are willing to pursue, God provides **New Mercies** every day for us to not only survive but thrive toward His likeness, His intent for our lives. *Breathe: New Life* in each and every one of your experiences as you seek to become everything God intends for it is there you will receive **New Mercies**, whatever is necessary, each and every time to overcome and inherit all things as promised.

## November 19

*How excellent is thy lovingkindness, O God!*
*therefore the children of men put their trust under the shadow of thy wings.*
*They shall be abundantly satisfied with the fatness of thy house; and thou shalt make them drink of the river of thy pleasures.*
*For with thee is the fountain of life: in thy light shall we see light.*
Psalm 36:7-9

With God, we can eat the fat of the land; we enjoy the abundance of life in our experiences toward our good. The abundance that is ours hinges on our ability to seek and pursue that which God has purposed for our lives, His calling, and as we press toward the higher calling God provides in abundance, to and for us. In the press, we will be challenged, and sometimes we will meet those challenges not at our best or operating at our full potential because of separation, intentionally or unintentionally, from God's direction; nevertheless, God provides **New Mercies**. The **New Mercies** are new because they are what we need when we need them, not because we deserve them, but because God wishes to reward our willingness to keep pressing toward our higher calling. You may or may not always make the mark for several reasons, mostly by your choosing, but do not give up on yourself or God's promises for your life. Press His lovingkindness, which produces **New Mercies** every day. Trust God and *Breathe: New Life*; get up, dust yourself off, and press, you will be satisfied, and you will eat of the fat of the land, **New Mercies** available to and for you to overcome and inherit the abundance God has promised, your springs of life-giving water.

## November 20

*I will exalt you, Lord, for you rescued me. You refused to let my enemies triumph over me. O Lord my God, I cried to you for help, and you restored my health. You brought me up from the grave, O Lord. You kept me from falling into the pit of death.*
Psalm 30:1-3 (NLT)

I will bless the Lord for the **New Mercies** I see every day, because if it had not been for His mercies, I would have been consumed. No one needs to tell me that it is amazing where I am and that I have recovered from some of the chaos and impossibilities I have faced; it definitely was not because of how good, right, capable, or worthy I was. When I look back on my life and think about the goodness of God to me, it makes me both humble and grateful. My humility and gratitude are transformed into Worship, which pushes me to *Breathe: New Life* into my present experiences, knowing that God can and will extend **New Mercies** to me. I believe that, with God's promises, He has already reinforced them with mercies revealed along my journey because of my willingness to stray and/or the onslaught of attacks to separate me from His plan for my life. Therefore, I have the assurance that I am well-equipped and supplied to overcome whatever I face and thus can *Breathe: New Life,* resurrected to press forward to God's higher calling for my life.

## November 21

*The LORD is my strength and my shield;*
*my heart trusted in him, and I am helped:*
*therefore my heart greatly rejoiceth;*
*and with my song will I praise him.*
*The LORD is their strength,*
*and he is the saving strength of his anointed.*
*Save thy people,*
*and bless thine inheritance:*
*feed them also, and lift them up for ever.*
Psalm 28:7-9

God rescues us because we diligently pursue, pressing toward the mark of His higher calling for our lives. Because we choose to press on, even though our circumstances are difficult and seem impossible, we are willing to focus and remain determined to achieve. God sheds His mercies upon us, giving us a leg up. These **New Mercies** are packaged within our promises and placed throughout our journey that awaits our press. Remember, the Lord is your strength, and the Lord God is synonymous with His Word for your life. Focus and process toward that Word, your higher calling, and all along the way are **New Mercies** that allow you to *Breathe: New Life* into your experiences. God, your Word is reinforced, equipped with all that is necessary to deliver, save you from being overwhelmed by you and/or life's challenges, to lift you beyond them all and land you in the place of your promise, your life, and life more abundantly!

## November 22

*O Lord, I give my life to you. I trust in you, my God! Do not let me be disgraced, or let my enemies rejoice in my defeat. No one who trusts in you will ever be disgraced, but disgrace comes to those who try to deceive others. Show me the right path, O Lord; point out the road for me to follow. Lead me by your truth and teach me, for you are the God who saves me. All day long I put my hope in you. Remember, O Lord, your compassion and unfailing love, which you have shown from long ages past.*
Psalm 25:1-6 (NLT)

Our willingness to allow God, His Word of promises for our lives, to lead and guide us through life and its challenges releases God's mercy to and for us to endure and yet overcome. No one is immune to making bad and/or wrong choices in our lives as we seek to live in our promises. It is common for us all to yield to temptations that draw us away from the path of life God has ordained. However, we can be confident that our determination to live in God's Word, His promises, and with them, He has already provided sufficient grace, **New Mercies**, for us so that His strength and His will are made perfect in our weaknesses. Turn over the responsibility of getting over whatever tempts you and/or separates you from God's promises and arrive at where you are supposed to be, allowing God to lead and guide you. As you release to God's guiding Spirit, all along the way He provides **New Mercies** to combat your bad choices which cause you to miss the mark, positioning you to *Breathe: New Life* in and through them all.

## November 23

*The kings of the earth set themselves,*
*and the rulers take counsel together,*
*against the LORD, and against his anointed, saying,*
*Let us break their bands asunder,*
*and cast away their cords from us.*
*He that sitteth in the heavens shall laugh:*
*the Lord shall have them in derision.*
Psalm 2:2-4

As we face life and its challenges, if we choose the purpose and plan of God for our lives, all that which would be against us will be confused and eventually consumed by the power of our living in our Word.  God desires that you and I would be saved, delivered into what should be for our lives as He has purposed, and if we are willing to diligently pursue that purpose, God promises us whatever we need, including **New Mercies** to accomplish His intent.  The **New Mercies** are new every day because we are both tempted by our challenges and often fall for them, but God has provided a way of escape also that we might stand up under them, each and every one of them, every time; thus, **New Mercies** are made available.  Remember, God sits high and looks low, and as we choose to *Breathe: New Life* into our experiences and as required, He provides **New Mercies** for us to overcome and inherit all things!

## November 24

*For great is thy mercy toward me:*
*and thou hast delivered my soul from the lowest hell.*
Psalm 86:13

We are blessed beyond measure, not because of what we have done or can do, but instead because of the mercy of God that is greater and more than we would ever deserve.  It is God's compassion and love for us, despite and in spite of our failings and choices that lead us away from His intent for our lives, that we are not consumed.  To be honest, we sometimes are so intent on having our own way that we forge ahead, at speed, down pathways of eventual destruction rather than turn our lives over to the leading and guiding of God's Spirit. We knowingly, and sometimes unknowingly, reject the **New Mercies** of God for and in our experiences for what we believe is our better knowledge and will for our lives. However, God patiently and lovingly awaits our coming to ourselves, and when we do, He makes **New Mercies** available to and for us to *Breathe: New Life*.

## November 25

*To you, Lord, I call; you are my Rock, do not turn a deaf ear to me. For if you remain silent, I will be like those who go down to the pit. Hear my cry for mercy as I call to you for help, as I lift up my hands toward your Most Holy Place.*
Psalm 28:1-2 (NIV)

Because of God's willingness to provide **New Mercies** to us every day, in every experience of our lives, we have the privilege and right to call on Him. God welcomes you and me into an intimate relationship with Him, in which He takes responsibility for supporting and assisting us in accomplishing His intent for our lives. Do not fail to access the privileges that are made available to you in *Breathe: New Life*. Feel free to ask for help, cry out to the Lord, and God will answer you, whether you deserve it or not. God provides sufficient grace, **New Mercies**, to suit your circumstances for you to live in the fullness of His intent for your life. God is a very present help wherever you are, and for whatever, they will answer with **New Mercies**, positioning you to *Breathe: New Life* and seize God's opportunity for your life and life more abundantly in your circumstances.

## November 26

*Answer me, Lord, out of the goodness of your love; in your great*
*mercy turn to me.  Do not hide your face from your servant;*
*answer me quickly, for I am in trouble.  Come near and rescue me;*
*deliver me because of my foes.*
Psalm 69:16-18 (NIV)

Your life is determined not only by your willingness to be focused
and press toward your higher calling but also by your willingness
to invoke the Lord, His Spirit embodied in His Word, in and over
your life.  Speaking the truth of God and His Word releases the
difficulties and impossibilities of your journey to the One who
foreknew, predestined, and called you.  In your silliness to invoke
God, His word in and over your life, you are simply responding to
God's call; releasing the responsibility to God, who releases **New
Mercies** as required for you to get over yourself and the
challenges of life to live in the fullness of His Word, His intent for
your life.  Be free to press toward your higher calling and ***Breathe:***
***New Life*** because God shoulders His responsibility of fulfilling His
promises for your life, and when you need rescuing, He is there to
lift and push you higher to His intent.

## November 27

*Be careful for nothing; but in every thing by prayer and*
*supplication with thanksgiving let your requests be made known*
*unto God.*

Philippians 4:6

One of the ways to the heart of God, to the place in which His loving compassion springs, is our sincere show of gratitude to Him simply for being God, Creator, Redeemer, and Sustainer of all life. And with thanksgiving, we can reach God at His core, releasing whatever we need, as we need it, to live in God's content for our lives.  Please know that God has already provided a pathway to our fullness of joy, and with that promise, He has given us guidance and direction to ensure that neither you nor external forces permanently separate you from Him and His promise.  It is along the pathway of life that God has reinforced your pathway with **New Mercies** each and every day because He is well aware that, because of your flesh, you will be tempted and sometimes stray; nevertheless, His loving compassion awaits the opportunity to rescue you.  Therefore, despite and in spite of us and the things of our life, God is there for us, which should spur our gratitude to Him, just simply for being.  And with thanksgiving, we have a release for life's challenges, whether internal or external, because of a relationship with God defined by our lived experiences that continues to give us access, opportunity, to *Breathe: New Life* in and through all things!

## November 28

*Cast thy burden upon the LORD, and he shall sustain thee:*
*he shall never suffer the righteous to be moved.*
Psalm 55:22

As believers, you and I have a release valve that allows us to let go of the yokes and burdens of our lives and be free to press forward in God's higher calling. Life's challenges, internal as well as external ones, have come to separate you from the fulfilled promises of God for your life and thus keep you wandering around aimlessly, and the more we give them all of our energy, the more we will wander. Focus on your promises and pull your release valve, letting go of the pressure of life to God, who cares for you and stands ready and available to all the waves and storms of your life. God wants to sustain you and give you the space to press toward His higher calling, to respond carefree, but you must be willing to give it to Him, and in so doing, you can *Breathe: New Life*. The space given is new every morning; it is God's **New Mercies** that put space between you and your life's challenges so you can stay focused to go forward and higher, responding to God and releasing all things!

## November 29

*But to the saints that are in the earth,*
*and to the excellent, in whom is all my delight.*
Psalm 16:3

The Word of promises from God for your life must be your delight. Delight in the sense that it is something that you diligently seek after. As you are immersed in the joy of your promises, they consume you, releasing you from the chaos of your life's challenges. Understand that the challenges of your life are challenges to the truth of God's Word, His promises, and thus, the challenge seeks to separate you from the truth of God's Word.

Remember that the devil, evil, is a deceiver; deceiving you from the truth of God's Word for your life, and thus when darkness says that you can not and/or creates confusion so you feel you can not, it is a lie, and God is not a man who can lie. *Breathe: New Life* and embrace the truth of God's promises for your life; He will supply all your needs, no weapon formed against you shall prosper, and as you focus, you receive **New Mercies**, new opportunities of seeing and knowing God. Thus, to know God is to have eternal life; therefore, your **New Mercies** open up the way for you to live in the life and life more abundantly promised, *Breathe: New Life*!

## November 30

*Humble yourselves therefore under the mighty hand of God, that he may exalt you in due time: Casting all your care upon him; for he careth for you.*
I Peter 5:6-7

Because of God's **New Mercies** available to us in all of our experiences, we do not have to fear that somehow our shortcomings or failings will be the end of us and His Word for our lives. It is because of His **New Mercies** available in and through our experiences that we have not been consumed and should serve as the foundation for a heart and attitude of thanksgiving. And with Thanksgiving, a posture of humility sets us up to have direct access to the fullness of God's presence, power, and promise being made real, fleshed out in our lives. It is with this attitude of thanksgiving that we are afforded the **New Mercies**, space to *Breathe: New Life.* Therefore, instead of trying to face our challenges on our own, knowing that our spirit is willing but our flesh is weak, we can cast it all on God and with Him receive **New Mercies** to *Breathe: New Life* in our experiences to press forward in His higher calling.

# ALL THINGS HAVE BECOME NEW

## DECEMBER

## December 1

*Commit thy way unto the LORD;*
*trust also in him; and he shall bring it to pass.*
Psalm 37:5

As you press toward God's higher calling for your life, you press the release value, releasing the pressure of the guilt and shame you experience because you do not always get things right, whether willingly or because of external circumstances. It is you committing your way, your focus to that which you believe should be for your life as God intends, which serves as your mechanism to release you from what is to trust God for what can and should be for your life. Thus, no matter what you face, whether of your own doing or a direct result of circumstances beyond your control, commit your way, keep pressing forward, and **All Things will Become New**. Your ability to press forward amid the challenges you face requires that you *Breathe: New Life,* and as you breathe, you set in motion for your space, atmosphere, God to intervene on your behalf, and as a result, **All Things Will Become New**.

## December 2

*The steps of a good man are ordered by the LORD:*
*and he delighteth in his way.*
*Though he fall, he shall not be utterly cast down:*
*for the LORD upholdeth him with his hand.*
*I have been young, and now am old;*

*yet have I not seen the righteous forsaken,*
*nor his seed begging bread.*
Psalm 37:23-25

One thing we can count on in life is God's faithfulness, and it extends to everyone, becoming activated when we choose to respond to His call in our lives. As we respond, we do so not in perfection but in the reality of our imperfection, which God already knows. Thus, He has reinforced our journey with His goodness and mercy, ensuring that as we diligently pursue our calling, we will receive His reward for the fullness of our joy. The reinforcements along our journey ensure us that, as dark as things may become, whether because of our own doing or circumstances, All Things Have Become New, giving us the space to **Breathe: New Life** into our circumstances. Therefore, critical to our ability to **Breathe: New Life** is reinforced along the way, meaning we must be on the ordered path for the promises of God to be fulfilled in our lives. Remember, as you respond to God's calling, your steps have been ordered and reinforced with God's goodness and mercy; thus, you need not be careful about anything. God has your back and will provide for you to reach your place of fullness of joy.

## December 3

*Many are the afflictions of the righteous:*
*but the LORD delivereth him out of them all.*
Psalm 34:19

We can celebrate and face the challenges of our lives with the assurance that **All Things Have Become New** because the Lord God is our Shepherd. A shepherd, by definition, is a caretaker who does so not just in the moment of our experiences but also goes ahead to make sure that our pathway is cleared and/or strategic for our eating of the good of the land, of our experiences. The Lord who is our Shepherd has already ensured that whatever we face or that comes against us, built into the experience is our ability to overcome and win, to eat the good of the land. Thus, we know that **All Things Have Become New;** they work for our good. Your afflictions may seem overwhelming, and you may feel as though you will not be able to stand up to them. *Breathe: New Life* and respond by pressing to your higher calling.

## December 4

*Meanwhile, Saul was uttering threats with every breath and was eager to kill the Lord's followers. So he went to the high priest. He requested letters addressed to the synagogues in Damascus, asking for their cooperation in the arrest of any followers of the Way he found there. He wanted to bring them—both men and women—back to Jerusalem in chains. As he was approaching Damascus on this mission, a light from heaven suddenly shone down around him. He fell to the ground and heard a voice saying to him, "Saul! Saul! Why are you persecuting me?" "Who are you, lord?" Saul asked. And the voice replied, "I am Jesus, the one you are persecuting! Now get up and go into the city, and you will be told what you must do." The men with Saul stood speechless, for they heard the sound of someone's voice but saw no one! Saul picked himself up off the ground, but when he opened his eyes he*

*was blind. So his companions led him by the hand to Damascus.*
*He remained there blind for three days and did not eat or drink.*
Acts 9:1-9 (NLT)

It is through the encounters of our lives, the casual and unexpected experiences that we meet and come to know God, to realize the power in which **All Things Have Become New**. All of us tend to believe that the experience of meeting and knowing God has to come through some supernatural or miraculous experience, although that can and does happen, it is not normal. God is alive in our everyday walking-around experiences and thus present, omnipresent, everywhere, and in everything. The critical issue is not the presence of God, but the presence of the mind to be sensitive and know God, and that is only developed as a result of being in a relationship with Him, a relationship with your life, and what can and should be for your life. Saul, a scholar of the Torah, the Word of God, and in his heart a true believer in the Messiah's coming, did not accept Jesus as the one because He did not fit his preconceived notions. Nevertheless, God, Christ Himself was present even in Saul's breathing out threats and slaughters against Him, Saul's sin and chaos, to connect with Saul in a space where he was, casual and unexpected, in which God/ Christ was revealed. It is in the very space where you are in which you can see God that the challenges of your life make sense, and you see your way over them to the place of life and life more abundantly, not because you see in the natural but because you receive insight from God, His Spirit. *Breathe: New Life* by your sensitivity to see God everywhere and in everything, and in your very casual as well as unexpected life experiences, you will be empowered by His presence, positioned to believe **All Things Have Become New**.

## December 5

*The first thing I did was place before you what was placed so emphatically before me: that the Messiah died for our sins, exactly as Scripture tells it; that he was buried; that he was raised from death on the third day, again exactly as Scripture says; that he presented himself alive to Peter, then to his closest followers, and later to more than five hundred of his followers all at the same time, most of them still around (although a few have since died); that he then spent time with James and the rest of those he commissioned to represent him; and that he finally presented himself alive to me. It was fitting that I bring up the rear. I don't deserve to be included in that inner circle, as you well know, having spent all those early years trying my best to stamp God's church right out of existence. But because God was so gracious, so very generous, here I am. And I'm not about to let his grace go to waste. Haven't I worked hard trying to do more than any of the others? Even then, my work didn't amount to all that much. It was God giving me the work to do, God giving me the energy to do it.*
I Corinthians 15:8-10 (MSG)


No matter where you are in life, God offers to you and me to press higher from a perspective in which **All Things Have Become New**. God generously offers His grace, unmerited favor, to us in sufficient amounts that no matter what we have done or where we find ourselves, He will lift us and give us the necessary fuel to press toward His higher calling for our lives. Stop allowing life and all your detractors, within and without, to try to convince you what you do not deserve, accept that you don't, while simultaneously accepting the grace of God for your life, and *Breathe: New Life*. It is God who has made you, and it is He who will shepherd you through life and all of its challenges, despite and in spite of you, so that you appropriately respond to His calling and are rewarded with the fullness of joy and at His right-hand pleasures forevermore!

## December 6

*"So I am telling you: Hands off these men! Let them alone. If this program or this work is merely human, it will fall apart, but if it is of God, there is nothing you can do about it—and you better not be found fighting against God!"*
Acts 5:38-39 (MSG)

God opens up the way as a direct result of our encountering Him in our everyday walking-around life. We must make it a priority to seek God in the midst of whatever is going on in and around us, encounter God, and diligently pursue Him, and in so doing, we will see the hand of God moving on our behalf to push us into our exceeding, abundantly more than. **All Things Have Become New** because we seek to encounter God in and through the circumstances of our lives. Do not allow what appears to be overwhelming, wilderness, or desert experiences to hinder you from engaging them to overcome and inherit all things, just *Breathe: New Life* and encounter the power of God in and over your life.

## December 7

*"All Israel, then, know this: There's no longer room for doubt—*
*God made him Master and Messiah, this Jesus whom you killed on*
*a cross." Cut to the quick, those who were there listening asked*
*Peter and the other apostles, "Brothers! Brothers! So now what do*
*we do?"*
Acts 2:36-37 (MSG)

**All Things Have Become New** for those who would believe that
whatever is going on in your life is only a vehicle to get you to the
place of your prosperity, your living life and life more abundantly.
To see each and every life experience, even the challenges, as
vehicles that will transport you to the fulfilled promises of
abundant life is rooted and grounded in your belief in what can
and should be for your life. The challenges of life and your
everyday walking around experiences can and will cloud your
judgment and your focus on living abundantly, and it is up to you
to release the stress from the challenges and how to achieve your
expected end, and *Breathe: New Life*. Trust God to lead and
guide you through the vicissitudes of your life, navigating and
leveraging them for your good, not because you deserve it, but
instead because of the sufficient grace, unmerited favor, of God
for your life to ensure you get to your expected end.

## December 8

*About midnight Paul and Silas were praying and singing hymns to*
*God, and the other prisoners were listening to them. Suddenly*

*there was such a violent earthquake that the foundations of the prison were shaken. At once all the prison doors flew open, and everyone's chains came loose. The jailer woke up, and when he saw the prison doors open, he drew his sword and was about to kill himself because he thought the prisoners had escaped. But Paul shouted, "Don't harm yourself! We are all here!" The jailer called for lights, rushed in and fell trembling before Paul and Silas. He then brought them out and asked, "Sirs, what must I do to be saved?" They replied, "Believe in the Lord Jesus, and you will be saved—you and your household." Then they spoke the word of the Lord to him and to all the others in his house.*

Acts 16:25-32 (NIV)

The wonder of an encounter with Christ, with God's Word for your life and life more abundantly, is that the way has been opened for you and all of your space to be set on the pathway for your fullness of joy and pleasures forevermore. Although your encounter with Christ may be casual, right wherever you are, or unexpected, in the challenges of your life, God's intent is for you to see and seize the opportunity to press to His higher calling. God uses your everyday walking-around experiences and challenges to help you see and seize opportunities in which **All Things Have Become New.** You may be in prison to what may appear to be the status quo of your life, as well as to your life's challenges; however, rest assured that God is only getting your attention so you can be saved, delivered into His promises for your life. **All Things Have Become New.** Instead of allowing the pressure of figuring out the how to, trust God and release, *Breathe: New Life* and watch God bring about your salvation, deliverance, into your promised life and life more abundantly!

## December 9

*And I Daniel alone saw the vision: for the men that were with me*
*saw not the vision; but a great quaking fell upon them, so that*
*they fled to hide themselves.*
Daniel 10:7

When you are pressing toward your higher calling, responding to God's call on your life, it may not be very apparent to those around you, the vision, the promise; nevertheless, keep pressing. Often, we desire the confirmation of others to justify our pressing to a higher calling, but that does not always come and can not be allowed to be a hindrance for you moving into your life and life more abundantly. What God is calling you to, **All Things Have Become New**, may not be apparent to others, for it is not their Word. Be assured that your Word is God, and as you diligently seek to be in His presence, your Word is made flesh, real. ***Breathe: New Life***, not based on what others may or may not see, but on what you see and respond to your call, your Word, and with your Word is God's presence, power, and promise for your new life, **All Things Have Become New**!

## December 10

*Are they servants of Christ? I can go them one better. (I can't*
*believe I'm saying these things. It's crazy to talk this way! But I*
*started, and I'm going to finish.) I've worked much harder, been*
*jailed more often, beaten up more times than I can count, and at*

*death's door time after time. I've been flogged five times with the Jews' thirty-nine lashes, beaten by Roman rods three times, pummeled with rocks once. I've been shipwrecked three times, and immersed in the open sea for a night and a day. In hard traveling year in and year out, I've had to ford rivers, fend off robbers, struggle with friends, struggle with foes. I've been at risk in the city, at risk in the country, endangered by desert sun and sea storm, and betrayed by those I thought were my brothers. I've known drudgery and hard labor, many a long and lonely night without sleep, many a missed meal, blasted by the cold, naked to the weather.  And that's not the half of it, when you throw in the daily pressures and anxieties of all the churches. When someone gets to the end of his rope, I feel the desperation in my bones. When someone is duped into sin, an angry fire burns in my gut. If I have to "brag" about myself, I'll brag about the humiliations that make me like Jesus. The eternal and blessed God and Father of our Master Jesus knows I'm not lying. Remember the time I was in Damascus and the governor of King Aretas posted guards at the city gates to arrest me? I crawled through a window in the wall, was let down in a basket, and had to run for my life.*

II Corinthians 11:23-33 (MSG)

**All Things Have Become New** in your life because you are willing to step back from the present state of your life and *Breathe: New Life*, discern the pros and cons of your situation and what you bring to the table, especially your expectations, your future, to choose life.  We all stand at the crossroads of life in every experience, because it challenges us to choose whether to maintain or expand our pursuit of our higher calling.  Critical to our choice is our confidence that, though it may stretch us to the limit, our record is that, in each and every experience we have chosen, we have overcome.  In our overcoming **All Things Have Become New**, a higher position that opens up our pathway to our fulfilled promises, God's intent for our life, and life more abundantly.  Please be assured that our pathway will not always be easy or without challenges; it is the uneasiness and challenges that cause us to *Breathe: New Life* that **All Things Have Become New** in your mind first and then made real in your life.

## December 11

*Circumcised on the eighth day, of the people of Israel, of the tribe of Benjamin, a Hebrew of Hebrews; in regard to the law, a Pharisee; as for zeal, persecuting the church; as for righteousness based on the law, faultless.  But whatever were gains to me I now consider loss for the sake of Christ.  What is more, I consider everything a loss because of the surpassing worth of knowing Christ Jesus my Lord, for whose sake I have lost all things. I consider them garbage, that I may gain Christ and be found in him, not having a righteousness of my own that comes from the law, but that which is through faith in Christ—the righteousness that comes from God on the basis of faith.  I want to know Christ —yes, to know the power of his resurrection and participation in his sufferings, becoming like him in his death, and so, somehow, attaining to the resurrection from the dead.*
Philippians 3:5-11 (NIV)

The very thing we are all looking for in the transformation of our present circumstances into that which will bring us life and life more abundantly is not new to God.  God has already provided and established that which is the outcome of our pressing toward our higher calling, His intent for our lives. The process of our pressing is our process of discovering, the uncovering of God, including His presence, power, and promises seen and experienced as real in our lives. Therefore, God, who has established our new invites us into a co-creator relationship with Him where we bring our lived experiences, the deposits along our life's journey of what we have come to understand as truth, as well as our own desires, to bear for His glory. God invites you to join Him by taking a step back from your circumstances to **Breathe: New Life**, which allows you to see and seize God's opportunities with new mercies available to you to come up higher, the place where **All Things Have Become New**.

## December 12

*Still, it's what God had in mind all along, to crush him with pain. The plan was that he give himself as an offering for sin so that he'd see life come from it—life, life, and more life. And God's plan will deeply prosper through him. Out of that terrible travail of soul, he'll see that it's worth it and be glad he did it. Through what he experienced, my righteous one, my servant, will make many "righteous ones," as he himself carries the burden of their sins. Therefore I'll reward him extravagantly—the best of everything, the highest honors—Because he looked death in the face and didn't flinch, because he embraced the company of the lowest. He took on his own shoulders the sin of the many, he took up the cause of all the black sheep.*
Isaiah 53:10-12 (MSG)

**All Things Have Become New** because of the process of your lived experiences that are focused on responding to God's calling for your life and life more abundantly. Whatever you experience on your journey has already been processed by God for your good. Through the process of your lived experiences, you discover who God is and who God created you to be in collaboration with Him to achieve your life and life more abundantly, your fullness of joy. Choose to take on the circumstances of your life for the good and *Breathe: New Life*, taking on life and its challenges head-on, conquering your fears, and dispelling the darkness so that the light of God's truth, His Word, becomes flesh, real in your life.

## December 13

*This is what the Lord says: "Don't let the wise boast in their wisdom, or the powerful boast in their power, or the rich boast in their riches. But those who wish to boast should boast in this alone: that they truly know me and understand that I am the Lord who demonstrates unfailing love and who brings justice and righteousness to the earth, and that I delight in these things. I, the Lord, have spoken!*
Jeremiah 9:23-24 (NLT)

**All Things Have Become New,** not because of how good or wise we are, but instead how good and powerful our God is. Although God uses what we bring to the table to execute His intent and the plan for our life and life more abundantly, never think that what we bring does the job. We, without question, are inadequate, lack the capacity, physically, mentally, and spiritually, to stand against the wiles of darkness and evil; we are only able to stand

368

and overcome because of the senior partner of our lives, God. Therefore, we put on the whole armor of God, more of God; occupying Him; His presence, power, and promises, and He causes things to swell so that we are in abundance and can eat of the fat of the land. **Breathe: New Life** by doing your part and understanding that God's presence, power, and promise make up the difference, fill the gap, and put us over the finish line to win and win big!

## December 14

*Brethren, my heart's desire and prayer to God for Israel is, that they might be saved. For I bear them record that they have a zeal of God, but not according to knowledge. For they being ignorant of God's righteousness, and going about to establish their own righteousness, have not submitted themselves unto the righteousness of God. For Christ is the end of the law for righteousness to every one that believeth.*
Romans 10:1-4

Deliverance from that which hinders your living life in the fullness of joy is also your deliverance to the presence, power, and promises of God released in your life. God getting the glory and revelation in our lives, and through their challenges, is the very mechanism by which we are delivered from our challenges and to our deliverance to God. Thus, your willingness to come to yourself in your life's challenges is the vehicle that reveals God to you and opens up your way to willingly follow the pathway to more of Him; His presence, power, and fulfilled promises for your life, that **All Things Have Become New** space of life. **All Things**

**Have Become New** because you choose to see and seize the pathway of life in and through your life's challenges; your evening experiences, knowing that where you are is only the beginning of your Word of life; deliverance from so you can get to. Release yourself and be delivered to the presence, power, and promises of God's Word for your life, stepping back from where you are to *Breathe: New Life* and receive clarity, deliverance, and be delivered to your fullness of joy.

## December 15

*For therein is the righteousness of God revealed from faith to faith: as it is written, The just shall live by faith.*
Romans 1:17

**All Things Have Become New** because you dare to believe that what exists now is not it and/or there is more that produces your life and life more abundantly. One can always find fault with oneself as well as all the people, places, and things around you to justify limiting yourself, but when you believe, have faith, that God's promises of abundance are beyond your righteousness, you fuel your press forward. Pressing forward entails an expectation of the more and that it will be greater than what you have now. As you go forward *Breathe: New Life,* fueled by your belief in what can and should be for your life and life more abundantly, over and over again, it is from faith to faith!

## December 16

370

*Know ye not, that so many of us as were baptized into Jesus Christ were baptized into his death? Therefore we are buried with him by baptism into death: that like as Christ was raised up from the dead by the glory of the Father, even so we also should walk in newness of life. For if we have been planted together in the likeness of his death, we shall be also in the likeness of his resurrection:*
Romans 6:3-5

Being fully immersed in that which can and should be for your life as God intends is a choice to die in order to live, to be raised to the fulfillment of God's promises for your life and life more abundantly. Our belief in God is made real as we willingly give ourselves up for His intent to be fulfilled in our lives, and the very things we fear are conquered, with us receiving all power and redefining our lives in which **All Things Have Become New**. The resurrection of Christ with all power is also available to you and me if we are fully immersed in God's Word of truth for our lives, entering a space in which our lives are transformed into God's intent for our life and life more abundantly. Step back from the evening and chaos of your life and its challenges and ***Breathe: New Life***, fully immersing yourself in God's intent for you, and be raised, resurrected anew, transforming you and your space in which **All Things Have Become New**.

## December 17

*For as many as are led by the Spirit of God, they are the sons of God. For ye have not received the spirit of bondage again to fear; but ye have received the Spirit of adoption, whereby we cry, Abba, Father. The Spirit itself beareth witness with our spirit, that we are the children of God: And if children, then heirs; heirs of God, and joint-heirs with Christ; if so be that we suffer with him, that we may be also glorified together.*

Romans 8:14-17


**All Things Have Become New** because you choose to operate from a perspective that defies your present reality for that which can and should be for your life as God intends.  To live and operate in that which defies your reality, you must be immersed in the Spirit of God, baptized with the Holy Ghost.  Baptized with the Holy Ghost is allowing the Spirit of God, His Word of truth for your life, to totally consume you; focused and engaging God in each and every experience of your life, and you will be led and guided into your pathway of life as God intends.  The Spirit of God seeks to reconcile you to God, to His Word of truth, and thus, landing you into the place of your fullness of joy and at His right hand pleasures forevermore, no matter where you are or what is going on, to ensure **All Things Have Become New**.  *Breathe: New Life* by allowing yourself to be totally consumed by the Spirit of God, which is available to you, and as you are immersed by the Spirit, you will arrive, in your experiences, at your life and life more abundantly!


## December 18


*Wherefore henceforth know we no man after the flesh: yea, though we have known Christ after the flesh, yet now henceforth know we him no more. Therefore if any man be in Christ, he is a new creature: old things are passed away; behold, all things are become new. And all things are of God, who hath reconciled us to*

372

*himself by Jesus Christ, and hath given to us the ministry of
reconciliation; To wit, that God was in Christ, reconciling the world
unto himself, not imputing their trespasses unto them; and hath
committed unto us the word of reconciliation.*
*Now then we are ambassadors for Christ, as though God did
beseech you by us: we pray you in Christ's stead, be ye reconciled
to God. For he hath made him to be sin for us, who knew no sin;
that we might be made the righteousness of God in him.*
I Corinthians 5:16-21

Experiencing God in your everyday walking around life is key to
living in the abundance of God's intent. As you go about life,
especially its challenges, diligently seek God; sense His presence,
power, and promises for your life. Remember, there is absolutely
nothing that happens by happenstance or accident, causal or
unexpected, that is not Divinely ordered. Your experiences are
God's opportunity to get your attention, and if you are willing to
occupy Him in your experiences, engage God, you will have an
experience that will yield the exceedingly, abundantly, more than
you can ever ask or think by the power that is working within you.
**All Things Have Become New** for you because you are willing to
experience God in your circumstances, and as a result, God will be
revealed, He will get the glory. Your experiences are always about
the development of your inner being, the very spark of life within
you. If that internal spark, the breath of God, is ignited, the spark
will cause the life God intends for you to spring forth and immerse
you; your mind and thoughts, and thus your actions, leading and
guiding you into the promises of God. See and seize your
experiences by reflecting, reacting, and reimagining; ***Breathe:
New Life,*** and you will see God's revelation of not only Him, but

also of you, and as a result, you become His ambassador to the people, places, and things of your life for His glory.

## December 19

*Ye are my friends, if ye do whatsoever I command you. Henceforth I call you not servants; for the servant knoweth not what his lord doeth: but I have called you friends; for all things that I have heard of my Father I have made known unto you. Ye have not chosen me, but I have chosen you, and ordained you, that ye should go and bring forth fruit, and that your fruit should remain: that whatsoever ye shall ask of the Father in my name, he may give it you.*
John 15:14-16

Because we have chosen to experience God in and through our everyday experiences, we have become friends of God, engaging Him in response to our calling, which reveals His anointing and His chosen-ness for our lives.  Although we have free will, God's intent is fulfilled because He has chosen us.  When God calls, and we respond, it is because God called us to Him for His purposes. Therefore, we never have to worry about being alone or feeling as though we have to do it all. We are God's friends because He chose us, and as a result, He will be with us, providing whatever is needed to ensure that **All Things Have Become New**.  Our experiences are God's experiences, and thus the outcome is His glory, His revelation. ***Breathe: New Life*** for you are a friend of God, chosen by Him to reveal Himself in and through your experiences.

## December 20

*Then I saw "a new heaven and a new earth," for the first heaven and the first earth had passed away, and there was no longer any sea. I saw the Holy City, the new Jerusalem, coming down out of heaven from God, prepared as a bride beautifully dressed for her husband. And I heard a loud voice from the throne saying, "Look! God's dwelling place is now among the people, and he will dwell with them. They will be his people, and God himself will be with them and be their God. 'He will wipe every tear from their eyes. There will be no more death or mourning or crying or pain, for the old order of things has passed away." He who was seated on the throne said, "I am making everything new!" Then he said, "Write this down, for these words are trustworthy and true."*
Revelation 21:1-5 (NIV)

The result of our experiencing God, internalizing our everyday walking around experiences in which we perceive God and His Word in the process of His revelation, we can see and seize the new. The process to **Breathe: New Life** demands the ability to reflect on what is and what can and should be, and allow God to show you how to connect the two, leading and guiding you in the pathway of life. It is in the pathway of life, led by God's Spirit, that always leads us to the presence, power, and promises of God made real in your lives for God, scattering the darkness that exists so that **All Things Have Become New**. Allow God to come and dwell with you and you in Him, experiencing the fullness of His presence, power, and promises to **Breathe: New Life,** and with your inhaling His way and exhaling the toxic, perceive and receive that **All Things Have Become New**.

## December 21

*By entering through faith into what God has always wanted to do for us—set us right with him, make us fit for him—we have it all together with God because of our Master Jesus. And that's not all: We throw open our doors to God and discover at the same moment that he has already thrown open his door to us. We find ourselves standing where we always hoped we might stand—out in the wide open spaces of God's grace and glory, standing tall and shouting our praise. There's more to come: We continue to shout our praise even when we're hemmed in with troubles, because we know how troubles can develop passionate patience in us, and how that patience in turn forges the tempered steel of virtue, keeping us alert for whatever God will do next. In alert expectancy such as this, we're never left feeling shortchanged. Quite the contrary—we can't round up enough containers to hold everything God generously pours into our lives through the Holy Spirit! Christ arrives right on time to make this happen. He didn't, and doesn't, wait for us to get ready. He presented himself for this sacrificial death when we were far too weak and rebellious to do anything to get ourselves ready. And even if we hadn't been so weak, we wouldn't have known what to do anyway. We can understand someone dying for a person worth dying for, and we can understand how someone good and noble could inspire us to selfless sacrifice. But God put his love on the line for us by offering his Son in sacrificial death while we were of no use whatever to him. Now that we are set right with God by means of this*

*sacrificial death, the consummate blood sacrifice, there is no longer a question of being at odds with God in any way. If, when we were at our worst, we were put on friendly terms with God by the sacrificial death of his Son, now that we're at our best, just think of how our lives will expand and deepen by means of his resurrection life! Now that we have actually received this amazing friendship with God, we are no longer content to simply say it in plodding prose. We sing and shout our praises to God through Jesus, the Messiah!*
Romans 5:1-11 (MSG)

**All Things Have Become New** because it is to reveal God, His glory, and in so doing, the darkness of our lives is scattered and is obvious not only to us but to everyone and everything in our space. Remember, God's primary purpose in your and my life is to reveal His glory; thus, He has chosen us to be the crown of His glory. So the process to **Breathe: New Life** will take us through our tribulations, knowing that they produce patience and patience, experience; experiencing God's presence, power, and promises in and over our lives. The very experience of God fuels our hope, our expectancy, and not just the ordinary but also the extraordinary in which God will be revealed. **All Things Have Become New** for it is the space in which God takes center stage, showing up at the right time to do what is required in our lives for us to live in the abundance of life as He intends, and the more we **Breathe: New Life,** the more He gets the glory!

## December 22

*Even though you were once distant from him, living in the shadows of your evil thoughts and actions, he reconnected you back to himself. He released his supernatural peace to you through the sacrifice of his own body as the sin-payment on your behalf so that you would dwell in his presence. And now there is nothing between you and Father God, for he sees you as holy, flawless, and restored, if indeed you continue to advance in faith, assured of a firm foundation to grow upon. Never be shaken from the hope of the gospel you have believed in. And this is the glorious news I preach all over the world.*
Colossians 1:21-23 (TPT)

**All Things Have Become New** for our life because we receive God's offer to co-create with Him that which He intends, despite and in spite of our failings, shortcomings, or inabilities in the flesh. God invites all of us to choose to be in partnership with Him to reveal Him; His presence, power, and promises for life and life more abundantly, and no matter our position in life, good or bad, guilty or not, He will reconcile us if we choose to ***Breathe: New Life***. As we come to the end of the year on the verge of the new, choose to be reconciled, made one with God, and His promises for your life. Just give yourself up to God, to His Word being fulfilled, and respond to that call of His intent, and God will do the rest, reconciling you: uniting your heart, mind, and soul to Him while also advancing you in faith to grow to full maturity in His intent for your life. **All Things Have Become New** because you continue to believe, hope in the fulfillment of God's promises for your life by continuously positioning yourself to ***Breathe: New Life*** into and for your experiences in which God gets the glory, the revelation!

# December 23

*And for me, that utterance may be given unto me, that I may open my mouth boldly, to make known the mystery of the gospel, For which I am an ambassador in bonds: that therein I may speak boldly, as I ought to speak.*
Ephesians 6:19-20

**All Things Have Become New** attitude demands a boldness in which you face your experiences with confidence that no matter how fierce the opposition is, you will *Breathe: New Life*. Life-changing experiences are born of adversity, and when change happens, it takes confidence in what can and should be. As a result, the change you envision is translated into your reality, causing friction and eventual transformation. Remember, be ye transformed by the renewing of your mind; thinking and thus acting with confidence and boldness, which bumps up against your reality to birth the promises of God's intent for your fullness of joy. Although you may not be where you can and should be today, be bold in your mind for the change that brings into existence your life and life more abundantly, which is the mystery of the gospel, the good news of Christ. Thus, as you think so will your actions align with your confidence, a renewed mind; experiencing God in the fullness of His presence, power, and promises, and behold, **All Things Have Become New**, transformed for your good.

# December 24

*That if thou shalt confess with thy mouth the Lord Jesus, and shalt believe in thine heart that God hath raised him from the dead, thou shalt be saved. For with the heart man believeth unto righteousness; and with the mouth confession is made unto salvation.*
Romans 10:9-10

**All Things Have Become New** because of your confidence in the Word of truth for your life; that which can and should be as God intends.  Having faith in what you believe can and should be is the necessary fuel to press toward the higher calling of God in your life.  Do not allow what is the reality to prevent and/or detour you from responding to God's promises for your life and life more abundantly, press by confessing, declaring your confidence in that which can and should be.  As you confess, speaking into your life and atmosphere, you position yourself to be sensitive to seizing those opportunities God has provided, not because of how good you are, but instead because of God's intent to fulfill His promises, your Word of truth.  Thus, as you engage life and its challenges, ***Breathe: New Life*** by confessing and declaring your confidence in what can and should be, so that your heart, mind, and thus your actions will align with God's intent, evoking His presence, power, and promises fulfilled in your life.

## December 25

*God grabbed me. God's Spirit took me up and set me down in the middle of an open plain strewn with bones. He led me around and among them—a lot of bones! There were bones all over the plain —dry bones, bleached by the sun.  He said to me, "Son of man,*

can these bones live?" I said, "Master God, only you know that." He said to me, "Prophesy over these bones: 'Dry bones, listen to the Message of God!'" God, the Master, told the dry bones, "Watch this: I'm bringing the breath of life to you and you'll come to life. I'll attach sinews to you, put meat on your bones, cover you with skin, and breathe life into you. You'll come alive and you'll realize that I am God!" I prophesied just as I'd been commanded. As I prophesied, there was a sound and, oh, rustling! The bones moved and came together, bone to bone. I kept watching. Sinews formed, then muscles on the bones, then skin stretched over them. But they had no breath in them. He said to me, "Prophesy to the breath. Prophesy, son of man. Tell the breath, 'God, the Master, says, Come from the four winds. Come, breath. Breathe on these slain bodies. Breathe life!'" So I prophesied, just as he commanded me. The breath entered them and they came alive! They stood up on their feet, a huge army. Then God said to me, "Son of man, these bones are the whole house of Israel. Listen to what they're saying: 'Our bones are dried up, our hope is gone, there's nothing left of us.' "Therefore, prophesy. Tell them, 'God, the Master, says: I'll dig up your graves and bring you out alive—O my people! Then I'll take you straight to the land of Israel. When I dig up graves and bring you out as my people, you'll realize that I am God. I'll breathe my life into you and you'll live. Then I'll lead you straight back to your land and you'll realize that I am God. I've said it and I'll do it. God's Decree.'"
Ezekiel 37:1-14 (MSG)


Today is Christmas Day, and we gather with family and friends to celebrate the coming of the new, new Spirit for a new life that is unrestrained by what is. With the birth of Christ, we not only get an enduring King but also, with Him, new life and new hope, harmony with the will of God for our life and life more abundantly, and it is available to all, no matter who you are or where you are in life. Although we do not know the exact date of Jesus' birth, we celebrate at the end of our calendar year, on the threshold of the New Year. Interestingly enough, the King of Kings and Lord of Lords is born in a manger, a trough for which animals eat, because there was no room in the inn; the place perceived as "appropriate" and/or "acceptable." The good news of Christ's birth, the coming of new life, and new hope directly contradict everything we thought, yet it is exactly what we desired: unexpected possibilities. Today, celebrate your gift of unexpected possibilities by choosing to **Breath: New Life**; inhaling possibilities and exhaling the constraints of your life, life's toxicity which prevents you from expecting and living in God's promises for your life and life more abundantly. Speak to your bones, the foundation and fragments of your life, the what is and cause the Spirit of God's presence, power, and promises to come and you will see, **All Things Have Become New**; an exceedingly great army, power to live in God's promises for your life. MERRY CHRISTMAS!

## December 26

*And the slain shall fall in the midst of you, and ye shall know that I am the LORD.*
Ezekiel 6:7

Because of the gift of Christ, He is not only 'Emmanuel"- "God with us," but also He is the fulfillment of the Word of God becoming flesh, evidence of God's presence, power, and promises. Thus, our Christmas celebration encompasses the faith that our Word from God will come to pass, and although we may not see it right now, we are renewed in our hope and expectations that His Word does become flesh, real.  Our renewed hope empowers us so that whatever challenges our progress toward our higher calling is diminished, and, as a result, all things will fall amid our press.  Today, *Breathe: New Life* because God is made real in your life, including His Word of truth, thus celebrate for **All Things Have Become New**!

## December 27

*Be glad then, ye children of Zion, and rejoice in the LORD your God:*
*for he hath given you the former rain moderately, and he will cause to come down for you the rain, the former rain, and the latter rain in the first month.*
*And the floors shall be full of wheat, and the fats shall overflow with wine and oil.*
*And I will restore to you the years that the locust hath eaten, the cankerworm, and the caterpiller, and the palmerworm, my great army which I sent among you.  And ye shall eat in plenty, and be satisfied,*
*and praise the name of the LORD your God, that hath dealt wondrously with you:*
*and my people shall never be ashamed.  And ye shall know that I am in the midst of Israel, and that I am the LORD your God, and none else:*
*and my people shall never be ashamed.  And it shall come to pass afterward,*
*that I will pour out my spirit upon all flesh;*

*and your sons and your daughters shall prophesy,*
*your old men shall dream dreams,*
*your young men shall see visions:*
Joel 2:23-28

Amid life and its challenges, it is critical to our enduring and pressing forward in that which can and should be for our lives to be glad, to celebrate in the midst of it all. Our celebration is triggered because we choose to be led and live in the Spirit of God, His Word of truth for our lives. Every day and in every experience, seek to live in the Spirit of truth, allowing the Spirit to dominate, suppressing the negative, and lifting the positive, causing you to celebrate despite and in spite of it all, and as a result, **All Things Have Become New**. God's presence, power, and promises are reinforced with His Spirit, and if you choose to be baptized in His Spirit, totally consumed, the Spirit will dominate even in your chaos and confusion, allowing the Word of God to prevail. ***Breathe: New Life*** and allow the Spirit of God to brood over your deep, pouring out the power to prevail, overcome, and press forward in that which is your life and life more abundantly!

## December 28

*The LORD also shall roar out of Zion, and utter his voice from Jerusalem;*
*and the heavens and the earth shall shake: but the LORD will be the hope of his people,*
*and the strength of the children of Israel. So shall ye know that I am the LORD your God dwelling in Zion, my holy mountain: then shall Jerusalem be holy,*

*and there shall no strangers pass through her any more.  And it*
*shall come to pass in that day, that the mountains shall drop down*
*new wine, and the hills shall flow with milk,*
*and all the rivers of Judah shall flow with waters, and a fountain*
*shall come forth of the house of the LORD, and shall water the*
*valley of Shittim.*
Joel 3:16-18

Our hope, expectation, for the fulfillment of God's Word for our life, is simply our having faith.  According to God's Word, faith is the very thing that pleases Him.  By no means do I suggest that our right kind of living according to God's intent is not important; however, our faith, our willingness to believe His Word, is paramount.  The more we are willing to believe in what God has declared for our lives, it not only transforms us and aligns us with His way of living but also transforms the circumstances, the experiences of our lives, reflecting His promise in which **All Things Have Become New**.  As you are on the verge of an old year passing and a new one coming, build your faith to *Breathe: New Life* into the circumstances of your life.  It is in building your faith that you not only transform your life, exhaling your toxicity, but also transform your atmosphere, inhaling that which will cause you to grow and be rewarded with the promises of God.

## December 29

*And after three days and an half the Spirit of life from God entered*
*into them, and they stood upon their feet; and great fear fell upon*
*them which saw them. And they heard a great voice from heaven*

*saying unto them, Come up hither. And they ascended up to*
*heaven in a cloud; and their enemies beheld them.*
Revelation 11:11-12

**All Things Have Become New** as a direct result of God getting the glory. The experiences of our lives are opportunities to reflect on God's presence, power, and promises. The more you are willing to put God's Word of truth for life, in particular for you, center stage, you set up the opportunity God has given for Him to be revealed and, as a result, reveal and reward you as the crown of His glory. There is a process, and it may appear like death, hell, and the grave, God has shown through the death and resurrection of Christ, a three-day process, that He does raise from the dead, *Breathe: New Life,* it is your promise and reward!

## December 30

*I will ransom them from the power of the grave;*
*I will redeem them from death:*
*O death, I will be thy plagues;*
*O grave, I will be thy destruction:*
*repentance shall be hid from mine eyes.*
Hosea 13:14

Our willingness to *Breathe: New Life* by inhaling that which God has spoken as truth to and for our lives is reinforced by the power of His Spirit consuming and abiding with us. It is the Spirit of God that provides the wind as we stretch forth, press toward that which God intends for our life and life more abundantly. Although life and its challenges can and will be contrary winds, we are empowered by God, in and through His Spirit, to lift and propel us forward and higher, in which **All Things Have Become New**. God's Word, reinforced by His Spirit, the wind of God lifts us from the death, hell, and the grave of our experiences, giving us new life. Be not deceived by what may appear as the end; it is only the beginning of the new. ***Breathe: New Life***, and with the power of God, transform you and your space in which **All Things Have Become New**.

## December 31

*Balaam said, "Build me seven altars here, and prepare seven bulls and seven rams for me." Balak did as Balaam said, and the two of them offered a bull and a ram on each altar. Then Balaam said to Balak, "Stay here beside your offering while I go aside. Perhaps the Lord will come to meet with me. Whatever he reveals to me I will tell you." Then he went off to a barren height. God met with him, and Balaam said, "I have prepared seven altars, and on each altar I have offered a bull and a ram." The Lord put a word in Balaam's mouth and said, "Go back to Balak and give him this word." So he went back to him and found him standing beside his offering, with all the Moabite officials. Then Balaam spoke his message: "Balak brought me from Aram, the king of Moab from the eastern mountains. 'Come,' he said, 'curse Jacob for me,' come, denounce Israel.' How can I curse those whom God has not cursed? How can I denounce those whom the Lord has not denounced? From the rocky peaks I see them, from the heights I view them. I see a people who live apart and do not consider themselves one of the* nations.  Who can count the dust of Jacob or number even a fourth of Israel?  Let me die the death of the righteous, and may my final end be like theirs!"  Balak said to Balaam, "What have you done to me? I brought you to curse my enemies, but you have done nothing but bless them!"  He answered, "Must I not speak what the Lord puts in my mouth?"  Then Balak said to him, "Come with me to another place where you can see them; you will not see them all but only the outskirts of their camp. And from there, curse them for me."  So he took him to the field of Zophim on the top of Pisgah, and there he built seven altars and offered a bull and a ram on each altar.  Balaam said to Balak, "Stay here beside your offering while I meet with him over there."  The Lord met with Balaam and put a word in his mouth and said, "Go back to Balak and give him this word."  So he went to him and found him standing beside his offering, with the Moabite officials. Balak asked him, "What did the Lord say?"  Then he spoke his message: "Arise, Balak, and listen; hear me, son of Zippor.  God is not human, that he should lie, not a human being, that he should change his mind.  Does he speak and then not act?  Does he promise and not fulfill?  I have received a command to bless; he has blessed, and I cannot change it.

Numbers 23:1-20 (NIV)


The last day of the year is here, and we are positioned to **Breathe: New Life**.  However, being in a position to experience our new life is not sufficient in and of itself; we must also bring a positive mindset, vibe, and life to it.  Without a doubt, we will experience difficult, complex, and downright damning experiences in the coming year.  Nevertheless, we do have new life, and thus, we come to our experiences with a new attitude, despite and in spite of it all, which is positive and illuminating for us to walk right

388

through our valley and shadows of death and yet fear no evil. Our positive attitude serves as our light in our experiences, which does not diminish our expectations but instead increases them for the more, the exceedingly, abundantly, more than we can ever ask or imagine. Thus, seeing ourselves and our experiences through the lens of positivity and inspiration, we are invited as well as our space to a *Most Favored Status* in which **All Things Have Become New**. This is the impact of breathing new life, inhaling the Spirit of God, which makes us living souls.